AMERICAN EDUCATION

Its Men,

Ideas,

and

Institutions

Advisory Editor

Lawrence A. Cremin
Frederick A. P. Barnard Professor of Education
Teachers College, Columbia University

AMERICAN EDUCATION: *Its Men, Ideas, and Institutions*
presents selected works of thought and scholarship that have
long been out of print or otherwise unavailable. Inevitably, such
works will include particular ideas and doctrines that have been
outmoded or superseded by more recent research. Nevertheless,
all retain their place in the literature, having influenced educational thought and practice in their own time and having provided
the basis for subsequent scholarship.

IN QUEST
OF KNOWLEDGE

A HISTORICAL PERSPECTIVE
ON ADULT EDUCATION

By C. Hartley Grattan

ARNO PRESS & THE NEW YORK TIMES
New York * 1971

Reprint Edition 1971 by Arno Press Inc.

Copyright © 1955 by National Board of Young Men's
   Christian Associations
Reprinted by permission of C. Hartley Grattan

Reprinted from a copy in The Newark Public Library

American Education:
   Its Men, Ideas, and Institutions - Series II
ISBN for complete set: 0-405-03600-0
See last pages of this volume for titles.

Manufactured in the United States of America

Library of Congress Cataloging in Publication Data

Grattan, Clinton Hartley, 1902-
   In quest of knowledge.
   (American education: its men, ideas, and
institutions. Series II)
   1. Adult education--History. I. Title.
II. Series.
LC5215.G68 1971   374.9   77-165738
ISBN 0-405-03608-6

IN QUEST OF KNOWLEDGE

IN QUEST
OF KNOWLEDGE

A HISTORICAL PERSPECTIVE
ON ADULT EDUCATION

By C. Hartley Grattan

ASSOCIATION PRESS   NEW YORK

IN QUEST OF KNOWLEDGE

Library of Congress catalog card number: 55-7412

Printed in the United States of America
American Book–Stratford Press, Inc., New York

Preface

THIS BOOK was made possible by the financial support of The Fund for Adult Education. The work, however, and the opinions set forth are those of the author alone; in no sense do they purport to be those of the Fund.

The book is addressed to all persons who are interested in any phase of adult education or who desire to gain some degree of familiarity with its background or development. It is not specifically addressed to specialists in the field, but it is hoped that it may prove more than casually interesting to them simply because the approach, unlike that of the greater part of the voluminous material on adult education, is through its history. The writer felt that what had happened in the history of adult education would throw valuable light on present-day problems.

There is, of course, an enormous "literature" of adult education, but as far as the writer could determine no book like this one has ever been written before. This is, he thinks, a pioneer effort to establish that adult education is one of the interests of mankind that has persisted since the beginning of history. Yet the book is neither a formal nor a complete history; it is, rather, a long essay using historical materials.

In the present state of historical studies in adult education, therefore, it was necessary to fix upon some selective approach. The material available was weighed for intrinsic significance, illustrative value, and the accessibility of sufficient information to make a discussion meaningful. The author decided to begin the book with a short sketch of the Western European background from primitive man to the industrial revolution, chiefly to emphasize the often overlooked point that adult education has such deep roots. Even an elementary understanding of the story—about all that can be achieved until more research is done by culture-historians—would, the author felt, help get recent history into a reasonable perspective.

The focus of the book is, however, the American story. Surveying the histories of adult education in other countries, mostly, it must be confessed, on the basis of tantalizingly sketchy accounts, led to the conclusion that it would be most profitable to support the American focus with a brief resume of British experience. This decision was enforced by two considerations: (1) the British story amply illustrates the problems of adult education in an industrial society, the evolution of which is not entirely unknown to American readers; and (2) the British story contains the major precedents for American action, insofar as foreign precedents have played any role. The British story, however, is not recounted inclusively, but selectively, with a view to serving the purposes stated.

The American story then follows, but notwithstanding the relative length of the report, it is still but a sketch rather than an exhaustive review. For one thing—and very important it is—after a reasonably diligent search, the author was, in this Part as in the others, exceedingly handicapped by the scarcity of specialized monographs analyzing particular episodes in satisfactory detail. It was clear that the contribution of the study would have to be as perceptive a survey of the field as was possible with the materials in their present underorganized state. It was hoped, of course, to achieve a result interesting in itself. If it also provided provocative reading for research-minded specialists in adult education, so much the better.

What had to be left out of this account entirely was the story of adult education on the continent of Europe since medieval times. It would be wrong, and indicative of a false sense of values, to suggest that that story contains little of value. It contains, as a matter of fact, much that is profoundly interesting to all concerned with adult education. But, it is generally agreed, the impact of continental experience in this field on American practice has never been very great, and the same generalization may be made about the British background.

Present indications are that it will be a long time before a comprehensive, inclusive history of adult education in the West can be written.

For the reader who seeks an introduction to adult education in the world today, with bibliographies by countries, the *International Directory of Adult Education,* published by UNESCO (Paris, 1952), may be helpful. No "brief list of selected titles" from among the great number consulted in the preparation of this book seems to the author to be likely to be useful to many readers, but those mentioned in the text and the Notes (pages 311-332) can, of course, serve as a partial bibliography.

Grateful acknowledgement is made to the following publishers and copyright owners for permission to include brief quotations from several works: to Beacon Press for *Greek Historical Thought,* edited by Arnold Toynbee, and *Socrates,* by A. E. Taylor; to Columbia University Press, for *Leisure: A Suburban Study,* by Lundberg and others, copyright, 1934, and *A History of Adult Education at Columbia University,* by J. A. Burrell, copyright, 1954; to *Encyclopaedia Britannica* for its article on Socrates by A. E. Taylor; to Alfred A. Knopf, Inc. for *Poetry and the Age,* by Randall Jarrell, copyright, 1953; to Harvard University Press for *General Education in a Free Society,* copyright, 1945; to Longmans, Green & Co., Inc. for *Platonism,* by A. E. Taylor, copyright, 1924, and *Aristotelianism,* by John L. Stocks, copyright, 1925; to The Macmillan Company for *Henry M. Leipziger,* by Ruth Frankel, copyright, 1933, and for the articles on Elkanah Watson and Christian Socialism in the *Encyclopedia of the Social Sciences,* copyright, 1934; to Oxford University Press for a passage translated by W. D. Ross in *The Basic Works of Aristotle,* edited by Richard McKeon, copyright, 1941, and *Social and Economic History of the Roman Empire,* by M. I. Rostovtzeff, copyright, 1926; to Paul R. Reynolds & Son for *Talks to Teachers,* by William James, copyright, 1899, 1900; to University of Illinois Press for *Mass Communications,* edited by William Schramm, copyright,

1949; and to Yale University Press for *Daily Life in Ancient Rome,* by Jerome Carcopino, copyright, 1940.

The author wishes to thank warmly for their comments, advice, and shared knowledge those numerous persons both inside and outside the Fund with whom he has held discussions of adult education in general and the problems of this book in particular. He is under obligation to Professors I. L. Kandel and H. G. Good for comments on the earlier sections of the book and to Professors Cyril Houle and Lyman Bryson for their observations on the book as a whole. None of the gentlemen mentioned is, however, in any sense responsible for the version of the story the writer finally determined upon. An obligation of a different kind is owed to Mr. Howard Mahan. For many months he acted as the writer's research assistant and was very efficient at "digging up" facts. He was, moreover, a most stimulating speculator on what the facts might mean. In his dual capacity his assistance was invaluable.

C. HARTLEY GRATTAN

Contents

Educating the adult in colonial New England. Benjamin Franklin as an adult education hero. Thomas Jefferson's views. George Washington epitomizes early views. Religion and literacy in early 1800's. Science bridges religious and secular emphases. The library-lecture, vocational-training institutions. Timothy Claxton as an examplary figure.

PART I

ADULT EDUCATION

AND ITS SOCIAL CONTEXT

1

Definition and Implications

THIS BOOK approaches adult education by way of the historical
background. Nearly twenty years ago, Lyman Bryson defined adult
education as "All activities with an educational purpose that are
carried on by people engaged in the ordinary business of life." [1]
Other definitions have been suggested before and since, but none
seems strikingly better. Adult education does not lend itself readily
to succinct summary and efforts at greater precision than Professor
Bryson achieved have ordinarily resulted only in the elaboration
of commentaries on the basic ideas he expressed.

The essential points are all there: that the activities be purposefully educational, that they be engaged in by adults, and that at the
time the adults also be engaged in their ordinary routine. The definition correctly suggests that there are no limitations on what subject matter adults may study—the range can be from a most intimate personal problem to the operation of the universe—and that
how they deal with the subject matter can be equally various, the
way being wide open to experimentation. Adult education is normally a highly fluid, flexible, multiple-faceted operation in all
its aspects.

Although adult education by definition takes place after formal
education, or what we call "schooling," is over, it is obviously re-

lated to it in many ways. Not only are opportunities for adults to pursue their education often offered by the schools, from the public schools through the universities, but the level of formal educational attainment of the adults participating directly influences the nature of the educational adventures in which they can profitably share. Since at any given time the members of a community will vary considerably in level of completed schooling, it naturally follows that adult education can usefully be organized at various levels. Moreover, the progressive rise in the average number of years of formal schooling characteristic of the populations of modern democratic societies—an increase which has as yet by no means achieved its peak—is a highly significant fact for adult educators; and adult educators must be alert to the content of the education received by the successive school generations.

It should not be assumed, however, that adult education is rigidly bound to the school system, or any level of it, and least of all that it must in the final analysis only aspire to repair the deficiencies in the formal education of adults. Adult education can adventure on its own, for the adult mind is fed and conditioned by forces other than public education. Far more important than adult education simply calculated to bring adults up to some chosen mark of formal schooling, is that kind of adult education addressed to *adults as adults* and designed to assist them to live more successfully. This is the real field of *adult* education.

This observation gets us fairly close to what adult educators believe is the heart of their target, but immediately we are confronted with a variety of suggestions about how to hit it. The multiplicity of these suggestions, when translated into activities, accounts for the vast jungle of adult education that confronts us today. This jungle can be variously analyzed and classified. One set of categories, suggested by Lyman Bryson, is remedial, occupational, relational (understanding ourselves and our relations with others), political, and liberal. Still another possible classification is by sponsorship: school and college, community, trade union, etc. Any classification must inevitably include a "miscellaneous" category into which to group items that fit nowhere else. Many of the miscellaneous items are, on any reasonable showing, as important as items more elegantly classified. But with the risks recognized, it may be suggested that adult education activities can with more or less justice be sorted out into four groups: vocational, recreational, informational, and liberal.

In the United States, the vocational courses have predominated and for that reason many people see adult education as a road to an improvement in pecuniary status. "Know more, earn more." Many observers appear to think that adult education *is* vocational education. Such announcements of adult education as they see from time to time tend to confirm this view, whether the advertisements specify the offerings of public-school systems, colleges, universities, private schools, or correspondence schools. There are excellent reasons why, in the United States, vocational education should bulk so large; and the reasons entirely justify its extensive development, as we shall see later on. Nevertheless, vocational education is not the whole of adult education.

Recreational *education* may cause some eyebrows to rise, especially the eyebrows of persons not at all sure that instruction in recreational techniques is legitimately an activity of educators. Many people identify recreation with fun and appear to think that, if people can't find their own way to fun, it is no part of the work of educators to help them to it. Truly, a large part of recreation, both commercial and noncommercial, *is* fun. Very many Americans can see no use for recreation that is not, in their view, simply fun. The "fun complex" pervasively influences the way in which Americans employ their leisure.

To define exactly how recreation finds its proper place in adult education requires close analysis of the many kinds of recreational activities, including those ordinarily assessed in terms of the fun they give. It is necessary to determine, among other things, which of these activities make a creative contribution to personal development and which do not. We cannot pause here to carry through such an exercise. But we can point out that serious errors may result from too hasty dismissal of forms of recreational activities identified with fun and fun alone in the minds of many. One man's fun can be another man's meat and drink. Many arts, serious and lively—the movies, the dance, music, the graphic arts, photography, and others—run a wide gamut; instruction in the higher expressions of them is readily justifiable. So, too, with sports. Moreover, one must think about such complicated considerations as how the particular recreational activity fits into the total life-regimen of the individual; his motive for seeking to master the particular recreational activity; and the social consequences sought or unconsciously achieved. Recreational adult education has a far larger frame of reference than at first glance appears. Nevertheless, the teaching of recreational techniques can never be more than a fraction of the whole field of adult education.

The informational activities of adult education are enormously complex; to report them adequately would require the compilation of an encyclopedic handbook. Many are quite outside the area persons not closely informed ordinarily think of as adult education. They range from efforts to provide club members with specialized information on gardening, photography, natural history, stamps, and the innumerable do-it-yourself activities currently flourishing, to efforts to inform citizens at large on foreign and domestic affairs and issues, or on health, child guidance, conservation of natural resources, science, books, and so on; and they run off into propaganda for special-interest points of view. They are most obviously adult education when they involve courses, discussion groups, or lectures; but whatever the vehicle used, the motive is to inform and instruct adults—the intent is educative—and whether or not those carrying on the work use the term, the effort is one in adult education. Consciousness of that fact increases responsibility and improves skill; the awareness is growing, though hardly fast enough yet in view of the enormous growth of propaganda activities.

We come finally to liberal adult education, today not too conspicuous a part of the variegated whole, but nevertheless a part which history ratifies as supremely important and to which many wise contemporary analysts believe increasing attention must be given. Liberal adult education is ordinarily concerned with the humanities and the social sciences and should also include the natural sciences, music, and the plastic arts. Its primary objective is to deepen the understanding of the human predicament and put men in the way of making relevant judgments and sensitive discriminations among values. It is not concerned, in the first instance, with improving the prospect of greater pecuniary rewards like most vocational education, nor with improving competence in recreation, nor with information of any specialized kind, but with those varieties of knowledge and understanding that somehow underpin wisdom. Liberal adult education is calculated to assist in the maturation of the individual as an individual—not simply as a factor in the economic equation or as a political citizen, but as a Man. It is more concerned with helping men *to be,* than *to be something* —the distinction is that of Henry James, Sr.—on the theory that if this can be achieved, all else will be on a higher plane. It is concerned with the great and enduring thoughts, deeds, and creations of the past on the one hand; on the other it adventures on the frontiers of knowledge. It is concerned with literature and philosophy, political science and economics, the behavioral sciences and the arts, dealing with them as only adults can deal with them and on the theory that adults are precisely the ones who can most fruitfully wrest their meaning and significance from them.

None of these categories is "pure." A program, whose predominant characteristics place it under the heading "liberal," may in some of its aspects be recreational, in others informational, and for some participants (e.g., school teachers) possibly even vocational. Even if the elements were not inevitably mixed in the categories, they could be mixed by the customers, because of the wide range of motivations and reactions. Moreover, there is nothing to prevent anybody from undertaking work in all the categories. Everybody wants vocational competence, should covet information, needs recreation, and can profit from the liberal studies. A specialist in liberal studies, however, may well shy away from more of them in adult education, but he may be perfectly content to take a course in what the schools call "shop," leaving the liberal studies to the man whose daily work is "shop" or something like it. The possible permutations and combinations are endless.

The point that adult education is education "carried on by people engaged in the ordinary business of life" is more important than may appear at first glance. "People engaged in the ordinary business of life" are persons upon whom all those forces which go to influence and condition people's minds and emotions play with full force. Many efforts vigorously to express this truth have been made, but here we can be satisfied with one relevant quotation. In his inaugural address as Chancellor of St. Andrews in Scotland, delivered in 1867, John Stuart Mill declared:

Education, in its larger sense, is one of the most inexhaustible of all topics. . . . Not only does it include whatever we do for ourselves, and whatever is done for us by others, for the express purpose of bringing us somewhat nearer to the perfection of our nature; it does more: in its larger acceptation it comprehends even the indirect effects produced on character and on the human faculties, by things of which the direct purposes are quite different; by laws, by forms of government, by the industrial arts, by modes of social life; nay, even by physical facts not dependent on human will, by climate, soil, and local position. Whatever helps to shape the human being; to make the individual what he is, or hinder him from being what he is not—is part of his education. And a very bad education it often is; requiring all that can be done by cultivated intelligence and will to counteract its tendencies.[2]

A contemporary statement of the point would be only superficially different. It would, without a doubt, include a reference to the influence of the mass media of communication: press, radio, television; it would bring in propaganda; but what Mill said would not be fundamentally changed. The essence of the matter is that an adult mind is continually being fed and formed by the total environment in which it has its being. The general context of adult life and work embraces the educational world; the latter is, on any reasonable showing, but a fraction of the former; and the influence of education on the adult mind is less than educators like to admit. This is especially true of adult education, which in relation to the total adult world is, by accurate definition, but a peripheral influence. (Progress in adult education is to move from the periphery toward the center; today there is a vast distance to go.) The actual situation is well presented in the Harvard report of 1945, *General Education in a Free Society:*

Adults, not young people, set the tone of a community. Almost inevitably, school people, and also the general public, overestimate the importance of the influence of schools and colleges in forming the individual's character, beliefs, and habits of thought. The community outside the schools has a weight and influence the schools cannot possibly have. If life in the community fails to illustrate the teaching of the schools, the individual is more apt to conform to the community mores than he is to hold fast to the teaching of his school or college.[3]

To clarify this rather confusing situation, it may be helpful to draw a distinction between education of adults and adult education. This is more than a bit of semantic jugglery. All those influences which have an impact on the adult mind, and which "condition" it, may on this distinction be called the education of adults, while those activities which are educational *by intent* may be called adult education. Both must be taken into account to gain a complete view of what is moving and influencing adults at any given time, but it is helpful to discriminate between the two aspects of the picture for the purpose of understanding. The two do, of course, interpenetrate and should do so to an even greater extent, but for purposes of discourse the distinction has its usefulness.

The time for adult education is almost always the time of leisure. (The great exception is the increasingly common on-the-job adult education.) Historically, as we shall see, adult education began its modern career in a period when leisure was largely an upper-class possession, and the fact that most people had little leisure made their use of any part of it for adult education highly remarkable. There is a sense in which the prospects of adult education improve in proportion as the average work day and work week shorten— as leisure time increases—but that adult education has been able fully to profit from the historical changes is difficult to argue. Adult education was and is but one of many competitors for the leisure time of people. It early came into competition with commercialized entertainment and still competes with it. Few things interest a student of adult education more than how people use their leisure and the significance of the uses in psychological, sociological, and cultural terms.[4]

It should be kept in mind, of course, that leisure is at the free disposal of those who possess it. Economically it is one way in which the fruits of progress can be enjoyed; the coming of extensive leisure to the masses of the people is a measure of how far economic progress has gone in technologically advanced societies. But the availability of leisure is no guarantee that it will automatically be used creatively. Neither the classes, when leisure mostly belonged to them, nor the masses, as they came into possession of it, have unassailable records in the use of leisure. The failure of the masses to use their leisure creatively has been, indeed, the subject of a good many articles and books.

It is easy for adult educators to claim a considerable share of available leisure on the ground that what they offer is of high moral value. This has regularly been done, though without appreciably affecting the tone of life in most societies. It may be nobler to attend adult education lectures than beer parlors or dance halls or the movies, or than to listen to the radio and look at TV; to say as much, however, does not appear to dissuade those who prefer these things from continuing in their course in overwhelming numbers. After all, how people employ their leisure is pretty much their own business and many individuals who respond readily to social pressures in other phases of their lives are conspicuously stubborn in asserting the right to spend their leisure as they please.

If, then, there is reason to think that some uses of leisure are uncreative, while others are creative, people must be persuaded to share this evaluation, not coerced into appearing to do so. Participation in adult education, for example, is and must remain a voluntary act. Adult educators have long been seeking means of persuading more people to spend at least part of their leisure in the ways they recommend. The final answers as to the most effective techniques for such persuasion have not yet been found.

Why, after all, do we need adult education? The world is well supplied with answers to this question, most of them rather eroded of novelty by repetition. It would be extremely difficult to invent an absolutely original answer; a person acquainted with the literature of the field has a feeling that in repeating the established answers he is once again threshing well-threshed straw. Some answers, once highly compelling, were "of their time" and have disappeared as the social and intellectual climate changed. At any moment in history the real problem is not so much to demonstrate that adult education is a vital necessity, as it is to get more people to accept and act upon one or another of the several arguments advanced.

To confine ourselves here to currently valid answers (since the historical arguments will appear later in their places), we may properly turn to Mary L. Ely's compilation of 1936, *Adult Educa-*

tion in Action, made up of selections from the old *Journal of Adult Education.* Here we find in the opening pages eighteen brief statements by eighteen different individuals (including Nicholas Murray Butler, Dorothy Canfield Fisher, Charles A. Beard, H. A. Overstreet, Harry Elmer Barnes, and Alvin Johnson) under the general heading, "We Need Adult Education—"

> To Educate the Whole Man
> To Keep Our Minds Open
> To Base Our Judgments on Facts
> To Meet the Challenge of Free Choice
> To Keep Abreast of New Knowledge
> To Be Wisely Destructive
> To Return to Creative Endeavor
> To Prepare for New Occupations
> To Restore Unity to Life
> To Insure Social Stability
> To Direct Social Change
> To Better Our Social Order
> To Open a New Frontier
> To Liberalize the College Curriculum
> To Improve Teachers and Teaching
> To Attain True Security
> To Enlarge Our Horizons
> To See the View

Taken collectively, this is a heavy load for any field to carry, and in attempting to carry all, a certain amount of wobbling has inevitably resulted. Underlying all the variant readings is a basic thesis: Adult education is needed because only through it can the full development of man's potentialities be achieved. X may approach this end for one reason, Y for another, but consciously or unconsciously, with a high conception of the meaning of the phrase or a mediocre understanding of it, they both aim to improve their chances of living successfully.

No matter how persuasively the arguments for adult education are put, the obstacles to the free use of its opportunities are formidable for many people. Since the late eighteenth century, when modern adult education began, most of those who have profited

from it have been middle-class people. Many enterprises aimed
originally at the working class have ended up serving the middle
class, as we shall see, and some of the most striking and famous
enterprises were of, by, and for the middle class from the beginning. Historically speaking, adult education has drawn the greater
part of its audience from the great middle group situated intellectually between those hopelessly immersed in the "slums" of the mind
on the one hand and the intelligentsia—whether institutionally
trained or self-educated—on the other. The audience, furthermore,
has never thus far, even within the broadly defined limits, embraced
all who might reasonably be expected to find a place in it. The
obstacles which have prevented adult education from reaching its
maximum imaginable audience are many and varied, some trivial,
some profound.

Conspicuous among the obstacles are (*a*) the failure of acceptance as a rule of general conduct of the idea that education should
be lifelong; (*b*) a widespread sense of cultural inadequacy; and
(*c*) a failure of adult educators successfully to meet adults on their
own intellectual ground.

The idea that education should be lifelong—an idea which must
gain wide acceptance if adult education is to function in full measure—has been held for long periods by the small class that was
educated at all. It originated in Greek times, and as long as, and
whenever, classical learning has been cultivated as the basic ingredient of education, it has had wide acceptance. Unluckily, nobody seems ever to have written a history of the idea and it is
hard to say why and when it ceased generally to be accepted as a
guiding principle of life. In a way, of course, it never completely
died out, for most intelligent people have continued to recognize
it as good sense when it was stated to them, but it certainly lost
its significance for the generality of men. It has been suggested by
Professor Cyril Houle that this may have been because, in the long
struggle for a comprehensive system of education, the idea of
terminal points came to be overemphasized. Education was talked
of as education *for* life, and once one was launched upon life,
education was thought of as over. This was true whether the
launching site was at the end of four, eight, twelve, sixteen, or
even twenty years of formal education. Curricula were shaped to
the termini immediately in mind. Childhood and adolescence were

the times legitimately devoted to education; life was something else again. If mentioned at all, the idea of lifelong education was occasionally used by speakers at commencements, or by college presidents on state occasions, but their direct influence on popular thinking has never been very remarkable. Rather the idea that there was a point at which education ended and life began became fixed in the minds of most adults. This did adult education no good.

Some adults in every generation acted on the older principle, for systematic or catch-as-catch-can self-education has never really ceased and adult education on a social basis has long had its partisans. Many, moved by the idea that even as adults they could be educated, were nevertheless estopped from action, or discouraged from persistence in it, by a feeling of cultural inadequacy which may or may not have been objectively justified. Illiteracy, actual or functional, has long kept many adults out of adult education. Much more potent, once literacy has been won, is the acute consciousness of the gap between the high culture of the course and the popular culture familiar and comfortable to the customers. This can be both a real and a fictitious obstacle; to hurdle it requires a realistic recognition of its existence and some technique of inducing the people who feel or express it to "take the plunge" into adult education and profit from the effort to dissolve their insecurities.

One aspect of the matter is the "language bar," or the fact that the very words used in a text or by a speaker are barriers to understanding by the pupil, even when the vocabulary is not "technical." [5] As often as not, also, it is in this area that the problem of relevance has its roots. People stay away from adult education because they fail to see a connection between what they would like to know, or obscurely feel the need for knowing, and what is offered to them. Often the customer is right. Not only do adult education offerings sometimes have a shockingly narrow range, but often the customer just does not have the power to relate offering to need, through ignorance of the meaning of the "course titles." This points toward the need for collaboration between sponsors and prospective customers in matching wants and offerings, either at the planning level or through counseling. To the extent that this is not done, an obstacle remains.

These considerations bring us into the question of teaching

methods, including the physical availability of opportunities. From the modern beginnings in England in the late eighteenth century there has been a fairly constant awareness of the point that to teach adults successfully, methods understandingly adapted to adults must be employed. This phase of adult education still remains "wide open" today, for how best to translate the perception into practice is still not finally settled in spite of the immense amount of attention given to methods by adult educators. Poor teaching methods have continued to trip up many adults who have attempted to go on with their education.

Closely allied to teaching methods is the problem of where the teaching shall be done. To an astonishing extent adult education has been conducted in makeshift quarters. How many prospective customers have been put off by unattractive or psychologically disturbing quarters nobody will ever know. Nor will anyone know how many have been put off by quarters, not necessarily unattractive, which were simply off the beaten paths of the prospective customers. Traditionally, opportunities have been more numerous in urban than rural areas, and more numerous in the centers of towns and cities than in the suburbs. Where the opportunities are tends to determine what people, and how many, will take advantage of them, and what subject matters it will prove worth while to offer. Some people will attend adult education courses in public schools, but some will not; some will be attracted to courses given in libraries but not in schools, some only to courses sponsored by colleges or universities; and some only to courses not obviously related to any formal educational institution. The absence of courses enticingly sponsored will keep some people out of adult education; others will be put off by an inconvenient location.

Finally, many adults are reluctant to attempt really serious adventures in adult education by a nagging feeling that, after years out of school, they can no longer learn, or cannot readily learn. There is something of a tradition which supports this notion. We have all heard that men learn little or nothing after some arbitrary age, say forty. Even flexible-minded psychologists of past times, like William James, have supported the idea. In recent years, however, this idea has begun to lose its force among informed people, with especial rapidity since Professor Edward Lee Thorndike published *Adult Learning* in 1928. Given correct teaching methods and a favorable environment, adults can learn, if not quite as rapidly as adolescents, nevertheless just as thoroughly and in many instances with greater satisfaction. Adults who today still cling to the older notion are simply putting an unnecessary obstacle in their way. There is no doubt that many still do. It is up to adult educators to contrive ways of removing it.

On the record—and this book is in large part an impressionistic transcript of the record—the impulse to find ways to educate themselves is a strikingly persistent impulse among adults. The roots of the impulse are in the nature of life itself. Although there is the popular satirical observation that so-and-so "has learned nothing from life," it is obvious that nobody can work his way through all the chances and changes from birth to death without learning "something." Some people manage to learn remarkably little, but at minimum they achieve some kind of adjustment or tolerable maladjustment to the cultural pattern into which they are born and to the changes which occur in it during their lifetimes. The schools, from kindergarten to university, are largely concerned with giving their pupils competence in their culture and with diffusing the kinds of knowledge which are more the products of self-consciousness than custom. After formal schooling is over most men learn from experience only. "The trouble with the school of experience," Henry Ford is reported to have said, "is that the graduates are too old to go to work." Nevertheless, some few adults do undertake self-education, and a proportion in each generation turns to the adult education with which we are concerned in this book.

Societies have differed in the extent to which they utilized education as a technique for diffusing knowledge; they have differed also as to the proportion of members it was considered worth while to educate. Until industrialism and democracy developed, the educated class was always a small elite. Both industrialism and democracy by their inherent nature require the education of all. This was not immediately recognized; when recognized, it was resisted by some; and the problems posed by its eventual acceptance have not yet been solved. Adult education began before a state-supported school system was accepted as a legitimate charge upon the public revenues and it has continued ever since, no matter

how elaborate the school system has become. As time has passed,
it has been recognized, and never more widely than today, as a
necessary and vital extension of the educational process, not merely
as a repair service to the process. The need for adult education
cannot be eliminated by improvements in the school system; rather,
the cultivation in the schools of better attitudes toward learning
can lead more and more people to embark on lifelong education.

This is true because no education that has a terminal point can
ever fully meet all the needs of life, whether the terminal point is
reached at fourteen, eighteen, twenty-two, or twenty-six. Ideally,
the person who has completed his schooling, no matter at what
level, should be so thoroughly imbued with a sense of the need for
elaborating his education that he will unfailingly continue it on
his own. This would be self-education, the kind that has supported
numerous careers of great distinction, and perhaps the best kind
of adult education. Experience has demonstrated, however, that
little reliance can be placed on self-education as far as the generality
of men are concerned. Many adults find it more profitable to satisfy
their need for education in association with their fellows, whether
formally or informally. They turn to adult education of one or
another variety.

Those who have thought most deeply about the contemporary
situation are convinced that the need for adult education was never
greater than it is today. The reason is simple: It has rarely been
more obvious that the future of mankind depends upon the decisions of those now adult. To make these decisions soundly will
require knowledge, and beyond knowledge, wisdom. At any and
all levels of thought and action, adults today can hardly be expected to manage with what has survived from their school days.
To broaden, deepen, supplement, and elaborate their knowledge
and to put them in the way of being wise is the largest and highest
task of adult education. Success at it will do more than guarantee
survival; it will guarantee that those who win through will emerge
at a higher level of understanding than is today common.

Let us now look at the historical background of adult education.
It is suggested that adult education is not finally understandable
apart from the education of adults—that the general intellectual
climate in its successive historical changes has conditioned adult

education. It is obviously impossible to sketch the changes in intellectual climate in this book, so only token indications of the changes are here offered. It is impossible because to do so would require a book many times as long as this one; moreover, since most of what has been written about past intellectual climates is largely the history of climates experienced by the high intelligentsia, its relevance to the climates known to average, common, wayfaring men is not at all certain. Certainly it is elementary that there has always been a cultural gap between the two groups. One way of trying to close the gap has been by the diffusion of knowledge; and one way of diffusing knowledge has been through schemes for adult education.

We know too little about the mechanisms of culture-diffusion in complex civilizations to be absolutely certain about how culture moves from the culture-creators to the intelligentsia and then to the wayfaring men. The intellectual history of our segment of humanity is in its entirety a story of what adults have thought and said about the human condition, about the material environment of humanity, and sometimes about what should be done to improve or change the one, or more effectively to understand and control the other. Our concern here is not with the story of man's thinking, talking, and writing at this high level, but rather with how wayfaring men have come by the knowledge and understanding they have needed in their lives, with specific attention to adult education as one of the possible mechanisms.

PART II

ADULT EDUCATION

HAS DEEP ROOTS

CHAPTER

2

Preliterate Man Leads the Way

ALTHOUGH MAN has spent more time on this planet as an illiterate
than as a literate, the accomplishments of preliterate man are often
overlooked. If we are to gain any worth-while historical perspective
on adult education, a brief glance at them is necessary. We should
at least revive our appreciation of the point that it was while men
were innocent of letters that they established their character as
learners and discovered the advantages and at least some of the
basic techniques of transmitting knowledge.

The methods of dealing with traditional knowledge, innovations,
and borrowings are known to anthropologists by the terms *enculturation* and *acculturation*. Enculturation is the process by which
man achieves competence in his own culture. It is not, says Herskovits, "terminated at the close of infancy. As an individual continues through childhood and adolescence to achieve adult status,
he is continuously exposed to this process of learning, which can
be said to end only with his death." [1] Here we have an idea basic
in all thought about adult education: that education should be a
lifelong process. Acculturation is defined by Herskovits as "the
study of cultural transmission in process" when the transmission
is from one culture to another rather than within a single culture.
Enculturation and acculturation between them cover most of the

21

22

ground we know as education, including adult education. They have, of course, been going on for untold ages. They still go on today.

How impressive a success preliterate man was can be illustrated by a cursory glance at the accomplishments of Neolithic man, the immediate precursor of literate man. Specialists speak of the "Neolithic Revolution" as at least as impressive as the "Industrial Revolution" of modern times. Basically, it was a substitution of systematic food production for food gathering. Men began to plant and cultivate edible grasses, roots, and trees; and either simultaneously or fairly closely in time, to domesticate animals. This led to the establishment of small agricultural villages and to the sedentary, as contrasted with the nomadic, life. In the villages the crafts developed: carpentry (with the wheel as its greatest prehistoric triumph), pottery making, and the production of textiles. Lore gathered around agriculture and the crafts and was accumulated and transmitted from generation to generation. A rudimentary commerce developed between the villages, and the benefits and difficulties of culture-contacts were experienced.

The rate of progress achieved by Neolithic man between 6000 and 3000 B.C. was by far the most rapid in human history up to that time. From the standpoints of creation and assimilation, this was a most remarkable demonstration of man's educability. The basic work in invention and innovation was done by adults and the original assimilation of the creative changes was by adults. Only when the changes had been thoroughly accepted by adults did they become embodied in the culture passed on to the children. The role of the adult in cultural change—or "progress"—is therefore central.

Man's story for the next five thousand years is basically an account of how he has dealt with the problem of social living in all its multifarious aspects. Since the efforts to manage the human adventure have been made by adults and the adults have been mostly average wayfaring men, how they gained access to the cumulating knowledge is a matter of vital importance to our comprehension of the extraordinary story.

Unfortunately, the principle is easier to state than to illustrate from the historical record. Until the late eighteenth century it is hardly possible to identify and discuss institutions which, by intent, were designed for the education of adults. Adult education has its roots far back in history, but it got its present general shape during the last two centuries under the conditions of industrial society. In all the earlier centuries it was rarely thought of self-consciously. Rather it appears to have been left to the operation of those forces at large in society at all times and places which tend to form the minds of mature people. It is not until we come to the Greeks that we have much to consider that directly bears upon adult education as it is thought of today. From the Greek period to the nineteenth century, it is possible to identify and discuss a very few innovations that are both interesting and relevant to modern concerns.

In the period before the Greeks, attention will be given to certain aspects of the great civilizations of the Nile and Tigris-Euphrates valleys. These river-valley civilizations, based upon peasant agriculture, irrigation, and the working of metals, were among the first to develop an economic surplus—a surplus of goods and services from which persons not directly engaged in production could draw their support. Those able to appropriate a portion of the surplus gained the leisure necessary to cultural pursuits. This leisure was available chiefly to city-dwelling priestly, administrative, commercial, and intellectual groups—a small minority of the total population and, culturally speaking, apparently divided from the masses of the people by an even wider gap than existed in later societies. These river-valley societies are said to have been literate after about 3000 B.C., but they were so only in the sense that relatively small groups within them were capable of making written records.

The art of writing first appeared in Mesopotamia and spread from there to Egypt and the Indus Valley. (Systems of writing were also devised independently in China, Central America, and elsewhere.) It developed to meet the needs of the account-keepers in the temples. Mesopotamian agriculture was largely under the control of the priesthood. The land was the property of the heavenly hierarchy and was managed by its earthly representatives. The management involved record-keeping on a large scale. The society was dominated by middle-class conceptions and the sense of private property was acute, as is shown in the Code of Hammurabi of

2100 B.C. Putting together the available facts, Professor E. A. Speiser of the University of Pennsylvania has speculated that "writing was not a deliberate invention but the incidental by-product of a strong sense of private property." [2] In dealings with the temples, as well as between private individuals, goods were marked with personal devices by using cylinder seals. The account-keepers could, by examining the seal marks, credit the goods to the proper accounts. Out of such operations a system of writing developed.

The script developed in Mesopotamia was cuneiform and was impressed on clay tablets which have proved remarkably durable. The overwhelming bulk of the tablets thus far found deal with economic transactions, not only because the temple records deal mostly with such matters, but also because the most numerous class to achieve literacy after the clerical and civil government workers was the trading class. This class was larger and more powerful in the Mesopotamian civilizations than in Egypt and it is thought to have been the dominant class in the Harappā civilization of the Indus Valley. Literacy thus spread most widely where a large trading class developed, for this class early discovered writing to be useful in keeping accounts and conducting communications. Therefore, if Professor Speiser's speculation is correct, we can argue that the economic motive was powerful in beginning the spread of literacy. It was the business class which later encouraged the development of an alphabetic mode of writing, and it is altogether appropriate that the earliest alphabetic script was devised in Phoenicia, a trading center par excellence.

In these early civilizations, literacy reached neither the craftsmen nor the peasantry. Crafts could be transmitted only by direct instruction under an apprenticeship system and provisions governing apprenticeship were included in the Code of Hammurabi. Crafts were spread by the migration of the workmen themselves, either voluntarily or as prisoners of war. Technical knowledge was not exportable apart from the individual possessing it. The failure to apply the new literacy to the crafts—really a failure to direct any of the best-trained minds to the problems of technology —led to the slowing down of the rate of technological change, as compared with what had been achieved in the Neolithic age preceding, and accounts in part for the unprogressive nature of these societies.

The failure to spread literacy did not mean, however, that the elements of the culture failed to reach the ordinary wayfarers. Mores, folkways, and conceptions and practices on a higher level of consciousness are transmitted by methods even subtler than the written word. Acceptance of the pattern of culture of one's group is in large measure a matter of sub-literary habituation.

Traditions, lore, and facts, transmitted orally, have moulded the adult mind in all ages. Oral transmission of knowledge was the only method available to preliterate man and even after a literate elite developed, information and knowledge of the highest import long continued to be transmitted and dispersed by word of mouth. In Athens and Rome, where the percentage of literate citizens is believed to have been quite high, oral modes of communication (quite apart from lectures and discussions in formal education) played a very large role in adult education. This has continued to be true right down the ages. Few things can falsify more quickly one's sense of how wayfaring men have acquired their knowledge and information than neglect of the role of word-of-mouth communication even in eras and places of high literacy. Talk, both informal and purposive, is and always has been a pedagogical instrumentality of immense significance to adult man. To many adult minds, talk is the most significantly educative of all communications.

There are two additional points about these early civilizations to which special attention may profitably be directed. First, the civilizations of the Nile and the Tigris-Euphrates took a poor view of the nature of man, especially of the man who was not a member of the ruling group. Second, the characteristic mode of thought was such that it did not lend itself to education in any proper sense, but rather to indoctrination.

The ruling classes looked upon the individual man as of little or no importance in himself. The Egyptians looked upon men as the "cattle" of the gods, the Mesopotamians as the "slaves" of the gods—persons told off to do the dirty work of the gods' inscrutable scheme. By a simple extension of ideas, they were also the "cattle" or "slaves" of the very worldly civil authorities. Since the Egyptians developed a fairly high ethical sense, the Pharaohs, as "herdsmen" of the "cattle," did at times exhibit a sense of responsibility to their "cattle" and attempted to force their subordinates to show a comparable sense. In Mesopotamia, the Code of Hammurabi embodied the idea of justice as a right, not merely as a concession. But in both places idea and reality diverged. The fundamental rule of survival in both civilizations was unquestioning submission to authority. The wayfarer's lot was perhaps a bit more harsh in Mesopotamia than Egypt, because of the Mesopotamian emphasis on the role of force in the universe. In neither case was any provision made, either in theory or in practice, for the development among the masses of a civic consciousness or a sense of personal responsibility.

These peoples embodied their wisdom in myths. The possibility that man could penetrate the secrets of nature by the exercise of critical intelligence and experiment, and attain mastery over nature by such means, could not occur to men living in this kind of intellectual climate. Their minds looked, not for *how,* but for *who.* The universe, of which they conceived themselves to be inextricably a part, was run, not by impersonal, objectively assessable *forces,* but by anthropomorphized figures called gods. The myths of the doings of the gods—major and minor, good and bad—explained what happened in the observable universe. Therefore, knowledge of the gods was the indispensable basis for such understanding of the universe as men could hope to attain. The myths were not simply pleasant (or unpleasant) stories to beguile an idle hour, entertain children, or decorate literary creations; they were basic knowledge. But whose knowledge? Full knowledge of the myths was the peculiar privilege of the literate intelligentsia, especially the priests. The masses of the people understood them but crudely, only as they were symbolized, and perhaps narrated, in the great popular festivals.

It is obvious, therefore, that the indispensable conditions for anything resembling an adult education program aimed at average, wayfaring men were not present. It is axiomatic, surely, that a fairly high and optimistic view of man and his potentialities is needed as a foundation for education. It is also axiomatic that the development of judgment and critical powers is basic to successful education. If the one is absent because the prevailing view of man contradicts it, and the others because the prevailing mode of thinking precludes their development, adult education is unlikely, if not impossible.

Before turning to the Greeks, among whom some of the pre-conditions first developed, a glance at the Hebrews is necessary, chiefly to make the point that the teaching emphasis is conspicuous in the great religions of history. Religious teaching has ordinarily been addressed in the first instance to adults. Moses was certainly a teacher, transmitting to the people the Ten Commandments and a considerable body of law besides. So also were the great prophets whose exhortations are so conspicuous an element in the Old Testament. The same is true, later on, of Jesus and his disciples and great successors, like Paul, and of all Paul's successors in the never ending task of adapting Christianity to the exigencies of time and place.

The great religions have been motivated as powerfully as one can imagine by the wish, on the giving side, to guide men to salvation and, on the receiving side, to attain salvation. Once established, the teaching emphasis has remained constant, whether its expression has been formalized ritual, pulpit oratory, missionary activities, the construction of vast and intricate systems of theology, or the composition of popular "books of faith and power." Any or all of these may be thought of as adult education, and surely it requires only the saying of it to recall that a primary objective of almost all religions has been to reach the average man. From the historical standpoint, the importance of religious instruction, and religiously motivated instruction, in adult education cannot be overstated.

The Greeks on the Educated Adult

THE GREEKS believed, as Sophocles put it, that of all the many wonders in the world "none is more wonderful than man." Their central intellectual concern was the full realization of the potentialities of man. They believed that the universe was a moral universe and that the great questions of life were in essence moral. The answers to the questions were to be sought by the untrammeled operation of the mind, proceeding by free questioning and fearless criticism.

Their preoccupation was with the achievement of moral excellence, but it was not, they thought, to be gained through changes and adjustments in the material environment. Rather it was to be sought in knowledge and understanding of the individual person. "Know thyself."

Two Greek words taken together—*areté* and *moira*—convey much of the Greek outlook. *Areté* ("excellence"), says Werner Jaeger in *Paideia*, was "the central idea of all Greek culture." [1] Excellence could be of many kinds. Socrates said it was excellence of soul. *Moira*, often rendered as "fate," really referred to the "fixed order of the universe." J. B. Bury writes, "It was this order which kept things in their places, assigned each [including man] its proper sphere and function."

28

What Greeks may be considered to have shared in the intellectual adventures which followed the discovery of man and freedom
of thought? In this respect, as in others, the Greek city-states
differed markedly from one another, Athens from Thebes, Corinth
from Sparta. There was also a contrast between town and country.
Most of the Greeks we hear about were urban intellectuals. We
know there was a gap between what the intellectuals believed and
what the common citizens believed—in the sphere of religion, for
instance—and that demagogues were quite capable of exploiting
it. It was this petard that hoisted Socrates. We know what is meant
by the statement, "to turn from the civilized perfection of Sophocles
and Plato to Greek life in the raw is to experience something like
a mental dislocation." [2] We know, of course, that Greek intellectuals took a critical view of common men who followed what they
were pleased to call mean occupations. These people they considered to be mean people who thought meanly because their work
left no time for the life of the mind. Worse off still were the slaves,
to whom few Greeks gave any very sympathetic thought. Aristotle
dismissed them as mere animated machines. A surprising proportion of the people either lived in places, or followed occupations,
or occupied positions in society which made it unnecessary for
anybody to concern himself to any degree with their intellectual
and moral condition. Classical Greek culture was the creation of
a small leisure class of upper- and middle-class origin. Only those
who also had some leisure could freely share in it.

It is believed that a high percentage of the citizens of Athens
were literate. What the situation was in the other Greek cities is
not clear, but it can be assumed that Athens was the most advanced.
In Athens there were schools; state regulations about the responsibilities of parents for schooling dated back to the laws of Solon.
Elementary education consisted of letters, music, and gymnastics.
Neither the elementary schools nor the higher schools were state
supported; they were state-regulated private enterprises dependent
upon fees. The state paid the fees of sons of men killed in battle.
Elementary education was widespread, but more elaborate training was progressively limited by the economic resources of the
parents. Higher education was available. The Sophists were famous
suppliers of it. What they offered was sharply criticized, by Soc-

rates, for example. Skepticism about the quality of education currently offered has a very long tradition.

The existence of a large business class in Athens, Corinth, and other Greek cities makes it certain that basic literacy was supported widely by the economic motive. The high culture of Greece was founded upon lively commercial activity. The relatively high standard of living is inexplicable without a recognition of the central contribution of the business classes, for the natural resources of Greece were extremely meager. International trade made possible the Greece of culture-history. It was impossible to carry on the widely ramifying import-export trade of Greece without easy methods of record-making and communications. Like all business classes, the Greek developed a jargon of its own—*Koine.* This was widely spread through the eastern Mediterranean in the wake of the conquests of Alexander the Great. The New Testament was written in *Koine,* not classical Greek.

The Greeks used books, known to them as bibles, which were handwritten on papyrus or parchment. There were bookshops in Athens and books were hawked in the theater by the remote ancestors of the "news butchers" on our trains. Libraries, however, were either strictly personal possessions or located in private institutions. No public library was established in Athens until the time of the Roman Emperor Hadrian (117–138 A.D.) Books played a much lesser role in adult education than the spoken word.

The mild climate allowed the Greeks to spend most of their time out of doors. As a notably sociable people, they thoroughly enjoyed conversation; in the hands of a genius like Socrates talk became a fine art. In Athens and some of the other cities the citizens obtained much of their education from talk in the market place, colonnade, gymnasium, the law courts, or the political assembly, at the theater, at the public recitals of Homer and other literary readings, and at religious ceremonies. Talk was the "breath of life" to the Greeks, not because they especially delighted in idle chatter, like some fantastic nation of indefatigable gossips, but because they chiefly learned by oral communication and liked to discuss what they learned as they learned it. Adult Greeks were educated by the spoken word.

Let us tick off some of the ways in which the Greeks were educated orally, aside from general conversation:

1. *Public Recitals of Homer.* Homer was the "Bible of the Greeks." All through Greek history from the time of the tyrant Pisistratus (about 560 B.C.), who made Homeric recitations a feature of the Panathenaic festival, Homer was a basic element in the education of the Greeks, not really displaced until the Christian Bible began to be widely read. Homer, says Werner Jaeger, "is the first and greatest creator and shaper of Greek life and character." The reciting of Homer aloud for public audiences was not only a custom; it was a recognized profession. The Greeks, whether literate or not, were familiar with Homer and his teachings.

2. *Tragedy and Comedy.* The tragedies and comedies first came to the knowledge of the people through their public production in annual dramatic competitions. Writers on Greek tragedy point out its educative effect along the lines sketched above in dealing with idea of the moral universe. The comedies, too, had an educative effect.

3. *Literature in General.* T. W. Hall points out in *A Companion to Classical Texts:* "The literature of early times in Greece was not composed in order to be read. It was composed for recitation in public or private and consisted essentially of the spoken word." [3] Public reading of literary compositions was a regular practice throughout Greek history and was taken up by the Romans. In the introduction to his *Greek Historical Thought,* Arnold J. Toynbee writes:

> Where "write" and "writer" or "read" and "reader" occur in the English translation, the English reader must not forget that "recite" and "composer" or "hear" and "hearer" are generally the equivalents in the Greek. Oral transmission was a more natural method of communicating the contents of a literary work in a society in which the reproduction of copies was a slower and more costly business than it has latterly been in the West since the comparatively recent introduction of printing. From Herodotus' day to Simocatta's a public recital to a select audience by the author himself was the ordinary method of publication. [4]

4. *Politics.* The knowledge, experience, and understanding of the mature citizens were supposed to be brought to focus in carrying out political duties. All a man learned, or failed to learn, found

expression in his contribution to the management of public affairs. In an important sense, the political records of the Greek democracies are indices to the success or failure of Greek adult education. A study of the record from this point of view would tell us much about the kinds of issues that were met by the Greeks with wisdom or stupidity and the conditions and leadership under which they were met. We know that Greek democracy had tremendous successes; we know also that it had appalling failures; and we know that in the long run it collapsed and disappeared.

5. *Religion.* Greek religion was without a sacred book, theological dogma, a corporate ecclesiastical organization, or a closed community of priests. There was, however, a close relationship between worship and the symbolisms of glory and power of the cities. While Greek governments were secular, they commanded religious support. The religious observances and ceremonies would appear to have enforced upon the minds of ordinary citizens the reality of the existence of the officially recognized gods. They thus enforced the same point of view as animated the tragic dramas.

6. *Things seen.* While we must not suppose that the average Greek was perpetually environed by great art, he nevertheless had numerous opportunities to see a good deal of it. Recalling that Greek art was characterized by its humanism, simplicity, balance and measure, naturalism, and idealism, it is a reasonable supposition that the art and architecture the Greek saw conveyed to him a reinforcement of the belief in these qualities he had gained by other means. He was thus educated visually along the same lines in which he was educated orally.

The Greeks are usually credited with being the founders of Western science. What knowledge they borrowed from the Egyptians and the Mesopotamians they "transmuted." While this is not the place for an exposition of Greek science, a few words must be said of the place of the mechanic arts in education. Herodotus says in Book II of his history:

I have remarked that the Thracians, the Scyths, the Persians and Lydians, and almost all other barbarians, hold the citizens who practice trade, and their children, in less repute than the rest, while they esteem as noble those who keep aloof from handicrafts, and especially honour such as are given wholly to war. These ideas prevail throughout the whole of Greece, particularly among the Lacedaemonians. Corinth is the place where mechanics are least despised.

The craftsmen were held in low esteem because, by reason of their occupations, they were unable to devote themselves to achieving the kind of *areté* most valued by the intellectuals and because they were physically unfitted to serve in the armies. They were, it was thought, debarred by the nature of their status and occupations from becoming ideal citizens. Very often they were slaves. The craftsmen were men largely without honor in Greek society and their preoccupations were given small attention by the intellectuals. What the craftsmen had to know to do their work was not regarded as true education. This point of view, not unheard of today, makes it completely understandable why vocational education, or the teaching of the mechanic arts, was largely left to an oral tradition peculiar to the craftsmen themselves.

There are at least four great documents which are not only basic to an understanding of education as the Greeks, at their best, conceived it, but also basic to one's thinking about adult education at any time. These are, in order of time, Homer's great epic poems, the celebrated funeral oration by Pericles, certain books of Plato's *Republic,* and the first book of Aristotle's *Ethics*. Homer's place has been indicated. To complete the record a quick look at the others is in order. To the discussion of the documents will be added a short statement of the significance of the work of a great teacher who, as far as we know, wrote nothing, namely Socrates.

Pericles' funeral oration, reported or reconstructed by Thucydides, was delivered in 431 B.C. at the end of the first year of the Peloponnesian War. That war was to last twenty-seven years, with interludes of uneasy peace, and in the end destroy the very society which Pericles was either eulogizing or portraying as an ideal toward which to strive. We must view the speech as a favorable report on, or ideal of, a society which was about to pass away.

The basis of Athenian greatness, said Pericles, was its democratic constitution under which the administration favored the welfare of the many, not the few, and under which also a career in the public service was open to all men of talent, regardless of their economic background. As the government was founded on the idea of freedom, so the social life of the people was characterized by mutual respect and tolerance. Out of their freedom the Athenians drew their happiness; and they sustained their freedom-supported happiness by their valor.

Athenians cultivated and celebrated certain virtues, conspicuous among which were refinement ("without extravagance"), thought ("without effeminacy"), courage, sense of duty, and sense of honor. An education, also founded in freedom, supported these virtues. There was no regimentation in Athens, nor any of that ridiculously over-severe discipline favored by the enemy Spartans. It was not a disgrace to be poor, but it was a disgrace not to struggle against poverty. However, the purpose of wealth was use, not accumulation. No citizen was supposed to be so preoccupied with private business that he had no time left for public business. Those who failed correctly to apportion their time were adjudged "useless." But the jaded mind must have its refreshment, and Athens provided for this. "We celebrate games and sacrifices all the year round, and the elegance of our private establishments forms a daily source of pleasure and helps to banish the spleen." (Oddly enough, Pericles is not reported as making any reference to recitals of Homer, performances of tragedies or comedies, or to "things seen," to the latter of which he made, of course, striking contributions.)

Under these conditions, Pericles asserted, the average Athenian was able to judge public issues soundly. Best in judgment were fathers who saw not only their own interests, but bethought themselves of the future in which their children must live. They achieved a nice balance in their decisions between daring and deliberation, after a full discussion of alternatives. They always sought to be fair, generous, and just. But even that citizen whose ordinary conduct stopped short of ideal could redeem himself in battle. Every true Athenian, Pericles said, was always ready to meet "legitimate danger," and there was "justice in the claim that steadfastness in his country's battles should be as a cloak to cover a man's other imperfections; since the good action was blotted out by the bad, and his merit as a citizen more than outweighed his demerits as an individual." Happy is the man who dies in the military service of his country, or, as Horace put it for the Romans, *Dulce et decorum est pro patria mori.*

Such was the ideal citizen of Pericles. Athens, he insisted, was "the school of Hellas," and no better man could be expected than the graduate of that school. All the more tragic, then, that this ideal man, or ideal of man, was about to perish in the holocaust of war, never to rise again in quite the shape envisioned.

Socrates (*ca.* 470–399 B.C.) is described by Jaeger as "the greatest teacher in European history." As he was concerned exclusively with the teaching of adults, he must, on this evaluation, rank as the greatest adult educator of all time. As Socrates was a nonwriting teacher—a great and valuable kind currently shockingly underestimated in the American academic community—our knowledge of him is derived from what has been said of him by others, notably Plato and Xenophon.

As a young man Socrates is reported to have been keenly interested in science, especially mathematics, astronomy, and medicine, as well as ethical issues; but finding the fields a confusion of conflicting systems, the exponents of each able to demonstrate the error of all others without nevertheless being able to demonstrate the correctness of their own outlook, he became disillusioned. He did not become an opponent of such studies but a critic of the failure to establish a method which would lead to the discovery of firm truths. Socrates, therefore, felt driven to seek a method of inquiry better than any of which he had knowledge.

As a mature man, which is how he is most fully reported to us, Socrates' interest was in man as an individual and a social being. He was now chiefly interested in discovering how man can achieve *areté*. Man needed to do so to assure himself a happy life. It was also indispensable to politics, for the rulers of men should themselves possess it and should use their power to promote the conditions for excellence in others. Socrates sought to establish the "moral predicates" on which excellence of soul could be based.

This strange-looking man, "stout and not tall, with prominent eyes, snub nose, broad nostrils and wide mouth," pursued his inquiries not in formal lecture halls or fashionable drawing rooms, though he appeared and was welcome in both, but mostly out of doors in the market place, or the gymnasium. He was a city man by inclination, saying, "The fields and trees will not talk to me; it is only the human beings in the city that will." Talk was his peculiar

métier. But not idle talk, nor pointless argument, nor imbecile
wrangles, nor undirected exploration of issues. It was highly disciplined talk, though often disguised by what we would call "clown-
ing," aimed always at eliciting those "moral predicates" on which
he hoped to found excellence of soul. Professor A. E. Taylor
describes his method:

> . . . he resolved henceforth to consider primarily not "facts"
> but . . . the "statements" or "propositions" we make about
> them. His method should be to start with whatever seemed
> the most satisfactory "hypothesis," or postulate, about a given
> subject, and to consider the consequences which follow from
> it. So far as these consequences prove to be true and con-
> sistent, the "hypothesis" may be regarded as provisionally
> confirmed; if they are false or mutually inconsistent it is dis-
> credited. But it must be a strict rule of method not to confuse
> inquiry into the consequences of the "hypothesis" with proof
> of its truth. If the question of its truth is raised, the issue can
> only be settled by deducing the initial "hypothesis" as a
> consequence from some more ultimate "hypothesis" which
> both parties to the dispute are content to accept.[5]

Or, in the simpler terms of J. B. Bury, "His teaching always took
the form of discussion; the discussion often ended in no positive
result but had the effect of showing that some received opinion
was untenable and that truth is difficult to ascertain." [6] Socrates
called his method *dialectic,* "a name which properly means the
method of 'conversation.' "

> The thought which explains the use of the name is that truth
> has to be reached by dint of dialogue, or debate, which may
> be carried on between two inquirers, or also within the heart
> of a single inquirer, as his "soul" questions itself and answers
> its own questions. The truth, which is not to be discovered
> by any direct inspection of "facts," may be beaten out in the
> critical confrontation of rival interpretations of them. It comes,
> when it comes, as the conclusion to a debate.[7]

This procedure has been known ever since as the Socratic method.
Socrates gave a new direction to philosophical inquiry. He directed
men's attention to a close examination of their assumptions, ex-

pressed or unexpressed, conscious or unconscious. By examining all assumptions with unprecedented pertinacity, Socrates showed men what ramshackle ideas had, to the moment of their encounter with him, guided their lives.

This great man went about his peculiar business chiefly from 430 to 399 B.C., or from his fortieth to his seventieth year. He was thus most active during the years of the Peloponnesian War. As the war drew to an end, Athens was at a very low point indeed, with social passions running high. The resurgent democrats were determined to discredit their opponents—a familiar enterprise in troubled times. Socrates was haled into court and charged with corrupting the young, as well as "neglect of the gods whom the city worships and the practice of religious novelties." He was convicted by 280 votes to 220. A sentence of death was passed upon him by an even larger majority, for he had shown neither fear nor contrition, but rather a disposition to reiterate his principles. A month later he drank the cup of hemlock as the law prescribed, and so passed from the earthly scene "the greatest teacher in European history," victim of the very forces he had sought to bring under control.

Plato (ca. 427–347 B.C.) was a close associate of Socrates during the last decade of the latter's life and chief conservator of his reputation. He was forty years Socrates' junior.

A man of outstanding literary gifts, Plato devised the so-called Socratic dialogue as his chosen literary vehicle. Socrates figures as a participant in the dialogues and in certain instances is believed to express his own views, while in others he is thought to express Plato's views. Our interest in this is simply that the Platonic dialogues are superlative examples of adult education in written form. Professor Taylor points out that Plato's associates learned his thinking by word of mouth in the lectures he delivered at his famous Academy. The dialogues, on the other hand, were "addressed to the educated public at large"; they were, in short, popularizations of a very high order of excellence; and they were devices for adult education. (It should be remembered, however, that the "educated public at large" was not identical with "wayfaring men" in Greek society, nor has it been in any other. Plato's dialogues were high-level adult education when written and have remained so.)

Plato felt that reading was a poor incentive to thinking and he therefore never attempted a systematic treatise on his philosophy. He felt that philosophy was "the actual life of a mind engaged in the quest for truth," and that mere perusal of authoritative texts, allegedly containing truths, was but a shadow of actuality. The dialogues were marvelous by-products of his life as a thinker; they were designed to introduce educated adults to the questions and lines of inquiry in which Plato was interested by employing a sophisticated form which is highly sublimated talk.

Plato had ideas bearing directly on adult education, both negative and positive. He thought of education, at least for men and women at the highest social levels, as a lifelong process; he emphasized that in his opinion some subjects could profitably be studied only by mature men and women, not by adolescents; and he strongly advocated that all education be guided by, and toward the realization of, an ideal. His ideal has been lucidly summarized by Professor Taylor as follows:

Man's life is a perpetual search for something he has not got, though without it he can never be at peace with himself. This something is "the good for man," "that which would make any man's life happy," if only he had the fruition of it. If most men live and die without knowing what true happiness is, the reason is not that they do not desire it—at heart they never desire anything else—but that they look for it in the wrong place. They confuse it with the round of pleasures, with health and long life, with worldly wealth, or with that irresponsible power which, by lifting its possessor above all law enables him always to "do as he likes." But satisfaction is not to be found in any of these things. The pursuit of pleasures is self-defeating, and those who get most of them find that in the end they bring very little of what they promised; "excitement" really has more of the bitter in it than the sweet. It is not the having of strength, long life, health, wealth, but the right use of them which makes a man happy. "Doing what you like" is the most wretched life of all; it is because the "autocrat, who is above all law," always does as he likes that he never gets what all men's hearts are set upon. The ultimate source of human unhappiness is thus not "unpropitious circumstance" but the inner division of the soul, the conflict of "passion" which prompts us always to do as we like, with judgment, which bids us aim at true felicity. No one ever would choose anything because he saw that it was bad for him; we choose what is bad for us; and so are unhappy, because we mistake it for good. Sin is thus the real cause of misery, and the source of sin is ignorance and error, the mistaking of evil for good. Hence the need of "philosophy" for the direction of life; the whole object of philosophy is to lead us into a sure and abiding knowledge of good and evil, and so to make our judgment, and the conduct which ensues from it, sound, and to restore the soul to health and unity with itself.

Philosophy is, as Socrates had called it, the art of the "tendance of the soul," and the chief reason for prizing even the most "abstract" science is not that it amuses our curiosity, but that it is a discipline in thinking which makes us fit to judge rightly of good and evil.

Philosophy, then, delivers us from sin by delivering us from false judgment and guiding us to a true estimate of the various kinds of good. There are three main kinds, goods of fortune, goods of the body, goods of the soul. Philosophy teaches us that a man's soul is the most precious thing about him, because it is most peculiarly himself; the body, again, is more truly myself than any of my belongings. Hence the rule of right judgment is that the best of all goods is goodness of soul, virtue, and wisdom; goodness of body comes only second, and the "goods of fortune" third. A sound judgment will always prefer virtue to health or strength and these to mere wealth or rank or power. . . . But Plato is no enemy of human pleasure. He is fully prepared to argue the point that, even by the rules of the calculus of pleasure and pain, if you formulate the rules correctly and work the sum right, the life of the man who puts the soul first, the body second, and "fortune" only third, will prove to be the most truly agreeable as well as the most noble. He is at special pains to establish this result because, as he says, it is not gods but men whom we want to enlist on the side of right living, and so we must make allowance for the universal human desire for pleasurable existence.[8]

The ideal Plato formulated, in spite of the fact that he himself reserved its realization to a minority of the people, is a permanently significant ideal in adult education. Unluckily for clarity, it is mixed up with other ideas and ideals that tend to confuse the issue. Among other things, Plato believed that the state should be the educator, not merely the supporter of education. This idea is unacceptable to modern democrats, for it savors of totalitarianism. But it is nevertheless beyond question that Plato raised some of the central issues of education and that his general conclusions still demand the closest study.

Aristotle (384–322 B.C.) was born fifteen years after the death of Socrates, when Plato was forty-three years old. For twenty years, from the age of eighteen to the age of thirty-eight, Aristotle was associated with Plato's Academy, first as student, then as teacher. He left it only when Plato died. After some years away from Athens, during which he was for a time tutor of Alexander the Great, Aristotle returned to Athens and in 335 B.C. established his own institution of higher learning, the Lyceum. Plato had then been dead for twelve years.

It is extremely interesting that, while Plato is known today chiefly through the survival of the works he addressed to the educated general public, Aristotle is known chiefly through his lecture notes, which survived, and that *his* works addressed to the educated general public—also in the form of dialogues—perished. We know, then, that these great thinkers were all keenly interested in reaching the educated general public, Socrates by word of mouth alone, Plato and Aristotle by literary works calculated to teach it how to discuss great issues with profit.

All, too, had a closely similar aim with regard to what they wanted to teach adults. They aimed at teaching men—specifically, citizens in the Greek definition—how to achieve the highest "good," the basis of happiness, the only secure foundation of the state. For adult educators, perhaps the most indispensable document by Aristotle in this connection is *Nicomachean Ethics,* especially Book I.[9] As Aristotle put it:

... human good turns out to be activity of soul in accordance with virtue, and if there are more than one virtue, in accordance with the best and most complete.

But we must add "in a complete life." For one swallow does not make a summer, nor does one day; and so too one day, or a short time, does not make a man blessed and happy.

Of happiness he declared:

Happiness then is the best, noblest, and most pleasant thing in the world, and these attributes are not severed as in the inscription at Delos: *Most noble is that which is justest, and best is health; but pleasantest is to win what we love.*

For all these properties belong to the best activities; and these, or one—the best—of these, we identify with happiness.

... some identify happiness with good fortune, though others identify it with virtue.

... happiness seems, however, even if it is not god-sent but comes as a result of virtue and some process of learning or training, to be among the most godlike things; for that which is the prize and end of virtue seems to be the best thing in the world, and something godlike and blessed.

The investigation of these problems was, to Aristotle, differentiated from the exact sciences by the methods employed and the degree of precision achieved in the results. But he nevertheless formulated quite clearly the ideal he had in mind. It has been succinctly stated by the distinguished Aristotelian, Professor John L. Stocks:

... the problem of conduct ... Its solution is goodness of character, an established discipline which is in love with itself and continuously achieves its own reproduction through every change of circumstance. This achievement is its consistent purpose, the ruling consideration to which all others—of pleasure, wealth, honor, or the most precious results of man's productive skill—are strictly subordinated: it is itself the happiness which men are said to seek; for it is welcomed for itself and never for anything it may bring with it, while it is

independent so far as the human can be, of the favor of man
and circumstance. The various facets of this disciplined character are the familiar virtues—courage, temperance, gen-
erosity, and the rest—each of which stands for its happy
mastery over a particular kind of emotion or situation.

. . . .

. . . success depends on a quantitative adjustment of materials
with reference to time, place, and situation; that the product
as a whole attains its characteristic perfection so far as each
ingredient avoids excess and defect and exhibits a neutral or
mean quantity.

It is this Law of the Mean that is the secret of the virtuous
discipline.[10]

As for his fellows, so for Aristotle also, the questions of who
studied what and at what time of life were to be determined, not
by individual whim, but by the state. He mentions that some subjects should not be studied by some people at all—not necessarily
only those young in years, but those of any age who were inferior
in discipline. He also felt that some classes of persons—craftsmen
and merchants, for example—were not worthy of higher education
of any kind. But for those he was willing to educate, he advocated
an all-round education, because it produced the best balanced
man.

With Aristotle the great age of the Greek thinkers came to an
end. The kind of social-political world Aristotle, like his fellows,
envisaged as ideal for man perished with Alexander the Great.
Nor was Aristotle's personal fate a happy one. All his years in
Athens he lived there as a foreigner, subject to the disabilities that
status implied. The Athenians intensely disliked the outlook and
activities (and the consequences of both) of Alexander the Great,
Aristotle's erstwhile pupil. In the year 321 Aristotle, then over
sixty, left Athens because it was rumored he was to be prosecuted
for impiety. The suspicion is that he, like Socrates before him, was
really to be prosecuted for political guilt-by-association—in
Aristotle's case, association with the Macedonians. At any rate,
Aristotle fled, and within twelve months he died.

The Greek story shows conclusively that worth-while adult education must be based upon a reasonably optimistic view of man and his potentialities and upon freedom of the mind and spirit. The Greeks discovered the way out of the trap in which earlier civilizations had been caught. But they failed, nevertheless, to face the problem of how to educate all wayfaring men. They concentrated on citizens, as they specifically defined them, and often merely on the minority of citizens who would probably hold high political office, neglecting or excluding various large categories of persons within the community. Their answer to the question, "Who shall be educated?" was narrow. Within their special focus of interest, they clearly formulated ideals of moral excellence which they believed were the necessary foundation of happiness. Education was to serve this end and was to be lifelong. The favored method was discussion. The content was, of course, humanistic, not vocational or, least of all, technological.

4

Rome: A Problem in Cultural Diffusion

T HE ROMAN pattern of an ideal adult man was based upon values appropriate to the farming life and the farmer-as-soldier. It was enforced by the discipline of family upbringing, by formal rituals of obeisance to the gods, both household and state, and by the usual social pressures. While the ideal Roman appeals to us today as rather a limited person, it cannot be denied that at his best he achieved greatness. The Roman virtues were often cogently stated and were verbally adhered to for centuries, but they were not consistently practiced by every Roman at any given time. Indeed, there were some Romans who never practiced them at all. In the end they disappeared in the cloud of dust we call "the fall of Rome," and were replaced by the very different Christian virtues.

The virtues the Romans admired were supposed to be implanted in the home and the ideal home was the rural home. We have here a paradox the Romans never resolved. They celebrated rural-rooted virtues, but their civilization found its highest expression in the cities. This paradox has existed more or less since civilization began; the Americans of today are not free from it. The Romans were inveterate founders of cities; and in their best days they succeeded well with urban life. Yet they never succeeded in reconciling urban life with virtues of rural origin and they managed to destroy the kind of rural life that promoted their prized virtues in the first place. They followed public policies which debased the free peasantry, plundered the land, and while driving the free-born Romans into the stews of the cities, peopled the countryside with slaves and barbarians. The Romans failed both to keep their idealized countryside within the orbit of their culture and to bring it unsullied to the displaced peasants who found refuge in the cities. Nevertheless, the Romans did succeed in spreading their culture over a wider geographical area and among a greater variety of peoples than any nation in history to that time—indeed, than any nation up to our own time. The trouble was that they spread it patchily, on the surface only.[1]

The Romans built up a society in which literacy was extremely common but not quite universal. We do not know what percentage of the people were literate, nor when, exactly, literacy became widespread (probably not until well after the Punic Wars), nor whether the proportion of literates fluctuated with social conditions, as seems very likely. There are good reasons for thinking that the builders, the barbers, the fruit dealers, the porters, the muleteers, the garlic dealers, and many of the soldiers were literate. Tradesmen such as these painted electioneering slogans on the walls of Pompeii. Commerce stimulated literacy. We know, too, that Varro suggested that the basic rules of a farm be written out and posted up for the workers to read. Inscriptions on public buildings and monuments, of which many thousands still survive, must have been made on the assumption that there was a wide reading public for them.

If literacy was common among tradesmen, it must have been just about universal in the middle ranks of society, and certainly universal in the higher ranks. The culturally pretentious were often literate in two languages, Latin and Greek. Jerome Carcopino states that by the second century A.D. "education was more widespread than ever before. For a long time illiteracy had been identified with barbarism in Rome and the Italian cities, and those who could not read nor write were an insignificant minority. At the end of the second century such men were only to be found in backward provinces."[2]

It does not appear, however, that the state assumed any direct

responsibility even for elementary education. Cicero could find
no compelling reason why it should. Some emperors, like Hadrian,
"encouraged" elementary education by granting teachers exemp-
tion from taxes when they were working in areas directly under
the emperor's control. Farther than this no Roman government
seems to have gone. Higher education, however, was better treated.

To meet the needs of a literate population the publishing industry
and bookshops were quite elaborately developed, especially in the
Imperial period. A speech by Cato or Cicero would be taken down
in shorthand, copied out, and widely circulated. Histories—very
popular reading—and poems were also regularly published. Man-
uals of instruction in farming, water supply, military training, etc.,
were issued—ancestors of the "how-to" books still today a staple
of the publishing trade. Pliny the Elder set a fashion of encyclo-
pedia-making that flourished into the succeeding Middle Ages and
has continued into our own time. However, the works of no single
Roman writer had the formative influence of those of Homer,
though a case for widespread influence could be made for the
writings of Cicero, Quintilian's *Institutes,* and Virgil's *Aeneid.*

As books became reasonably common in Rome, so also did
libraries, both private and public. The public baths, those immensely important facilities for social life in Rome and the provincial cities, almost invariably included a library consisting of special
rooms in the walls of which niches were hollowed out to hold
wooden chests in which the books were kept. Private libraries
then, as now, were often accumulated by the well-to-do for display
as much as for love of learning. In the later Imperial period there
were twenty-eight separate public libraries in Rome. There is,
however, no way of estimating what role they actually played
in adult education.

If the Romans were more addicted to reading books than the
Greeks were before Aristotle's time, they still depended to a great
extent on the spoken word for the communication of what we
today would normally read. The art of speechmaking, or rhetoric,
was very highly valued, and the spoken word in law courts and
political assemblies was a powerful educator. Moreover, manu-
scripts were usually given a trial run by being read before they
were published; "readings" by authors were fashionable events in
Rome, often staged with elaborate ceremony. Some of the well-to-

do had rooms especially designed for readings. The Emperor
Hadrian capped the system by providing a building exclusively
for the purpose. An *auditorium* provided space for a visible audience and also allowed room for a curtained-off retreat for those
who wished to listen without being seen. The author-reader sat
upon a dais and dressed for the occasion as impressively as he
could manage. If distinguished or fashionable authors were be-
sought to grace private auditoria, less favored writers could hire
rooms for readings, and truly desperate scribblers could stalk
possible audiences in the streets and the baths.[3] When the best
authors read, the educative intention was clearly foremost. It is
indicative of the importance attached to reading that the high
literature of Rome has a bias toward the kind of rhetoric which
is most effective when spoken.

The Roman theater was not as educative as the Greek. The
Romans produced no dramas as profoundly moving as the Greek
tragedies, none as important as adult experiences. Under the republic certain very popular stage productions had a definite
political slant, often critical in tone, which reflected public opinion;
but under the emperors these same popular dramas were turned
into propaganda vehicles by the Caesars. At the same time, Roman
high literature was also used as a vehicle for imperial propaganda.
No doubt the Caesars thought this propaganda was educational, a
confusion which victimizes so many people in our own time.

In touching upon the theater we raise the whole discouraging
question of the vulgarity of Roman pleasures. The comic dramatist
Terence, who has enjoyed a great reputation during subsequent
ages, was not popular with his contemporaries, who are alleged
to have preferred "tightrope walkers and gladiators" to his works.
Everyone is familiar with the expression "bread and circuses"
which Juvenal used to characterize the pap fed the Roman masses
to keep them quiet. The entertainment was not, however, devised
exclusively for the masses; rather they were admitted to spectacles
the classes had already contrived for their own amusement. Like
modern American movies, they were classless entertainment. The
Roman spectacles included gladiatorial combats, naked men and
women fighting wild beasts, chariot races, cheap theatricals—all
violent, frequently bloody, often bawdy, always vulgar. The masses
liked these things no less than the classes. Some of the most im-

pressive surviving Roman structures were built to house these spectacles. It was in attending such entertainments that the average Roman consumed his rather extensive leisure. Under the Antonine emperors the working day in Rome was seven hours in summer and six in winter. Most of the afternoon was free.

There were Romans, including some emperors, who shuddered at the vulgarity of the entertainments and tried in one way or another to clean them up. One device was to schedule the worst of them in the mornings when most of the people were at work, thus confining them to the well-to-do and the unemployed. But no emperor or other influential person seems to have understood that the leisure of the people might in some part have been employed for their education. This failure was, as Professor Carcopino says, a major error of judgment in view of the difficult problems the Romans eventually had to face and which they so signally failed to solve. The opportunity of turning leisure to account educationally was lost to the Romans by their failure to solve correctly a standing dilemma of our own times: how properly to balance entertainment and instruction in the regimen of men.

In Rome, and in the cities of the provinces, "things seen" were obviously of educative importance. The Romans themselves seem to have thought of them that way. This applies not only to the vast public buildings which the Romans were so fond of erecting but also to the sculptures which were judiciously placed in the baths, forums, and other public places where even casual visitors could see and ponder over them. Not only were Roman originals displayed, but the "loot" of the East found its way to them. The Romans were indefatigable collectors of Greek art. The great buildings, the sculptures, and other constructions like triumphal arches, commemorative columns (of which Trajan's Column is a supreme example), plaques, equestrian statues, forums, baths, coliseums, aqueducts, and even roads must surely have conveyed at least two ideas to the meanest of Roman minds: the grandeur of Roman society and the vastness of its power to bind space and defy time. That the Romans themselves had some appreciation of the effect of their constructions is made clear by the energy they expended in the making of them, even in the latter days of their greatness when the labor and capital might have been more wisely employed. As ruins, they have impressed men of all ages since.

As Roman power was extended over the Mediterranean world there was a parallel extension of Roman culture. Since the conquered peoples differed widely in cultural development, the Roman impact also differed both in degree and significance. It could hardly be the same in the sophisticated Hellenistic countries of the East and in the far less developed countries of the West. In the West, Rome meant law, order, trade, letters, material prosperity. In the East, the emphasis fell more heavily on law and order. The wide dispersion of a knowledge of the Latin language was itself deeply significant, for there was thus made available a vehicle for the circulation of learning and general ideas to a very wide variety of peoples.[4]

We have no evidence that the Romans ever self-consciously pursued a policy of Romanization, comparable in assimilative intent to the policies of certain modern nations. On the contrary, the Romans cultivated a tolerance of local cultures which allowed them to persist and, with Roman elements added, emerge as national cultures in the modern world. Indeed, elements of the local cultures—religious cults for example—rolled back on Rome, not always to its profit. Distinguished intellectuals of provincial origin—Cicero, Catullus, Virgil, Horace, Ovid, Livy, Tacitus, Pliny, Juvenal, Martial—became important figures at Rome and undoubtedly infused their work with alien cultural elements. The Romans were inveterate cosmopolitans, ever ready to assimilate new ideas regardless of origin. Nevertheless, whether by design or accident, they did achieve a measure of cultural universality in their dominions sufficiently strong to give the expression "the Roman world" a substantive meaning.

What they emphasized, or used unconsciously, as Romanizing agents were things we today regard as characteristically Roman. The agents were the army, the bureaucracy, the law (including citizenship), and the cities they founded or took over. When Rome was rising, these instrumentalities were in a healthy state and did their work well, but when it was declining, the corruption was reflected in them and they ceased to function properly. This can be illustrated by a series of generalizations which can readily be tested against the well-known facts of Roman history.

In the early days when thoroughly Romanized citizens served in the army, the Roman armies in newly conquered areas, or posted more or less permanently on the frontiers, were very important as setters of standards for the alien local populations. As the army was "barbarized" in later days by inclusion of all kinds of non-Roman mercenaries—both in the ranks and at the command level —this was no longer true. Most of the barbarians absorbed into the army were men of rural origin; the rural areas of the empire were precisely those where the Roman cultural influence was weakest—where the assimilative forces failed to do their work at all thoroughly, even at the level of speech. The barbarization of the army was at once a consequence of, and a contribution to, the decline of Rome.

Similarly with the bureaucracy. At its best—when it was staffed, at least at the higher levels, by individuals representative of Roman culture—it served in the provinces, like the army, as a setter of standards of culture and conduct. It was a powerful force in the Romanizing of the provincials. But as the empire slid deeper and deeper into disorder, the bureaucracy became the chosen instrument of imperial exploitation of the people. A primary reason for joining the bureaucracy at a senior level became the search for personal enrichment by grafting. The final collapse of the bureaucracy as a creative instrument of Romanization came when the barbarized army took over the administrative task and thus barbarized the bureaucracy. This was done in the time of the Emperor Septimius Severus, who ruled from 193 to 211.

Roman law commands the admiration of men to this day. In the days of the empire, it was the law which organized the peace which the power of the Roman arms sustained. The civilizing, or Romanizing, effect of the law—of law as a search for justice under complex social conditions—must have been enormous, not only in the West but also in the East. But if justice was highly valued, the highest legal prize for the ordinary man was Roman citizenship, for generations an honor sought and esteemed by subject people. Equality of citizenship with the Roman, the most admirable man of the time and place, was more than a legal technicality; it was also a powerful exemplary conception of the mature adult. As the empire fell on evil days, however, the burden of citizenship in the way of taxes and other exactions began to outweigh the honors and benefits. When the Emperor Caracalla widely extended citizenship in 212, he had chiefly in mind the increase in the number of persons liable for taxes. Roman citizenship ceased to be a creative force.

The Romans focused their efforts at Romanization on the cities they planted, developed, or took over. They were quite self-conscious about this, firmly grasping the relation between urbanization and civilization. It was in the cities that all the Romanizing influences found their highest expression. True, we do not know how thoroughly the city-dwellers were Romanized. But it was in the cities that the official languages, Latin and Greek, were spoken by the aspiring middle class, while the rural peoples, less responsive to Romanization, still spoke their local dialects.

In their early stages, many of the future cities of the West (including here the Danube Valley) were army camps. It was the army that encouraged the building up of communities on the Roman pattern. It was the city-dwellers with whom the imperial bureaucrats chiefly and most directly dealt; and it was urbanized people who knew and cherished the law and who most expectantly aspired to citizenship. Even the great road system, so important an integrative instrumentality of the empire, was designed to link up the cities. The roads thereby played a role in assisting the dissemination of Roman culture which should never be overlooked. The cities were the sensitive points in the process. When the great emperors of the second century sought to find a secure foundation for the state, it was to the urban middle class that they turned. As long as this class was strong or, put in reverse, as long as the emperors were wise enough to protect the middle-class interests, the empire flourished. The second century A.D. was the high-water mark—the great era of the Roman Empire, of the cities, and of the bourgeoisie.

When the crack-up began, it worked itself out, as remarked earlier, in the barbarization of the army and the bureaucracy. We can now add another development to the sequence. The barbarized army was chiefly of rural origin. It was opposed to the urban middle class which it regarded (with some justice, too) as its traditional exploiter. As the barbarized army waxed in power and authority, it forced its prejudices and policies on the emperors. The urban middle class felt the weight of the antagonistic views of the army until in the end it disintegrated. In the third century the ruin became complete and the forces which were inevitably destroying the empire from within needed only to be complemented by an intensification of the pressures from without to bring about the so-called fall. In fact, it was to meet the external threats and pressures, notably from the Iranians and the Germans, that the army forced the emperors to follow the policy of plundering the urban middle class. Thus the urban populations, which in the early years of the empire the Romans had sought to build up as proper carriers of the Roman spirit, were in the end destroyed as the empire was barbarized from within.

Explanations of why Roman power finally disappeared in the West are both numerous and unsatisfying. No single, and least of all no simple, answer is likely to comprehend what was an immensely complicated historical development. But it is obvious that a contribution toward disintegration was made by a weakness in the processes which Romanized the people of the empire. The fatal flaw seems to have been the failure to carry the Roman culture deep enough into the society. It has been already pointed out that the urbanized masses were probably not fully within the cultural orbit. The rural people of the provinces were definitely not within it. In the provinces, Romanization was largely confined to the upper segment of the townspeople. As the men of the rural provincial areas, very imperfectly Romanized if at all, took over the army and then the bureaucracy, ultimately making and breaking emperors and dictating imperial policy, we see in effect an engulfment of the cities by the country—the triumph of the least Romanized segments of the population over those groups in which Romanization had been most successful. All the evidence points to the conclusion that a crucial failure of the Romans was in adult education. They could not carry Roman culture at its best even to those people they were prepared to admit to a share of government.

This conclusion in turn raises another question: Can a high culture be successfully carried to the masses of the people? Was the Roman failure peculiar to Rome, or was it a failure which has been, or may be, repeated? Here are Professor Michael I. Rostovtzeff's conclusions on the Roman story:

Why was the city civilization of Greece and Italy unable to assimilate the masses, why did it remain a civilization of the elite, why was it incapable of creating conditions which should secure for the ancient world a continuous, uninterrupted movement along the same path which our modern world is traversing again?

.   .   .   .

Our civilization will not last unless it be a civilization not of one class, but of the masses. The Oriental civilizations were more stable and lasting than the Graeco-Roman, because, being chiefly based on religion, they were nearer the masses. Another lesson is that violent attempts at levelling have never helped to uplift the masses. They have destroyed the upper classes, and resulted in accelerating the process of barbarization. *But the ultimate problem remains like a ghost, ever present and unlaid: Is it possible to extend a higher civilization to the lower classes without debasing its standards and diluting its quality to the vanishing point? Is not every civilization bound to decay as soon as it begins to penetrate the masses?* [*My italics.*] [5]

CHAPTER

5

Educating Medieval Man: Things Heard and Seen

CHRISTIANITY, the last great creative effort of antiquity, brought about a profound reorientation of the human mind and spirit. Originating among a people notably recalcitrant to Romanization, it won, by a complicated process of teaching, preaching, high-level intellectual adaptation, propaganda, and political maneuvering, the position of the dominant religion of the Roman Empire and became, in the West, its heir.

In the Greek version of the New Testament, Jesus is called "teacher" over forty times. His methods of instruction—His use of informal discourses, discontinuous, interspersed with lengthy pauses for effect; His employment of brief, pointed, wise, or gnomic sayings, or parables, usually in rhythmical language to assist the memory; and His performance of rituals of symbolic meaning for the same purpose—all are devices of a teacher well aware of the necessities of time and place. Jesus was consciously a teacher. And He was a teacher of adults.

The kind of teacher who disinterestedly communicates knowledge was not suited to the spreading of Christianity. The new beliefs were spread by a process of indoctrination. It was a question of communicating knowledge and belief on the assumption

54

that they made a crucial difference and involved what men needed for salvation. In this task the teacher was of necessity certain and therefore dogmatic. The intellectual life of the early Christians was dominated by dogmatism.

Up to the time of the Emperor Constantine (306–337), only about 10 per cent of the population of the empire had been converted to Christianity, but Pope Gregory the Great was able to assert less than three hundred years later the Church's claim to universal spiritual jurisdiction, a claim that had validity in the West for eight centuries thereafter.

As time passed, the Church's services for believers and its task of indoctrinating newcomers were differentiated. A person receiving rudimentary instruction was called a *catechumen,* the period devoted to instruction the *catechumenate.* The objectives of the instruction were the inculcation of Christian moral discipline, the acquaintance of the converts with the Christian traditions, and the intensification of their devotion to the new faith and way of life. Essentially, the instruction was designed to prepare for baptism. The catechumenical school was the outstanding adult education institution of its time.[1] The foremost Fathers of the Church— Tertullian, Cyprian, Origen, Augustine, Chrysostom, and Ambrose —prepared materials for use in it. It reached its peak of strength in the late fourth and early fifth centuries.

In part it faded away because infant baptism became common, but it is significant that it was not succeeded by any other school of doctrine for wayfaring men. For one thing, literacy declined, not only among the laity but also among the lower clergy who presumably staffed the catechumenical schools. For another, even among the higher clergy there was a shrinkage of culture and intellectual grasp. The contrast between St. Augustine (354–430) and St. Gregory (540–604) in these respects is very great. By the fifth century people were signing their names by an *X,* meaning "I cannot read and write, but I am a Christian." [2]

As the deterioration of literacy and general culture proceeded, there was a shift in the Church from an emphasis on instruction to an emphasis on worship; and worship became largely a matter of symbolic acts of ritual. Such instruction as remained in the services was, aside from the reading of the Scripture lessons, what could be conveyed by symbolism. Since the services were conducted in Latin, communication was at a minimum, especially in the case of a congregation speaking only a vernacular. Moreover, in the course of time many of the symbolic acts lost their meaning even to the clergy itself. The efforts in medieval times to correct this situation by comprehensible instruction were the adult education of those ages.

For most of the medieval centuries there was no economic penalty for illiteracy. As society simplified itself in late Roman times, the need for literacy in the material affairs of life faded away. In medieval society literacy became a monopoly of the clergy. Only when government made pretensions beyond the average did the need for a literate bureaucracy arise; then, as we know, the bureaucracy was normally filled by men in religious orders. Even when the modern nationalistic state began to emerge in late medieval times, the king's first minister was ordinarily a great cleric. Thomas, Cardinal Wolsey, servant of King Henry VII of England, is a classic example. As a rule, the clergy could meet all the needs of its own organization and of society in general for literate servants, leaving the literate layman ordinarily a person of high social rank and uncommon ambition. The wayfaring man felt no particular need to be literate.

Oral traditions necessarily played a very important role. We know that medieval lore, presumably transmitted orally for centuries and then written down by a monkish scribe, included bits and pieces from as far back as Babylonian times. A successful analysis of medieval lore, orally transmitted, would let in a flood of light on the composition of the popular mind.

Apprenticeship was adapted to the needs of men of high and low degree. In the upper ranks of society it was customary for sons and daughters to be sent to the households of others of comparable rank for training. Boys went at seven to be pages and at fourteen began training as knights—in later days, as gentlemen—cultivating the virtues of valor, loyalty, largesse, and personal honor. Girls got no less rigorous training for the station in life they would occupy as married women. Among the lower orders the apprenticeship system provided the framework for handing on the skills of the crafts, especially when they were differentiated as specialties rather than incidental competencies of farmers. The monks played some role rather difficult to define in instructing the lower orders in the crafts and, by providing an example of superior skill, in agriculture. In the higher skills directly useful to the church, like masonry and glass-working, the clerical influence was probably very great.

When it came to doctrinal instruction, the medieval need was for some way to simplify the symbolism which had become the essence of church services. This was eventually done in at least three ways: (1) by the use of drama; (2) by visual means, or the use of sculpture, wall paintings, and stained-glass windows in the churches; and (3) by the development of styles of preaching especially designed to reach the masses. The resort was, in modern terms, to audio-visual devices. These things are familiar enough to all who have read about medieval times, though it is perhaps uncommon to relate them to adult education.

Henry Adams in *Mont-Saint-Michel and Chartres* has a great deal to say about the stories told in the sculptures and the stained-glass windows. Lewis Mumford describes the cathedral as "more than the stone Bible of mankind, as Victor Hugo was finally to call it; for it was likewise the Grand Encyclopedia: the sum of medieval knowledge as well as medieval faith." That these "visual aids" did convey instruction to the illiterate is borne out by such evidence as the stanza in François Villon's poem, "His Mother's Service to Our Lady," reading, in Rossetti's translation:

A pitiful poor woman, shrunk and old,
     I am, and nothing learn'd in letter-lore.
Within my parish-cloister I behold
     A painted Heaven where harps and lutes adore,
     And eke an Hell whose damned folk seethe full sore:
One bringeth fear, the other joy to me.
That joy, great Goddess, makes thou mine to be,—
     Thou of whom all must ask it even as I;
And that which faith desires, that let it see.
     For in this faith I choose to live and die.

A. R. Myers has said that the friars—the Franciscans and Dominicans—"were skilfully trained as preachers—to go to hear a friar preach was a recognized holiday attraction; their racy stories, direct moral appeal, and emotional style gave them great power to move their hearers." [3] They were at the height of their power and influence in the thirteenth century. *Little Flowers of St. Francis* is from this point of view a primary document of adult education history.

The friars preached to all who would listen, but they gave especial attention to wayfaring men and spoke in the vernacular all could understand; they did not confine the illustrative materials in their sermons to religious sources, but used bits and pieces of secular learning as well. They drew on astronomy; they talked about healing herbs and their properties; they discoursed on minerals, the burning glass, and animals (drawing on the Bestiaries); they used fables; and they employed moralized anecdotes from secular history. G. R. Owst considers the medieval popular sermon, for which the friars set the pattern and the pace, as "almost" a forerunner of the "modern University Extension Lecture." [4] Yet their primary purpose always remained the interpretation of the Scripture and the teaching of the Creed, the Lord's Prayer, the Ten Commandments, the seven deadly sins, and the seven cardinal virtues—all integral to the "extension work" of the Church.[5]

The same purpose is seen in the use of the drama as a pedagogical aid. The medieval dramas called *mysteries* dealt with actual Bible stories (otherwise brought home in cathedral sculptures, windows, and paintings) and emphasized the Nativity, the Passion, and the Resurrection. The *miracles* were chiefly concerned with the lives of the saints. The *moralities* presented the Christian virtues in allegorical form. The mysteries were most closely attached to the Church and developed naturally from the inherently dramatic passages in the liturgy. Originally given in Latin, they were designed to heighten the vividness of selected episodes of crucial doctrinal importance. Miracles and moralities were, in the course of time, taken over by lay associations for performance; as they were always given in the vernacular, they "communicated" to all. Eventually they developed into cycles of plays lasting several days and in the end they became markedly secular in emphasis, especially through the development of the comic elements. They reached their height early in the fifteenth century.

6

Toward Modern Times

IN LATE MEDIEVAL TIMES, literacy began to spread again. By 1498 King Henry VII of England had to redefine "benefit of clergy" to distinguish between genuine clergymen and literate laymen, for literacy by itself no longer sufficiently differentiated the two. The new spread of literacy was stimulated and sustained by a variety of factors, including the expansion of economic activity which increased the social surplus; the spread of religious ideas which included an emphasis on individual judgment fortified by Bible and tract reading; and struggles for political power to protect these advances which called out rationalizations, usually printed as books and pamphlets. The new literacy is associated historically with a rich pamphlet literature. The pamphlet, after the Bible, became the chosen vehicle for propaganda and education. Literacy became indispensable to success in life. Society once again took a shape in which illiteracy was definitely a handicap. Henceforth those who remained illiterate were disadvantaged in the race of life.

The discovery and diffusion of the art of printing from movable type signalized the beginning of a revolution in communications which has not yet, in a world perspective, reached completion.[1]

There are still whole peoples yet to be brought into the communications community the printed word created.

The art was discovered in Europe around 1440, though it had been known earlier in China. It was first practiced on an important scale by Johann Gutenberg at Mainz, Germany, about 1454. From there it spread throughout Europe within two or three decades. Printing made possible the multiplication of texts, hitherto uncommon and expensive. Books became available to a wider public and thus both stimulated and sustained the art of reading.

Since printing began in a period of transition, the books produced faced several ways, so to speak. Large numbers of them simply brought into print works of interest to minds still fascinated by medieval interests; others were devoted to the texts demanded by those preoccupied with classical learning; and still others reflected the rising interest in science and the practical arts. Mc-Murtie says that in the fifteenth century 45 per cent of the books printed fell into the category of religion, 30 per cent were literary, 10 per cent legal, 10 per cent scientific, and 5 per cent miscellaneous.[2] An analysis of the mass of printed material produced in the fifteenth and immediately following centuries would take us very far afield, but it is worth noting that, as Bryson emphasized in his F.A.E. lectures, it was the books on the practical arts and science which played a large role in setting in train the developments that made the modern world.[3]

Literacy was spread at this time chiefly to the members of the rising middle class. There is reason to suppose that simultaneously the position of the masses of wayfaring men worsened in this respect. In medieval times, the lower classes were not barred from instruction and the Church's servants were recruited from all levels of society, even the "gutter poor." But as the social pattern shifted and the middle class enlarged and extended its power and position, it became rather more difficult for the poor to achieve literacy. The Belgian historian, Gonzales Descamps, is quoted as saying, "It is a remarkable thing that the nearer we approach the nineteenth century, in inverse ratio to material and political progress, the shades of ignorance [among the wage earners] seem to darken."[4] This came about in part because the workers in the new mines and industries were often isolated from the traditional educational opportunities, and also because the religious changes brought about a decline of the ancient Catholic schools, for which no substitute was soon found. Moreover, it has been suggested, some of the Protestant reformers were essentially anti-intellectual, emphasizing faith and disparaging reason. Even men of good will differed on whether or not the poor wayfarers needed education. While there were those who argued for schools, others, like Rousseau, saw no real need for them. In Britain, an early movement under the new conditions to educate the poor was the Charity School movement, aimed at children, which was launched in the early 1700's. With its appearance we have almost reached the point in history where modern adult education begins its rise.

That the printed word was a potent educator was early recognized. The masters of church and state early concluded that it must be kept within carefully defined bounds if their prerogatives were to be preserved. They therefore began to devise systems of licensing, censorship, and prohibition to control the new communications medium. This soon precipitated the never-ending struggle for the freedom of the press which, before the middle of the seventeeth century, inspired John Milton's classic defense of press freedom, *Areopagitica*.

The spoken word did not thereupon cease to be important. The English Puritans, for their part, placed great emphasis on preaching as a means of teaching. On the other side, Queen Elizabeth I agreed with them, though in reverse. Her government systematically discouraged preaching for fear it would lead to sedition.

The West of this era, teetering on the edge of modern times, is extremely interesting as illustrating how new interests stimulate people to acquire new skills which offer access to new and coveted ranges of knowledge. The adults who actively participated in the verbal arguments, who snatched up the printed discussions of religion and politics, who read the vernacular Bibles, the purposive books, the topical pamphlets, who heard the thundering sermons, and even on occasion shouldered arms to enforce one point of view or resist another, appear not to have gotten adult education of the kind we talk about today. Whether high-born gentlemen, aspiring middle-class persons, or wayfaring common men, they found their own way through the hubbub and the confusion.

Let us now narrow our focus in two respects: by directing our

62   IN QUEST OF KNOWLEDGE

attention to the story of one country, Britain; and by confining our attention very largely to enterprises which can be described definitely as conscious ventures in adult education. The wide frame of reference used up to this time does not now become irrelevant; to make the story manageable, however, it must be presumed that from this point on, the reader can supply its elements for himself. The task in this book is now only to deal with adult education in our modern sense.

PART III

THE BRITISH RECORD:

ADULT EDUCATION IN AN

INDUSTRIAL SOCIETY

Shall the Laboring Poor Be Literate?

BRITISH ADULT EDUCATION had its origin in sporadic, religiously inspired, philanthropic efforts during the eighteenth century to teach poor working people of all ages to read and understand the Bible and the Catechism. Usually the classes were held on Sunday, for that was the only day on which the poor had leisure. On weekdays they toiled from sun to sun.

The goal of the teaching was, in educational terms, strictly limited. The emphasis fell heavily, often exclusively, on reading. Writing might be added, but it was viewed by many with hostility, for it was feared that knowledge of the art would encourage the poor into forgery. Perhaps simple arithmetic might also be taught. But the three R's were by no means considered inevitable companions.

The larger object was always to save the poor in religious and moral terms. Reading was emphasized because it would enable the poor to read the Bible and thus insure their salvation. There was no thought of training the pupils for citizenship, for the poor then had no citizenship in our modern sense; nor of developing their faculties in general, for it was feared that that would declass them; nor of strengthening their characters in a secular way, for that was thought both unnecessary and irrelevant, and least of all of placing them on the lowest rung of an educational ladder, for none existed.

65

In the eighteenth century, the spirit of the age was alien to large conceptions about what should be done educationally for the poor. It was sufficiently novel to propose to teach them at all. There were numerous people who regarded this as a radical and dangerous innovation. Indeed, there continued to be people who were fundamentally skeptical of the wisdom of teaching the poor well into the nineteenth century; even when suspicion of teaching basic skills had subsided, there was a common fear of what the poor might do with them. The dominant classes occasionally deplored the darkness of the lower orders, but they were exceedingly cautious about the kind of light it was thought wise to admit to them.

Economic advantages for the nation were supposed to reside in an uneducated laboring class. This was implicit in the then prevailing social philosophy of mercantilism. As Eli F. Heckscher puts it, the mercantilist theorists argued "for wealth for the nation, but wealth from which the majority of the people must be excluded." By extension, the majority was excluded from education.

To be sure, Adam Smith, discoursing on "The Expenses of the Sovereign" in *The Wealth of Nations* (1776), clearly saw the social and economic utility of elementary education. Here, as generally, he opposed the views of the mercantilists. Smith persuaded himself that institutions for education were a legitimate charge on the whole of society, or proper expenses of the sovereign. But Smith's views were not accepted for some decades after he formulated them.

Another economist of the time, Thomas Malthus, usually thought to have taken a very dim view of the prospect of raising the poor out of their poverty, also believed that education was needed to insure social improvement. Malthus put his point as follows in his *Essay on Population* (1798):

We have lavished immense sums on the poor, which we have every reason to think have constantly tended to aggravate their misery. But in their education and in the circulation of those important political truths that most nearly concern them, which are perhaps the only means in our power of really raising their condition, and of making them happier men and more peaceful subjects, we have been miserably deficient. It is surely a great national disgrace, that the education of the low-

est classes of people in England should be left entire to a few
Sunday Schools, supported by subscriptions from individuals,
who can give to the course of instruction in them any kind of
bias which they please.

The first reference to adult education in modern England is to be
found in the minutes of the Society for the Propagation of Christian
Knowledge, founded in 1698 to combat "vice and immorality
owing to the ignorance of the principles of Christian religion" by
establishing catechetical schools, forming libraries, and distributing
sound books the world around. In an entry for March 8, 1700,
John Pierson and John Reynolds were praised for teaching poor
children during the day, and poor adults at night, to read and
understand the Church of England Catechism. The SPCK, however, was more interested in reaching children than adults.

A classic eighteenth-century campaign for literacy was that of
the Rev. Griffith Jones in Wales. The Welsh had benefited from
the work of the SPCK, receiving both Bibles and tracts, and having had four libraries for clergymen and no less than ninety-five
Charity Schools established in the country. This effort, however,
had not reached the root of the problem. In 1731, when Griffith
Jones, vicar of Llanddowor, then forty-eight years old, embarked
upon his campaign for literacy, he had a free field in which to
work. He contributed a new principle of organization and an abiding enthusiasm.

His scheme was simple. He trained teachers at Llanddowor and
sent them "itinerating" into parishes where preparations had been
made for their reception. The teaching was in the Welsh language
and was a preparation for reading Bishop William Morgan's Welsh
version of the Bible. Jones himself described his procedure as
follows: "Where a School is wanted and desired, or like to be
kindly received, no pompous Preparations or costly Buildings are
thought of, but a Church or Chapel, or untenanted House of convenient Situation, is fixed on; and publick Notice given immediately, that a Welch School is to begin there, at an appointed
Time, where all Sorts that desire it are to be kindly and freely
taught for Three Months; (though the Schools are continued for
Three Months longer, or more, when needful; and then removed
to another Place where desired)." [1]

That the schools were entirely free was an important point, for the Welsh were terribly poor in those days. Children and adults were gathered into the same school, though they were often taught in separate classes. Many of the adult classes were held only at night. Between 1731 and 1761, when Jones died, a total of 3,495 schools were held and 158,237 individuals attended them, not including an unknown number of adults who attended at night but who, for some queer reason, were not counted. The movement continued until 1779 when Madam Bridget Bevan, Jones's chief financial backer, finally died and nobody was available to carry on further.

A modern historian of Wales evaluates Jones's effort as follows: "it would be difficult to exaggerate the greatness of Griffith Jones's work. His conception of education was admittedly narrow, but he should be judged only on the basis of his motive, which was to save men's souls. Nor did he show any great originality in ideas. His greatness lay in his remarkable powers of organization and in his ability to translate his purpose into practical form on a grand scale. He helped to make the Welsh a literate nation, and his circulating schools were the most important experiment in religious education in the eighteenth century not only in Wales but in Britain and all the British dominions." [2]

At this same time, there still survived in England private schools where, for a fee of sixpence a lesson, adults could learn to read, write, and figure in evening classes. Such a school is vividly depicted in George Eliot's novel of those days, *Adam Bede* (1859):

Bartle Massey's was one of the few scattered houses on the edge of a common, which was divided by the road to Trelleson. Adam reached it in a quarter of an hour after leaving the Hill Farm; and when he had his hand on the door latch, he could see, through the curtainless window, that there were eight or nine heads bending over the desks, lighted by thin dips.

When he entered, a reading lesson was going forward, and Bartle Massey merely nodded, leaving him to take his place where he pleased. He had not come for the sake of a lesson tonight, and his mind was too full of personal matters, too full of the last two hours he had passed in Hetty's presence, for him to amuse himself with a book till school was over; so he sat down in a corner, and looked on with an absent mind. It was a sort of scene which Adam had beheld almost weekly for years; he knew by heart every arabesque flourish in the framed specimen of Bartle Massey's handwriting which hung over the schoolmaster's head, by way of keeping a lofty ideal before the minds of his pupils; he knew the backs of all the books on the shelf running along the whitewashed wall above the pegs for the slates; he knew exactly how many grains were gone out of the ear of Indian-corn that hung from one of the rafters; he had long ago exhausted the resources of his imagination in trying to think how the bunch of feathery sea-weed had looked and grown in its native element; and from the place where he sat he could make nothing of the old map of England that hung against the opposite wall, for age had turned it of a fine yellow-brown, something like that of a well-seasoned meerschaum. The drama that was going on was almost as familiar as the scene, nevertheless habit had not made him indifferent to it, and even in his present self-absorbed mood, Adam felt a momentary stirring of the old fellow-feeling, as he looked at the rough men painfully holding pen or pencil with their cramped hands, or humbly laboring through their reading lessons.

The reading class now seated on the form in front of the schoolmaster's desk consisted of the three most backward pupils; Adam would have known it only by seeing Bartle Massey's face as he looked over his spectacles, which he had shifted to the ridge of his nose, not requiring them for present purposes. The face wore its mildest expression; the grizzled, bushy eyebrows had taken their most acute angle of compassionate kindness, and the mouth, habitually compressed with a pout of the lower lip, was relaxed so as to be ready to speak a helpful word or syllable in a moment. The gentle expression was the more interesting because the schoolmaster's nose, an irregular aquiline twisted a little on one side, had rather a formidable character; and his brow, moreover, had the peculiar tension which always impresses one as a sign of a keen

impatient temperament; the blue veins stood out like cords
under the transparent yellow skin, and this intimidating brow
was softened by no tendency to baldness, for the gray bristly
hair, cut down to about an inch in length, stood round it in as
close ranks as ever.

"Nay, Bill, nay," Bartle was saying, in a kind tone, as he
nodded to Adam, "begin that again, and then perhaps it'll
come to you what d,r,y, spells. It's the same lesson you read
last week, you know."

Three of the students are described in fair detail and their motivations indicated: a twenty-four-year-old stonesawyer who wanted
to read because his cousin and his helper could; a Methodist brick-
layer of thirty who wanted to read his Bible; and a dyer of about
thirty who wanted to read the literature of his trade. Adam Bede
himself had been a student at the school—the best the schoolmaster
had ever had—and the novelist attributes to his education some
of his superior qualities of mind and character. Not the least interesting phase of the story is the role played by Methodists and
Methodism.

John Wesley took a marked, if narrow, interest in the teaching
of reading, writing, and arithmetic. This was done in night schools,
Sunday schools, reading circles, and other ways, and some effort
was made to teach children and adults separately. Wesley himself
was a thoroughgoing Tory and had no idea whatever of contributing to fundamental social change by education. Methodism
was a personal, not a social, religious philosophy. It was not "intellectual" in outlook. Wesley thought to make the Bible accessible
and to relieve, by improving their personal capacity, the economic
misery from which so many of his early followers—mostly town-
dwellers—suffered. His motivation was religious and humanitarian,
and he sought to effect a change in persons within the existing social pattern.

Having made men and women literate, Wesley then faced a
perennial problem of teachers: What, aside (in his case) from the
Bible and Methodist tracts, should they read? They might, left to
themselves, wander far from pastures approvable by Methodists.
There is evidence that they did: Tom Paine's writings (eventually

proscribed by the government) percolated widely through Methodist channels and contributed to the "democracy" of the proletariat. Wesley met the difficulty for his people by turning to popular writing, editing, and publication.

> The problem of providing suitable literature for popular consumption was solved by undertaking an extensive program of publication. Wesley was indefatigable, not only in writing but also in selecting and editing chosen extracts from a host of other writers. The chief interest was naturally religious and moral, but the range of the literature which poured from the Wesleyan publication offices was, considering the period, nothing short of extraordinary. It included biography, poetry, travel, subjects of daily utility, etiquette, school books, Christian casuistry, the writings of Locke, Spenser, Shakespeare, and Malebranche, as well as explicitly religious works. In addition, from 1778, a magazine was regularly published by the Connexion. Its pages, too, were devoted to biography, literature, practical advice, poetry, as well as religion. Its breadth of taste under Wesley's editorship was so wide that it even incurred criticism from stricter Methodists for including matter held to be too secular in nature. . . .

> The entire Wesleyan organization was then used to spread this literature throughout the membership of the societies . . . To achieve this end, every preacher, and indeed every society member, became a book agent. . . .[3]

Wesley's activity illustrates a point that remains valid to the present day: the popular press is or can be an educator of the highest power. Everything turns on what is popularly offered and what selection from the miscellaneous offerings literate men and women are moved to make.

This same discovery was also made by Hannah More (1745–1833) who, like Wesley, combined religion, philanthropy, education, and Toryism. Miss More was a second-rate writer who, like many of her kind before and since, enjoyed great popularity in her own lifetime. As she grew older, Miss More's piety increased apace. She became closely associated with the so-called Clapham Sect, an evangelical Church of England group which combined piety and practical politics. In Miss More's case this developed into the promotion of Sunday schools (like that she founded at Cheddar in 1789) in which children and adults, mostly women, were taught reading (the Bible, the Catechism, etc.) as well as household arts.

While engaged in this work Miss More saw the need for moral tracts for school use and general circulation. Since, from her point of view, the task she faced was to reconcile the poor to their lot, to discourage the notion that they could better it by concerted political or economic action, and to indoctrinate them with the accepted tenets of religion and morality, she turned to the writing of "straight" and semifictional hortatory works. At this she had a fantastic success; in at least one year two million of her publications were sold or given away. One of her greatest successes was *Village Politics,* a counterblast to Tom Paine and the prevalent ideas of the French Revolution.

Miss More was astute enough to realize that she must know her competition if her tracts were to reach their mark. She therefore made a close study of the ever-swelling stream of popular reading material that was pouring from the presses, including such items (all still with us in modernized versions) as stories of notorious murderers, thieves, and highwaymen, coarse ballads, lewd songs, and bawdy joke books, as well as antigovernment and antichurch propaganda publications. In an effort to counter these, she produced stories supporting moral conduct and demonstrating that crime does not pay; edifying ballads; and simply worded sermons, prayers, and Bible stories. Like John Wesley, Hannah More recognized that once you have taught people to read, the next step is to try to influence what they read.

The first school exclusively for adults appears to have been established at Bala in Wales by Rev. Thomas Charles in the summer of 1811. This is a landmark in the history of adult education. In a letter dated April 2, 1812, Charles stated his position:

Observing and bewailing the great number of the illiterate grown-up and old people in our poor country, I have in different places established Sunday Schools exclusively for them, having another in the same place for children; telling them at the same time, that we meant to be urgent upon them—never

cease to press them to attend until they came. By kindness
and importunateness we have succeeded far beyond our most
sanguine hopes. We have six of these schools for the aged
set up within these three or four months, and some hundreds
have learned, and are learning to read . . . their desire for
learning soon became as great as any we have seen among the
young people. They have their little elementary books with
them often whilst at work, and meet in the evenings, of their
own accord, to teach one another. The rumour of the success
of these schools has spread abroad, and has greatly removed
the discouragement which old people felt from attempting to
learn, from the general persuasion, that they could not learn
at their age. This has been practically proved to be false, for
old people of seventy-five years of age have learned to read
in these schools to their great comfort and joy. I dare not
vouch positively for the conversion of any of them; but I can
say, that they are much improved in their moral conduct and
attendance on the means of grace. They lament with tears
their former ignorance, and rejoice they can read, and repeat
memoriter a few verses of the Bible given them to learn.[4]

Some months later (January 4, 1814) he wrote:

What induced me first to think of establishing such an institution, was the aversion I found in the adults to associate with
the children in their schools. The first attempt succeeded
wonderfully . . . in many places the illiterate adults began to
call for instruction. In one county, after a public address had
been delivered to them on that subject, the adult poor, even
the aged, flocked to the Sunday Schools in crowds; and the
shopkeepers could not immediately supply them with an adequate number of spectacles. Our schools, in general, are kept
in our chapels; in some districts, where there are no chapels,
farmers, in the summer time, lend their barns. The adults
and children are sometimes in the same room, but placed in
different parts of it. When their attention is gained and fixed,
they soon learn; their age makes no great difference, if they
are able, by the help of glasses, to see the letters. As the
adults have no time to lose, we endeavour (before they can
read) to instruct them without delay in the first principles of

Christianity. We select a short portion of Scripture, comprising
in plain terms the leading doctrines, and repeat them to the
learners till they can retain them in their memories; and which
they are to repeat the next time we meet.[5]

Like his early successors, Charles focused on Bible readings and
did not dream of proceeding beyond that point.

In England itself, the pioneer adult school was that established
at Bristol in 1812 by William Smith, doorkeeper of a Methodist
chapel, in association with Stephen Prust, a Quaker. In the next
few years schools of this kind multiplied and went through various
permutations and combinations, even to once more trying to hit
two birds with one stone by mixing in children with the adults.
In 1815 there were adult schools for reading in at least seventeen
towns and cities in England, but not only were they short-term,
they were short-lived. The idea of establishing them was contagious,
for it was so obviously right in the eyes of religious philanthropists,
but the fever for them was not lasting. Within two or three years
most of the seventeen schools had ceased to exist; it was not until
the eighteen-forties that such schools again became common and
that the movement for them put down permanent roots, although
so obvious an idea continually found new expression here and
there as somebody found the energy to start a school.

Writing in 1851, Hudson concluded that the relative failure of
the early efforts was attributable to three causes: (1) want of
competent teachers; (2) the reluctantly abandoned error of mixing
children with the adults; and (3) the inability to settle finally the
argument over the teaching of writing.[6] As throughout the history
of adult education, the problem was not how to make a start—men
with imagination, energy, and a little money take care of that—
but how to keep going. On the scattered figures available, it seems
improbable that the early schools actually taught more than forty
to fifty thousand adults in their best single years.

A revealing account of adult education as it appeared to a
conscientious observer in 1816 is provided by Thomas Pole's book
grandly entitled (in the second edition used here) *A History of the
Origin and Progress of Adult Schools, with an Account of some
of the beneficial Effects already Produced on the Moral Character*

of the Labouring Poor; also Considerations on the Important Advantages They are Likely to be Productive of to Society at Large.[7]

Pole was a Philadelphia-born Quaker who went to England as a youth and studied medicine there. It is not clear how he got into adult education, beyond the fact that his sect had a strong interest in it, but in 1802 he was lecturing on "Chemistry, the Economy of Nature" at Bristol, particularly to audiences of women. His book (the first edition of which quickly sold two thousand copies) was a most effective combination of fact, argumentation, and propaganda.

In his introduction Pole said, "A few years since, it would have been deemed a whimsical and chimerical project to have collected a school of persons from twenty to eighty years, under the expectation of being able to teach them to read. . . ." He speculated that the need for adult schools was stimulated when the British and Foreign Bible Society was organized to distribute the Holy Scriptures. Obviously this was hardly worth while unless the poor could read. Hence the schools. To meet the objections against making the poor literate, Pole argued that the poor in certain sections of Scotland were "well-educated" but that "cheerful submission to their lot" was nevertheless characteristic of them and they were far from aspiring to equality with their masters and mistresses. He added that literacy made the poor more efficient as producers without being less interested in productive labor; that it reduced crime; that it gave those who possessed it a beneficial sense of personal worth and strengthened their morals; and, of course, it re-enforced religious principles. (Looking back from the vantage point of 1903, the Quaker historians Rowntree and Binns grimly observed, "Faith in the moral results of simple elementary education was at that time more widely spread than at present.") [8]

Considering writing apart from reading, Pole soundly remarked that, pedagogically speaking, writing improved spelling and hence facilitated reading, while writing out Scripture passages tended to "fix those religious truths in the minds." It was improbable that possession of the art would turn the poor to forgery, for the instruction, said Pole, without any sense of being sardonic, was not to be carried to high enough levels to turn out expert penmen. This seems highly likely, as Pole contemplated holding his scholars at their tasks no longer than two hours a week for two months. In that brief period they were to be taught not only reading and possibly writing, but also serious deportment, cleanliness, temperance, honesty, and the habit of regularly attending church!

Pole thought that if he could teach adults, they would teach their children, and thus in time cut down the need of schools for children; and he envisaged the day when schools for adults would no longer be needed either, for every adult would know how to read! This suggests that every generation of adult educators defines its own horizon; as it is reached, however, a new horizon is observed in the distance. Differently put, adult educators operate on a constantly advancing frontier.

8

The Utilitarian Approach: SDUK and Mechanics' Institutes

IN 1818 James Mill published an article on education in a supplement to the *Encyclopaedia Britannica* in which he expressed, clearly and forcibly, as was his talent, the Benthamite utilitarian thesis that "The end of Education is to render the individual, as much as possible, an intrument of happiness, first to himself, and next to other beings." Mill took a very comprehensive view of education indeed and argued that it included "everything which acts upon the being as it comes from the head of nature in such a manner as to modify the mind, to render the train of feelings different from what it would otherwise have been . . ." [1]

Naturally, then, James Mill believed in education for all: infants, children, adults, rich and poor alike. He and the Benthamite utilitarian party were almost universal reformers, attempting to reorder society in accordance with the dictates of abstract reason to produce the highest Benthamite good, the greatest happiness for the greatest number. Its social base was the rising middle class. Its influence on education, including adult education, was profound and it colonized certain ideas in the minds of educators which they have never since quite abandoned, notably the idea that adult education must be severely "practical."

In the campaign to promote a Benthamite education, many men took a hand, but none more conspicuously than Henry Peter, Lord Brougham (1778–1868), a Scotsman not bashful about invading a variety of fields of activity. Brougham was active in journalism, politics, the abolition of slavery, law reform, the promotion of infant education, state schools, adult education, university education, popular publishing, colonial reform, and the promotion of free trade. He believed that education, properly managed, could cure the ills of the industrial revolution. Brougham was deeply influenced by James Mill. The latter's son, John Stuart Mill, wrote that his father "was the good genius by the side of Brougham in most of what he did for the public, either on education, law reform, or any other subject." [2]

In 1825 Brougham published a pamphlet called *Practical Observations upon the Education of the People,* which ran through twenty editions in its first year. Brougham held the notion of his school that "knowledge is power" and shared what its enemies called its "education-madness." In his tract he expressed the opinion that "the question no longer is, whether or not the people shall be instructed—for that has been determined long ago, and the decision is irreversible—but whether they shall be well or ill taught—half-informed, or as thoroughly as their circumstances permit and their wants require." It was up to the rich to promote such education, but "the people must come forward to profit by the opportunity thus offered, and they must themselves continue the movement once begun."

Brougham identified the two great obstacles to success as want of money—the poor of England were so abominably poor—and want of time—hours of labor were then so long and exhausting. Yet he thought that the poor could make time and find money, if they were convinced that education was worth while. He therefore recommended Benjamin Franklin's *Autobiography* as an admirably convincing argument on that point. As to ways and means, Brougham had a good word for cheap publications, circulating libraries, reading clubs, conversation (i.e., discussion) clubs, lectures, and, above all, the mechanics' institutes which had been pioneered in Scotland, notably by Dr. George Birkbeck in Glasgow.

Since Brougham had been convinced by somebody—perhaps James Mill—that once the people were literate their chief need would be for proper reading matter, he promoted the Society for the Diffusion of Useful Knowledge and its numerous publications. Financially backed by sympathetic manufacturers, it was active from 1826 to 1846. In those two decades it published an encyclopedia, numerous small books, pamphlets, and a magazine. At first the emphasis fell on natural science and mathematics; it was this preoccupation, together with its backing, that led Thomas Love Peacock to refer to the SDUK as "The Steam-intellect Society." In time, however, the scope was broadened to include geography, history, and a variety of other matters, always excluding "controversial Divinity," moral philosophy, and politics.

Famous series issued were the "Library of Useful Knowledge," the "Library of Entertaining Knowledge," the "Farmer's Series," and the "Library for the Young." Equally well-known was the *Penny Magazine,* which contained illustrated nonfiction and ran from March, 1832, to December, 1845, and had at its peak a million readers; and the *Penny Cyclopedia,* issued in parts from 1833 to 1846 to a total of twenty-nine volumes, and for many years a standard authority. (The *Penny Cyclopedia* became eventually the basis for the *English Cyclopedia,* to which supplements were issued as late as 1873.)

The SDUK publications did not, of course, have the field of popular literature to themselves. The *Penny Magazine,* for example, had as competitors *Chambers' Journal* (founded 1832), consisting mostly of articles, but with a short story in each issue; and the *Saturday Magazine,* published by the Society for the Propagation of Christian Knowledge, which naturally had a religious tone. *Chambers' Journal* outlasted the papers of the SDUK and the SPCK. All of the "educational" publications were subjected to severe competition by the contemporary publishers of "blood-and-thunder" stuff. The adventure of the SDUK in popular educational publications was an early demonstration of a fact constantly being rediscovered: that the people will absorb great quantities of good books if they are properly priced.

On January 28, 1841, the London *Times* reported a speech made by the Prime Minister, Sir Robert Peel, at the opening ceremonies of a new library and reading room at Tamworth in Peel's constituency. The Prime Minister had given one hundred

pounds to the project and had accepted the presidency. The speech
was not particularly brilliant—it was conventional in its praise of
knowledge; it echoed sentiments that Bentham and particularly
Brougham had made familiar; and the only really remarkable
thing about it was that Peel, a Conservative, should have expressed
his essential agreement on the subject of popular education with
the utilitarians. The Prime Minister said, for example:

> Do not be deceived by the sneers that you hear against knowl-
> edge, which are uttered by men who want to depress you, and
> keep you depressed, to the level of their own contented ig-
> norance.

> . . . I believe that society is now in the position that increased
> intelligence and increased knowledge are absolutely essential
> to success in your worldly pursuits.

> · · · · · · · · · · · · · · · · · ·

> I cannot believe that there is any risk to religious impressions
> and religious belief by opening the avenues to literary acquire-
> ments.

> I am sanguine enough to believe that that superior sagacity
> will be the first to turn a deaf ear to objections and presump-
> tions against revealed religion, will be the first to acknowledge
> the complete harmony of the Christian dispensation with all
> that reason, assisted by revelation, tells us of the course and
> constitution of nature.

In all probability the speech would have passed with only casual
notice had it not been attacked by John Henry Newman, later
Cardinal Newman.

In a long letter to the editor of the *Times,* signed "Catholicus,"
Newman seized upon the speech as a particularly objectionable
statement of the secularist (or, in his terminology, "liberal") outlook, subjected it to a fiercely critical analysis, and concluded by
stating with fiery dogmatism his opposed religious and "conservative" view.[3] Thus a minor ceremony at Tamworth was raised into
the status of a major intellectual collision which to this day drama-
tizes a fundamental apposition in educational thinking.

Newman fired with all barrels at Peel, but he was really aiming at Brougham and, behind him, Bentham. Peel, Newman insisted, had "condescended to mimic the gestures and tones of Lord Brougham." This, he argued, was disgraceful in a Tory and a Prime Minister. "It is, indeed, most melancholy to see so sober and experienced a man practicing the antics of one of the wildest performers of this wild age; and taking off the tone, manner, and gestures of the versatile ex-Chancellor, with a versatility almost equal to his own." And what was Brougham's error that caused Newman thus to excoriate him? It was "a chief error of the day, in very distinct schools of opinion—that our true excellence comes not from within, but from without; not wrought out through personal struggles and sufferings, but following upon a passive exposure to influences over which we have no control." Yet, Newman admitted, it was unquestionably true that "the problem for statesmen of this age is how to educate the masses," but, he said, "literature and science cannot give the solution." Developing the theme, he went on:

It does not require many words, then, to determine that, taking human nature as it is actually found, and assuming that there is an Art of Life, to say that it consists, or in any essential manner is placed, in the cultivation of Knowledge, that the mind is changed by discovery, or saved by a diversion, and can thus be amused into immortality—that grief, anger, cowardice, self-conceit, pride, or passion, can be subdued by an examination of shells or grasses, or inhaling of gases, or chipping rocks, or calculating the longitude, is the veriest of pretenses which sophist or mountebank ever professed to a gaping auditory. If virtue be a mastery over the mind, if its end be action, if its perfection be inward order, harmony, and peace, we must seek it in graver and holier places than in Libraries and Reading-rooms.

Newman's remarks got to the heart of the controversy, the core of his purpose in picking a quarrel—for his action was really nothing less—with Sir Robert Peel. Newman seized upon Sir Robert's rather innocuous address to strike a blow for religion and against the secular orientation in popular education. "The Knowledge School [i.e., Brougham's crowd] does not contemplate raising man above himself; it merely aims at disposing of his existing powers and tastes, as is most convenient, or is practicable under circumstances." He continued:

> I consider, then, that intrinsically excellent and noble as are scientific pursuits, and worthy of a place in a liberal education, and fruitful of temporal benefits to the community, still they are not, and cannot be, the instrument of an ethical training; that physics do not supply a basis, but only materials for religious sentiment; that knowledge does not occupy, does not form the mind, that apprehension of the unseen is the only known principle capable of subduing evil, educating the multitude, and organizing society; and that, whereas man is born for action, action flows not from inferences, but from impressions—not from reasonings, but from Faith. . . . Christianity, and nothing short of it, must be made the element and principle of all education.

Newman's blast at Peel is memorable as one of the most remarkable and enduring statements of a position that has ever been occasioned by a problem of adult education. Very rarely has adult education been the subject of such vehement and lofty rhetoric; and only very uncommonly has one position been so eloquently advocated as against another. True, in the days that followed, the secularists, their outlook changed from that of Brougham, went from victory to victory, and Newman's party had lesser though continual successes. The religious motivation in adult education has persisted through all the years, but it has persisted in a predominantly secular environment.

In 1851, J. W. Hudson, Ph.D., an active worker in adult education, published in London an invaluable book entitled *The History of Adult Education*. A gold mine of information, it was nevertheless in large part a catalogue of brave adventures either dead or dying. Yet, as of 1850 Hudson had knowledge of 610 active adult education enterprises in England, 55 in Scotland, 25 in Ireland, and 12 in Wales. Total paid membership was 120,081. The institutions possessed libraries in which there were 815,510 volumes, providing the basis for 2,026,095 issues of books in a year. They supported 408 newspaper reading rooms. They scheduled 5,840 lectures. Over 18,000 persons received instruction in evening classes. Outstanding among the institutions were the Mechanics' Institutes. The reader will recall that these had the warm approval of Lord Brougham. They demand a close inspection.

Hudson selected the Birmingham Brotherly Society, established in 1796, as the earliest example of a mechanics' institution, for the Society aimed to teach mechanics reading, writing, arithmetic, drawing, geography, history, and morals. However, it was more usual, Hudson said, to give the credit to Dr. John Anderson, Professor of Natural Philosophy at the University of Glasgow, who left his fortune to found Anderson's University, incorporated on June 9, 1796. But it was not until 1800 that Dr. George Birkbeck, who had been appointed Professor of Natural Philosophy at Anderson's the previous year, opened lectures to mechanics. These lectures he continued for five seasons, until 1804, when he moved to London. In 1823, members of the Anderson's classes seceded and set up the Glasgow Mechanics' Institution, the first in Scotland to use the name. Two years before that, there had been founded in Edinburgh a School of Arts which was essentially a mechanics' institution. And also there was established in Liverpool in 1823 a Mechanics' and Apprentices' Library, suggested to the founder by such an institution in New York City. Even if it were possible to establish absolute priority in time, it could not be asserted that all the subsequent mechanics' institutions were lineal descendants of the first. They had diverse origins. Adult education is a happy hunting ground for believers in multiple causation and independent invention.

Today Dr. Birkbeck is perhaps the best remembered pioneer of mechanics' institutions. He gave his name to Birkbeck College in the University of London, the successor of the London Mechanics' Institution.[4] (Very often in British adult education history institutions established for adults have either been absorbed by, or have formed the basis of, a regular academic college or even university.) Birkbeck was one of those numerous persons in the history of adult education whose main career was outside the field. Born the son of a Yorkshire banker and merchant in 1776, he was trained in medicine at Edinburgh and London. At Edinburgh, a fellow university student was Lord Brougham. Birkbeck's experiences at Glasgow convinced him that lecturing to mechanics, or workers, was feasible and profitable to all concerned. When, therefore, J. C. Robertson and Thomas Hodgskin proposed in the *Mechanics' Magazine* in 1823 that a teaching institution for workers be set up in London, citing the Scottish examples, Birkbeck was quite willing to take a hand in promoting the project. He got Brougham to serve on a board of four trustees. Of the first twelve hundred members secured, eight hundred were men on weekly wages. This was the group the Institution was supposed to serve. But in a short while it was dominated by shopkeepers, law copyists, and attorney's clerks.

The Mechanics' Institutions seem to have been related to a need of the time, even if their promoters were unable permanently to engage the support of the class of people they set out to serve. The evidence for this is that they spread rapidly, not only over the British Isles, but over the whole world responsive to a British example—to the United States, Canada, Australia, India. They were also surprisingly durable; they lasted in many instances for years and years, long after the vital spark had gone out of them and they were only oddly persistent vestigial remains of a famous educational experiment. In such a widespread activity, the stated purpose naturally varied from place to place, but three fundamental propositions were that they should promote a knowledge of general science, diffuse rational information to the workers, and elevate character by providing worth-while "intellectual pleasures" and "refined amusements."

They tried to teach workers the scientific principles *behind* their vocational practices, not the vocations themselves.[5] They taught mathematics, chemistry, optics, heat, steam, astronomy, geology, mechanics, hydraulics, pneumatics, hydrostatics, arithmetic, French, stenography, botany. (In the long run the most durable Institutions got into vocational training in somewhat the modern manner and were only displaced when the state took over technical training; the Manchester Mechanics' Institute, for example, was eventually transformed into the modern Technological College.)

Popularizing science was Birkbeck's special forte. It will be instantly recognized that it takes high skill to lecture (or write) in the field in such a way that the audience is interested and truly instructed and the scientists whose work is being discussed are satisfied. Furthermore, that the effort was made at all illustrates two facts: that a high evaluation was placed on science as an intellectual discipline and liberator of the mind; and that communication was now considered possible between the scientist and the tradesman, a vast change from the situation in ancient Greece, of which we took notice earlier.[6] By insisting on these points, the utilitarians made a permanent contribution to adult education.

It is hard to say what "rational information" is at any time, and certainly it was not easy to define it in the troubled England of the time when the Mechanics' Institutes were being established. It is obvious from the comments available that contemporary pressures were against any free exploration of information or ideas. Too many people had fixed notions about both, usually repressive in essence. The nature of the difficulty is well illustrated by the fact that whereas at the London Institution Birkbeck and Brougham stood for economic individualism, Hodgskin and Robertson were economically heterodox. This caused an acute controversy between them which was entangled with a struggle for control of the Institution. Since Birkbeck and Brougham controlled the money for the venture, they eventually called the tune. The tune became economic individualism—"sound" views, as Brougham said. However, when Chartism appeared the conservatives took fright and the Institutes abandoned *all* political economy and confined themselves to science.

Many workers were interested in politics and were therefore great readers of newspapers. They appreciated the newspaper reading rooms attached to some of the Mechanics' Institutes, for what with the heavy tax on papers (instituted in 1819), they could not afford to buy them themselves. Some managers looked askance at this sort of thing and abolished the reading rooms, forcing the politically minded out of the Institutes altogether and into the drinking places where papers were kept for the use of patrons, causing the sardonic (who are always on the alert for foolishness among adult educators) to ask if the price of political education was addiction to alcohol.

As to the libraries, the Manchester Institute excluded books on party politics and controversial theology. Some of the restrictive ideas were even more remarkable. Hudson quotes the Reverend Doctor Forbes as warning the Aberdeen Institute that "Belles Lettres, Political Economy, and even History, were dangerous studies." How to deal with fiction was a thorny question at all the libraries, usually answered by leaving it out altogether. At Sheffield, Hudson tells us, "For many years the members annually agitated for the abrogation of the law which prevented them from reading novels of acknowledged excellence, but successive committees held that there is a real distinction between the tales of Miss Martineau illustrating some principle of political economy, and Sir Walter Scott's novels." [7] Since Sir Walter Scott used his novels to reinforce conservative principles, this is rather hard to follow.

Finally, the Institutes had difficulty in dealing with the matter of amusements, "refined" or otherwise. The educational activities either were corrupted by what Hudson calls "light and meretricious" subjects for lectures—he seems to have put the popular dramatic readings under this head—or amusement was driven out altogether, leaving a vacuum in the members' lives which they filled by going to casinos, gin palaces, and beerhouses, especially those that offered musical entertainment and vaudeville. Then the very people who had refused to face up to the problem of "refined" amusements deplored what the people got and, apparently, enjoyed. Thus did the urbanized workers early express preference for commercialized amusements over the "refined" and "improving" enticements of the adult educators.

The net result was, said Hudson, that "Ten years after the formation of the Mechanics' Institutions in the principal towns in England [i.e., by around 1833], it was proved, upon undoubtable testimony, that these societies had failed to attract the class for whom they were intended, by their founders, to benefit." Elsewhere he wrote, "The universal complaint is that Mechanics' Institutions are attended by persons of a higher rank than those for whom they were designed. . . ." The workingmen, whom it was originally intended to serve, objected to association with "the boss," or even the supervising employees or the office workers; they lacked suitable clothing for such company in any case; and they found the fees too high in relation to their incomes. So they stayed away.

In some towns it was assumed that the workingmen could be reached by something simpler. Lyceums, so-called, were therefore tried. These organizations, governed by their members, combined instruction and amusement at a low fee; admitted women; provided newspapers, musical entertainment, gymnastics, and dancing;

and offered to teach reading, writing, grammar, sewing, and knitting. Nevertheless, they quickly suffered much the same fate as the Institutes as far as the audience reached was concerned.

The cry against the workers was that they were apathetic—a cry still used. But were they? Some of Hudson's evidence shows that they were not apathetic to what they themselves knew they wanted, but they were to what "do-gooders" thought they ought to want. The actual situation, as reported by Hudson, was that the middle classes—particularly the lower middle classes of the white-collar and supervisory grades—had taken over the Mechanics' Institutes. Even among these people, however, the turnover in membership was enormous, indicating widespread dissatisfaction and restlessness. Perhaps the working people, manual or white-collar or both, would have been more appreciative if they had not been disturbed by the fact that the Institutes were a respectable charity of the aristocracy and the moneyed upper middle class. Hudson felt that the workers would have had more confidence in the Institutes if they had supported them themselves and thus claimed a direct voice in their management. As it was, the Institutes were bedeviled by the fallacy so commonly held at the time that the working people were incapable of constructive initiative on their own behalf, but had to be helped upward and onward by the "leading classes," particularly the philanthropically inclined among them.

But consider further. The teaching methods in the classes were careless and bad and, worse still, not adapted to adults (a perennial complaint right down to the present day). Not the least important difficulty in the classes was the language barrier between the teachers and the taught. It was about this time that Sir James Kay-Shuttleworth observed, "Those who have had close intercourse with the labouring classes well know with what difficulty they comprehend words not of a Saxon origin, and how frequently addresses to them are unintelligible from the continual use of terms of a Latin or Greek derivation . . ." [8] Nor were the libraries of the Institutes as good and useful as one might offhand assume from the figures quoted earlier. Samuel Smiles, surely not one inclined to take a dark view, commented, "Many of the books in Mechanics' Institutions are very unattractive; many of those books, for instance, which are given by way of presents, are books which nobody would think of reading nowadays; a large proportion of them are dull, heavy books." [9] From our perspective it is obvious, moreover, that workingmen generally lacked sufficient preliminary education to take full advantage of the programs of the Institutes. Exceptional individuals could and, from the record, did do so, but the average members were not able to rise to the level on which the Institutes at first offered their work.

On the other hand, it is also obvious that the Institutes could have held their working-class customers if they had really set out to satisfy their wants; but what the workingmen chiefly wanted at that time—the kind of political and economic knowledge that would enable them to improve their status—was generally regarded as too dangerous for the Institutes, with aristocratic and upper-middle-class support, to attempt to supply. Precisely for political reasons the Institutes felt it necessary to handle cautiously, or to avoid, subjects which workingmen in very great numbers wanted to study and understand. Hudson hints at this when he writes of the Manchester Lyceum, "The newsroom has been its attraction from the thirst for political knowledge which exists amongst factory operatives, developing itself occasionally in chartist meetings, in appeals to the legislature for protection to labor, and gatherings to promote socialism and communism."

Writing in 1853, James Hole faced up to the problem and evolved clear ideas about how controversial subjects could be handled, though he recognized that few persons of influence would agree with him. Hole wrote:

> The question as to the introduction of any subject, whether of religion, politics, or political economy, may be determined by the answer to this question: Is it intended to hear both sides? You only wish to diffuse correct views on important questions. Granted. But what is correct? Who is to be judge? . . . Now, we believe the English mind has not reached this high standard; and it would therefore be impossible to unite any large support from men of all parties in behalf of an institution which permitted to all shades of thought the free expression of opinion . . . therefore the next best thing is, entire and strict neutrality. . . . Those who deplore the fallacies entertained by the working-classes on the subjects of machin-

ery, the poor-laws, etc., etc. must leave to other agencies the task of removing them.[10]

Differently put, since there was no agreed-upon technique for handling subjects in which the working class was keenly interested, the adult educators abandoned the working class to "other agencies." The working class did not abandon adult education; the adult educators abandoned the working class. This error has been repeated again and again in the decades since.

James Hole, by the way, seems to have been a man of uncommon understanding of the problems of adult education. Not only did he put his finger on the critical problem of how to deal with controversial subjects, but he clearly enunciated at least three ideas which are still being put forward as fundamental by adult educators: (1) "Education is not an affair of childhood and youth, it is the business of the whole life"; (2) ". . . to raise the workingman we must take hold of him where he is, not where he is not" (an idea often used nonsensically from a failure really to know "where he is"); and (3) teaching by discussion rather than exclusively by lectures.[11] There are very, very few "new" ideas in adult education.

Workingmen in those days, as today, would make great efforts to learn what they had a powerful incentive to learn. To learn about politics and economics they tried hard to jump the educational hurdles in their way. They felt no comparable incentive to master the "neutral" offerings of the Institutes. Therefore they abandoned the Institutes to those who could find some use for them. So completely did the audience change that sponsors, who knew perfectly well what class it was originally intended to serve, professed satisfaction that the *middle* class had been reached. Brougham declared in 1835 (*my italics*):

> I have no hesitation in saying that of all the improvements which have been made of late years in the condition of the people of this country, the diffusion of knowledge, both in science and in the other principles of their arts, *among the industrious portion of the Middle Classes, to whose use Mechanics' Institutes are more especially devoted,* stands in the first rank amongst the very foremost.[12]

What middle class? It is fairly clear from the record that it was that portion of the middle-class group which, but little advanced beyond the working class, was definitely "on the make" under the terms and conditions in society then prevailing. The upper middle class was getting what adult education it felt the need for in quite other institutions, like literary and philosophical societies and, at the highest level, Athenaeums. Now, whether the group referred to could be described as lower middle class or upper working class, it was in any case a social group that had definitely started up the economic ladder and seemed to require no great modification of the social terms and conditions to make a further advance. This has remained the steadiest audience for adult education to our day.

If working-class intellectual energies did not go into the Mechanics' Institutions, where did they go? The historians suggest the answer: They went into friendly, trade-union, and temperance societies, and into political clubs—enterprises, in short, completely under the control of workingmen, directed to ends they themselves regarded as important enough to make sacrifices to attain. While the management of such enterprises was educative, they are not normally considered part of adult education. We shall, therefore, not look closely at these undertakings with but one exception— the educational aspects of a political development of great importance, the Chartist movement.

Chartism was a many-faceted political and social movement which ran its course between 1836 and 1848. With a Right, a Center, and a Left, it was integrated around six famous points or demands: manhood suffrage, payment of members of Parliament, the ballot, annual Parliaments, equal electoral districts, and abolition of property qualifications for membership in Parliament. The fundamental objective was to gain for the working class a voice in the governing of the realm. It arose after it was clear that the 1832 reform of parliamentary representation was of little obvious benefit to the working class, but rather was a middle-class success.

Now one of the numerous ways in which the Chartists may be divided is into "Knowledge Chartists" and "Physical Force Chartists." Our concern is with the Knowledge Chartists, for what they wanted may be taken as an expression of the views of the moderate workingmen. Their leader and spokesman was William Lovett (1800–1877), a working-class radical with numerous ties to the middle-class reformers of the day, particularly the Benthamites. In 1840 Lovett (in collaboration with one John Collins) published a book called *Chartism: A New Organization of the People, Embracing a Plan for the Education and Improvement of the People, Politically and Socially*. It was designed to put the movement on an educational basis and frustrate those apparently willing to resort to force.

The basic argument was: "How can a corrupt government withstand an enlightened people?" Typical quotations are:

> Education will cause every latent seed of the mind to germinate and spring up into useful life which otherwise might have been buried in ignorance and died in the corruption of its own nature. . . . The ignorant man can never be truly happy.

The franchise is "the best of schoolmasters."

> . . . those who possess the power to elect must have knowledge, judgment and moral principle to direct them, before anything worthy of the name of just government or true liberty can be established.

The scheme proposed for the education of the people included a very wide range of amenities: the provision of public halls and schools, lectures, readings, discussion groups, dancing classes, musical evenings, public gardens, museums, libraries, baths, workshops and schools of agriculture, as well as a publishing house. All these were to be built up and operated on a *voluntary* basis, for Lovett had a keen suspicion of government control. Particular attention was to be paid to the publishing side, for Lovett was a firm believer in the power of the press as a popular educator.

While the Chartists failed to win either their general or specific points—the movement ended in 1848 in a rather farcical failure—most of the points they made were in the long run accepted by British and other democratic nations. The ideas of the Knowledge Chartists admirably illustrate two points specifically relevant to adult education: (1) that education can be thought of as a means to the end of social reform, and (2) that a free press is potentially an educative force of enormous power.

Search for a Firm Base for Adult Education

THE CHARTIST movement coincided in time with the "Hungry Forties," perhaps the most difficult period for wayfaring people in modern British history. Around 1850, however, historians usually mark a turn for the better. Not only was there an upswing in general economic welfare, but many environmental changes, mostly brought about by legislative action at the behest of middle-class reformers, provided a more hopeful background for life and for popular education. As the decades passed, aspiring wayfaring men had better and better chances to satisfy their wish for saving knowledge. Here we can but name some of the hopeful developments.

Edward Chadwick (later Sir Edward) and his friends conducted a successful campaign for a public-health system. This involved the compilation of a series of Blue Books on the appalling sanitary conditions in the industrial towns. Their circulation was in itself educational. Between 1845 and 1854 laws were passed which, in effect, revolutionized, but did not perfect, the environments of those dwelling in urban areas. About the same time men like R. A. Slaney and James Silk Bucking am supported legislation to allow the use of tax funds to provide public walks, playgrounds, parks, and baths, thus contributing not only to the improvement of health and welfare, but implicitly recognizing public responsibility for recreation.

Perhaps a bit more obviously relevant to our story was the work of William Ewart, Joseph Brotherton, and Edward Edwards in successfully advocating the use of tax funds for public libraries and museums. This effort achieved success between 1845 and 1850. Although there was some opposition to opening the new institutions—the first free public library was actually opened in 1848— to "the rough, uncultured democracy," the three leaders successfully insisted that they should be opened to all. Equally relevant was the campaign to abolish the so-called "taxes on knowledge," first imposed in Queen Anne's time, but increased in 1819 as an act of repression during the post-Napoleonic reaction. The taxes bore especially heavily on newspapers and made impossible a cheap press in any form. We have noted that people like the Knowledge Chartists believed that a cheap press would be of immense significance educationally. The tax on newspapers was reduced in 1836 and abolished entirely in 1855, although the last of the taxes on knowledge did not disappear until 1869. The way was finally opened to the use of the press as a popular educator.

As these opportunities for better and more intelligent living opened up, they inspired a campaign for a better chance to make use of them. This took the form of a fierce agitation, participated in both by workers and conservative reformers, for a law limiting the hours of labor. The first such law was passed in 1847. During the campaign, the Short Time Central Committee made the very point suggested here. It said: "Schools and libraries are of small use without time to study. Parks are well for those only who can have time to perambulate in them, and baths of little use to such dirty people as do not leave work until eight o'clock at night. We protest that it is a mere burlesque upon philanthropy to make provision for these benefits with a continuance of twelve hours' labour and fifteen hours' occupation for every manufacturing operative above thirteen years of age." [1] Restrospectively, the Hammonds, the economic historians, concluded that the 1847 law signified "the success of the contention . . . that the workman had a right to share in the culture and leisure enjoyed by other classes." [2]

Finally, on this point, it should be called to mind that improvements in education for children took place during the latter half of the century of the profoundest significance to adult education. After prolonged agitation and a period during which reliance for elementary education was placed on voluntary efforts, chiefly by the churches, a state system was established in 1870. In 1876 this was made compulsory and in 1891 it became entirely free. The development of the state elementary schools insured basic literacy to the people and progressively freed the adult educators for adventures on higher educational levels.

The transition from the characteristic emphasis on promoting literacy of the first half of the century to an emphasis on higher knowledge during the second half can well be illustrated by an account of the Adult School movement and the activities of the co-operators in education. They will provide a background for the experiments in bringing the cultural heritage to wayfaring people that the new environment encouraged.

In 1842 Joseph Sturge, a Quaker, discovered the Adult School of Nottingham and carried the idea it embodied back to Birmingham where he lived. He established such a school in Severn Street. However, it was not until 1852 that the men were separated from the boys, establishing a true adult school. Classes were of two hours' duration, one hour devoted to writing, the other to reading, with question periods interspersed. The motivation was still mixed, the evangelical and pedagogical purposes both being present. (At a later date the announced purpose was "to intensify the social spirit by associating men together for the free study of the deeper problems of life, viewed in relation to the ideal of manhood set before them in the Gospels.")

Sturge's school differed hardly at all from its predecessors of the same general kind, yet it became the basis of a widespread and enduring system. This was because of the presence of three factors: (1) The Quakers got behind the movement and were its chief sustainers for many years, both spiritually and materially; (2) the Friends' First-day School Association in 1847 dropped its preoccupation with children and thereafter gave its support to the adult schools, tending to the endless task of fund-raising; and (3) strong teaching leadership was available over many successive years.

The greatest teacher-leader was William White (1820–1900), who, after having taught in an adult school at Reading, joined Sturge in Birmingham and took over the teaching of the so-called "Number 1" class at Severn Street. He continued to teach until he was seventy-eight years old, always emphasizing reading and writing. "Reading" always meant to White the reading of the Bible. Freely available as a propagandist for Adult Schools, White traveled widely, spreading the word. His practicality made his help invaluable when new schools were being established. Like so many adult educators before and since, White lived on the "borderline at which adult education merges into social welfare," and campaigned for better local government—he was Mayor of Birmingham in 1882—for public-health measures, parks, and temperance. (There was long an affinity between an interest in adult education and an interest in temperance.)

The Adult School movement was preoccupied with spreading basic literacy from 1847 to about 1860. During these years schools were established in numerous industrial cities, including Sheffield, Leeds, Huddersfield, Bristol, and Leicester. From 1860 to 1900 the schools expanded their work in various directions: they sponsored savings banks (the thrift movement) and sick-benefits funds, built up libraries, promoted temperance societies, and encouraged school social life by teas and athletic contests. The curriculum, however, stayed within elementary limits and students were not expected, or encouraged, to climb an educational ladder. As a matter of fact none existed, though there was something R. H. Tawney was later to call the "greasy pole," up which the ambitious shinnied as far as they could. At Severn Street in 1879 there were 2,299 scholars and 50 teachers; in 1909 there were 1,662 schools with 110,000 scholars.

As the century drew to a close, it was apparent that a new and broader outlook was needed if the movement was to continue. The general educational environment had radically changed since the late forties and so had the political and social position and outlook of the prospective students. In 1897 Edward Worsdell wrote an article in the paper of the movement, *One and All,* in

which he made seven suggestions for the future of the Adult
Schools:

(1) that they encourage courses in literature, economics,
    physiology and other advanced studies;
(2) that the school libraries be strengthened and private
    reading encouraged;
(3) that reading circles be encouraged;
(4) that public lectures be offered;
(5) that the schools link up with the local University Ex-
    tension Movement;
(6) that educational tours and excursions be encouraged;
(7) that a publishing unit be established.[3]

The Adult Schools were asked, in brief, to adapt themselves to
the changing times rather than allow themselves to fade away,
while the new needs were met by new organizations, the more
customary development in adult education history.

The Quakers themselves, however, did not put the proposals to
the test, for in 1899 their Adult Schools were absorbed along with
the nondenominational Adult Schools of England, into a National
Council of Adult Schools Associations, of which William White
was chairman at his death. By 1909 the Quaker-founded schools
had been pretty completely taken over by the nondenominational
workers. Between 1900 and 1914, the movement slowly dropped
its reading and writing classes as the need for them was met by the
state schools.

Today, the Adult Schools are organized in a National Adult
School Union embracing about twenty-five county unions. The
emphasis now falls upon the pursuit of learning among compatible
friends dedicated to social service and inspired by religious ideals.
The studies ordinarily pursued are the social sciences and the
humanities. Discussion groups, correspondence courses, summer
schools, and sessions at residential guest houses are provided. The
Adult Schools, however, have ceased to occupy a central place in
the adult education movement.

Meanwhile the Quakers turned their energies into settlement-
house work, the WEA, the YMCA, and the founding of residential
guest houses for religious and educational purposes—Woodbrooke

in 1902, and Fircroft in 1909. They pursued adult education on new frontiers.

The modern co-operative movement, which has a lengthy and complex ancestry, dates from 1844 when a small group of working-men at Rochdale founded a co-operative store. This group had a background of Owenite socialism and Knowledge Chartism—some of the individual members were influenced by both movements. The Owenites and the Chartists were about equally convinced that education was indispensable to the improvement of the working-class conditions; from very early days the co-operators promoted education. The original rules of the Rochdale co-operative mentioned education as an approved area of action. In 1846 regularly scheduled discussion meetings were held in the Rochdale headquarters, in 1848 a reading room stocked with newspapers and magazines was launched, and books for a library were afterward accumulated. In the beginning persons wishing to use the reading room and library paid a small fee separately from any relations with the store, but in 1853 it was decided to make the service free and support it by allocating 2½ per cent of the trading surplus to that purpose. "Two-and-a-half per cent for education" thus became a famous slogan of the co-operators.

Yet, in the long run, the co-operators confined their particular educational efforts chiefly to the training required to sustain and operate the ever-expanding co-operative movement. Their own reading rooms and libraries were eventually abandoned as the cheap press developed, making every man a buyer of newspapers, and as the public libraries expanded. Rather than try to develop a full-dress educational system of their own, they participated largely in university extension, Ruskin College, and the Workers' Educational Association when they appeared. In fact, it was the limitations of co-operative education which suggested the WEA approach to its founder. In short, the educational interests of the social reformers found enduring lodgment in education at the university level for wayfaring men.

In the 1850's the most striking experiment was with the so-called "people's" or "workingmen's" colleges. The basic idea was to provide the people with culture through the study of modern and ancient languages and literatures, mathematics, logic, elocution, drawing, and so on, or humanistic as opposed to scientific (or vocational) subjects.

The first of the colleges was established at Sheffield in 1842 by the Reverend R. S. Bayley, a Congregationalist minister. Bayley called his school a "people's" college. It was held in a "ghastly, white-washed, unplastered garret," but it survived to become the nucleus of the present-day University of Sheffield. A similar people's college was established by George Gill at Nottingham in 1846. But the central event in this particular movement was the establishment of the Workingmen's College at London in 1854 by a group of Christian Socialists led by Frederick Denison Maurice. By 1862 there were colleges at Manchester, Salford, Ancoats, Leicester (which, as the Vaughan Memorial College, was the only one other than the London school to survive), Halifax, Liverpool, Wolverhampton, Oxford, and Cambridge.

No single explanation of the origin of the colleges is completely satisfactory. They were, in a sense, a link between the Mechanics' Institutes and the university-extension movement which follows next in historical sequence. But if linking them with the Mechanics' Institutes is sound, it is only because the people's colleges were organized along the lines of the Institutes. The content of their teaching was precisely that range of studies which the Institutes had professed to offer at their founding, but which they had immediately neglected in favor of a scientific emphasis. The link with the university-extension movement is easier to accept, for when it emerged its subject matter was cultural rather than scientific-vocational.

Vocational and scientific training passed, in large measure but not wholly, to the care of the public authorities, especially after the Great Exhibition of 1851 demonstrated vividly the crying need for it in England. Thomas Henry Huxley—ardent advocate of scientific education, who after 1855 regularly delivered the very popular "people's lectures" in science, especially Darwinism—worked from a base at the government-supported School of Mines in Jermyn Street, London. The history of technical education is complex, but it can be remarked that popular interest in and support of it fluctuated from 1850 with the depth of the worry about foreign-trade competition, especially German and American.

Technical education only belatedly reached the high development characteristic in Germany and the United States, whether at the popular or university level.

Whatever the historical linkages of the colleges, it is clear that they were established by men who felt that the salvation of the people of England lay neither in vocational training nor in Chartist agitation for political reform, but in the enrichment of the human personality through the same kind of studies as were pursued in the universities. As John Ruskin put it, "You do not learn that you may live—you live that you may learn." The big question was, "What should man learn?"

The motives of the London pioneers can be well delineated by taking a close look at the Christian Socialists. The great names in this movement were Frederick Denison Maurice (1805–1872), Charles Kingsley (1819–1875), and Thomas Hughes (1822–1896). As Christian Socialists these men aimed to socialize Christianity, that is, to identify the Church of England with the struggle for the well-being of the people; and to Christianize socialism, that is, to see to it that social reform was not left to the secularists. More precisely, the Christian Socialists believed "that the economic development and the social relations of the community could prove satisfactory only if they were consciously brought into obedience to the spirit of Christ and His purpose for mankind. . . . [They] banded themselves together therefore to proclaim the supremacy of Christian values over purely secular considerations, to expound the traditions and implications of Christianity in this light, to enlist the sympathy of the public for the efforts made by the workers to improve their condition and transform their status, and to initiate practical experiments in working-class education and co-operation of every kind." [4]

They began their work in the wake of the collapse of Chartism in 1848. Their efforts in co-operation—chiefly producers' co-operatives—quickly failed; their efforts in education lasted longer; but their general influence on the intellectual life of their time and subsequent decades was greater still, continuing both in England and America down to our own day. A very considerable part of their influence was gained through periodical, pamphlet, and book publications, including novels like Charles Kingsley's *Yeast* and *Alton Locke*.

All three of the Christian Socialists we have chosen to mention
had distinguished and important careers before and after their in-
cursion into adult education. Maurice was a professor of English
literature, history, and theology at King's College, London, before
he undertook the direction of the Workingmen's College, and professor of moral philosophy at Cambridge later on. Kingsley became
professor of modern history at Cambridge and a prolific and miscellaneous author. He wrote the children's classic, *Water Babies,*
for instance. Thomas Hughes had a career as a judge as well as
a social reformer and was author of the celebrated *Tom Brown's
School Days* (1857). "Tom Brown" was, in a sense, the personal-
ity-image that dominated these men's minds.

The London Workingmen's College opened on October 31,
1854, with Maurice as principal. On the teaching staff with Maurice were Kingsley, John Ruskin, Dante Gabriel Rossetti, and C.
Lowes Dickinson. In addition to holding that the education offered
should be humane and not technical, ethical and not practical,
Maurice also believed that it should be based on the previous interests of the students (and hence that social and political questions
should be explored), and that the students and teachers must have
a sense of a *shared adventure* if the work was to be truly educational. Or as A. E. Dobbs has put it:

> The new ideal was not information, but the enrichment of
> personality; a conception which at the outset tended to draw
> a hard distinction between liberal and technical studies. The
> development of individuality was approached through an
> appeal to corporate feeling. Lastly, following out the con-
> ception of social reunion and admitting the postulate of human
> brotherhood, it was claimed that education is a reciprocal
> process, involving an interchange of thought between teachers
> and learners and a persistent reaction of mind on mind.[5]

It was not believed that this kind of education should declass
the students, or facilitate their rise into a higher class, but rather
should make them better members of the working class from which
they came and in which they should remain. Charles Kingsley was
especially fierce on this point. This was a long way from the conception of education as a factor in increasing social mobility, so
characteristic in the United States. Yet Maurice had it in mind

that graduates of the college should be capable of passing the examinations for university degrees. The college's curriculum included classes in the Bible, Shakespeare, history, geography, art (Ruskin taught drawing), law, and grammar.

What Maurice and his collaborators were really seeking was a way to use education to reconcile the classes. Like so many British adult education ventures, this one was an effort to acculturate the economically and educationally underprivileged. Maurice and his friends were extremely conscious of the fact that the workingmen believed that knowledge was ordinarily class-angled, yet they felt that culture *qua* culture, especially if impregnated with religion, would prove a reconciling element. In 1855 Maurice declared:

> I know well how hard it is, and must be, to persuade working men anywhere, especially those intelligent working men who are likely to desire instruction, that we do not mean to make our teaching subservient to our own purposes, that we do not wish to make the history of the past and the experience of the present echo our own conclusions, and apologize for our own injustice. We have played falsely with the facts; we have bent and twisted evidence to the justification of our own school and party and class, and to the condemnation of every other. We must pay the penalty for these crimes. The expiation cannot be a very brief one.[6]

Yet somehow Maurice could not shake off the feeling that he and his fellows knew better than the students what was needed. He resisted anything that savored of student self-government, declaring:

> I would not let the pupils have the least voice in determining what we shall teach or not teach, or how we shall teach. We may have social meetings with them; we may have conversations with them individually; but no education will go on if we have tumultuous assemblies to discuss what has been done or what is to be done. We who begin the institution must claim authority over it, and not hostilely resign our authority, however we may admit others by degrees to share it, and however willing we may be to creep out of it when the institution can

stand without us. That we may preserve this position, I believe
it is necessary that our teaching should be gratuitous; all the
fees going at first to the procuring of the necessary machinery
for the institution.[7]

However well the colleges may have satisfied their students,
their reach was short and they could not meet the wants of more
than a tiny fraction of those working people who were keen to
better their education. The cheap press was still the one true mass
educator. At this very time, the most important single contributor
to popular education was John Cassell, a self-educated lecturer on
teetotalism, who in 1850 began the publication of the *Popular
Educator* in weekly numbers at a penny each. It quickly won a
very wide circulation. In 1852 this venture was described as follows before a parliamentary committee:

> I consider Mr. John Cassell is doing more at the present time
> than any other individual to supply the increasing demand of
> the operative classes for useful knowledge, and in supplying
> works peculiarly adapted to their circumstances and condi-
> tion. His popular mode of education is receiving an extended
> and an extraordinary circulation and is highly estimated by
> a large number of the operative classes. For a penny a week
> the working-man is supplied with lessons in grammar, arith-
> metic, mathematics, in Latin, French, and German; and he
> has had enquiries for some lessons in Hebrew and Greek,
> that the working-man may endeavour to read the Scriptures
> in the original text. In these penny numbers are also furnished
> lessons in ancient history, natural history, geology and physi-
> ology; and such lessons and such subjects are being entered
> into by many with great avidity.[8]

By 1862 Cassell was selling his publications at an annual rate of
twenty-five to thirty million copies. Even after his death in 1865,
they continued to be issued in revised editions.

Cassell's undertaking links back to the SDUK and forward to
the cheap originals and reprints of the modern publishing industry.
All down the years, the role of the cheap book in both self-education and adult education classes has been central. For the latter,
cheap originals and reprints have provided indispensable texts for

class use, and for the former they have provided much of the high-quality, low-priced grist without which the adventure might have been impossible. Some of the English series, both famous and enduring, are "Everyman's Library," founded in 1906 by J. M. Dent, the "World's Classics," put out by Oxford University Press, also from 1906, and the "Penguin Books," launched in 1935 by Allen Lane who, quite properly, was later knighted for his successful experiment with the paper-bound book. The kind of series which consists of relatively short original books intended specifically for use as self-educators has never been as successful as the books, originals or reprints, not so labeled. The "Home University Library," founded in 1911, is a case in point. It is interesting, however, that such series have consistently been more popular in England than in the United States, though the reason is not clear even to the publishers.

An important phase of the general concern with education at mid-century was the intensive examination of the place of Oxford and Cambridge in English life. Royal commissions, says a British government report, "stirred into active life a mass of sleeping endowments, threw the older universities open to the active minds of the middle classes . . ." [9] A phase of the change thus brought about was a concern with making the intellectual resources of the universities available to the persons—chiefly of the middle classes and including women—never likely to be regular students. Perhaps some of the thinking was stirred as much by Matthew Arnold's conviction that the English was the worst educated middle class in the world as by the concern over the correct use of university resources.

The movement that finally took to itself the name "university extension" originated with James Stuart, Fellow of Trinity College, Cambridge, who was active in experimentation and promotion from 1867 to 1875, but not thereafter.[10] Two ideas seem to have influenced Stuart: the knowledge that university education was much more widespread in Scotland than in England, and the idea that a "peripatetic university" could be evolved to serve all the principal towns of England.

Stuart got his chance to make a practical experiment in 1867. In that year he lectured to audiences of women at Manchester,

Liverpool, Sheffield, and Leeds under the auspices of the North of England Council for Promoting the Higher Education of Women, an organization chiefly concerned with the further education of governesses and schoolmistresses and having in view the establishment of educational institutions for them. Stuart's subject was astronomy. That same year he also gave his lecture before a Mechanics' Institute established at Crewe by the London and North Western Railway Company. Later he lectured for the co-operative society at Rochdale. It was when talking to the co-operators that he discovered the value of allowing time for discussion at each session.

After about six years of experimentation, Stuart concluded that there was a widespread demand for higher education in the country and that there was an obligation "on the two ancient Universities to come forward to supply the demand." He put his case to his own university and in 1873 there was established at Cambridge a Syndicate for Extension Lectures. London University followed in 1876 with a University Extension Society; and Oxford in 1878 with its Delegacy for the Extension of University Teaching. From these beginnings came the extramural activities so characteristic of the British universities of the present day, often carried on under the leadership of professors or directors of adult education and staffed with tutors.

The first period of the history of university extension runs from the beginnings to about 1900, when it was apparent that, as Basil Yeaxlee put it in 1925, "Despite all that the movement accomplished before the end of the century . . . it could not be acclaimed as the fulfilment of the desires either of the universities or of the adult students, and particularly of working-class students, throughout the country. Except in a few well-marked districts it became a middle-class movement, with more women students than men, apt to be discontinuous in choice of subjects for successive courses, and necessarily unable to accomplish really effective class work with more than a tithe of those who attended the lectures." [11] The principle that university extension must be self-supporting excluded all who could not pay for their education out of their own pockets. It seemed to be a soundly based approach to a fundamental problem, but the secret of making it work in full measure had not been found.

Before continuing with the story of the effort to bring education of university standard to wayfaring men, let us glance at a differently based effort to achieve much the same end. It involves the story of an exemplary career and the invention of an institution which eventually became common in both Britain and the United States.

Arnold Toynbee, uncle of the author of *A Study of History,* was a late Victorian friend of the masses, full of sympathy for human suffering. Inspired by John Ruskin, whom he knew personally, he believed in the dignity of human labor and first tried to demonstrate his belief by helping to repair a village road near Oxford. Assiduous reading of the Bible gave him a longing for God and a fervent belief in the forgiveness of sins.

As a young man of twenty-three, Toynbee spent a few months doing good works in the parish of St. Jude's, Whitechapel, in the East End of London. Thereafter he spent much time lecturing on political economy and public affairs to audiences of working people, but while he was "zealous for the diffusion" of such knowledge, he saw its use as but preliminary to "quieting the animal appetites" and "satisfying the nobler aspirations" through religion.

Toynbee thought men of "culture and public spirit" should lead the way in both areas. He persuaded some of his friends at Oxford to join him in writing and delivering lectures like those he had himself been giving. His personal high-point in this effort was a paper he delivered before the annual meeting of the co-operative societies at Oxford in 1882 on the subject of "Education of Co-operators," a plea for political and economic education for better citizenship. The big difficulty was, Toynbee asserted, the "apathy of those who were to be instructed"; and he offered his solution of this: "Languor can only be conquered by enthusiasm and enthusiasm can only be kindled by two things: an ideal which takes the imagination by storm, and a definite intelligible plan for carrying out that ideal into practice." Toynbee died in 1883, at the early age of thirty-one. He became a symbolic figure.[12]

Two years after Toynbee's death, Canon Samuel A. Barnett established a "settlement house" in the East End of London to which he gave the name Toynbee Hall. It became the spiritual ancestor of all subsequent settlement houses in Britain and the United States. A value was supposed to inhere in the reciprocal influence for good between the "classes" (as represented by the settlement-house workers) and the "masses" (i.e., the slum-dwellers round about).

The Toynbee Hall educational experiments proceeded from mixed motives: religious, class-reconciliation, and education-as-such. The work was carried on at several levels: evening classes—the Bible, morality, literature, natural science, the arts and handicrafts—all informal and at a fairly elementary level; university-extension classes (later WEA classes) at the standards demanded by their supervisors; and activities like extempore debates, lectures (religious subjects on Sundays), a library, and many semieducational clubs.

On this basis, and with variations down the years, there has always been a tie-up between the settlement houses and adult education, permanently illustrating the close connection constantly to be found between adult education and good works.

CHAPTER

10

Educating Wayfarers at the University Level

Around the turn of the century, several striking attempts to bring university-level educational opportunities to adults were made.[1] All have proved enduring and in due course they became the "core" of British adult education. The stories of the various enterprises are linked with one another and together they have provided wayfaring men and women with "higher" education under varying conditions, animated by varying motives. After World War II the results were skeptically examined, and while inadequacies were identified and resolutions for improvement made, there was little doubt that, in general, a very great deal had been accomplished.

The first enterprise to be launched was Ruskin College. All who are familiar with the writings of John Ruskin are aware that much of his writing in the field of political economy had what we would today call a prolabor bias. We have noted that Ruskin himself was associated with Frederick Denison Maurice and the London Workingmen's College and that his outlook inspired Arnold Toynbee to experiment with bringing saving knowledge to the working class.

It was, therefore, altogether fitting and proper that when a labor residential college was established at (but not *in*) Oxford in 1899, it should have been named after him.

Much of the money needed to establish the school was supplied by Mr. and Mrs. Walter Vrooman, and Mr. Vrooman was chairman of the trustees and president of the college. The trustees were drawn from the trade unions, the co-operatives, and the Ruskin Societies (dedicated to preserving the memory of John Ruskin). The Vroomans were Americans. Walter Vrooman was, in his time, well known as a fierce critic of municipal corruption and as an advocate of public parks. In the venture at Oxford, another American, Charles Austin Beard, was closely associated with him—so closely that he is often called a cofounder. Later, in America, Beard had a profoundly influential career as historian, political scientist, and writer on public affairs, punctuated by excursions into adult education. It had originally been intended to establish the college in America, but that was not done because the American Federation of Labor was not enthusiastic about the idea and because it was felt that there were a "number of educational means of reaching the intelligent labouring classes . . ." already in existence in America.

The rationale and aims of the college were set out in a statement which read as follows:

> Hitherto the opportunity of gaining an educated insight into the problems of our life and generation has been beyond the hope of most working men. Yet these men are our citizens, our voters and the makers of our laws. Whether they will use their powers with judgment or under the influence of prejudice born of ignorance, depends upon their knowledge. It is in order that they may be able impartially to study the great social and political problems of the day that Ruskin College exists.

> The endeavour is to create in each student a feeling of responsibility. He is taught to regard the education which he receives, not as a means of personal advancement, but as a trust for the good of others. He learns in order that he may raise and not rise out of the class to which he belongs. The work is carried on in two ways:

(a) By the education at Ruskin College, Oxford; this is intended for those who show special promise, who may become working-men Members of Parliament, and officials of Trade Unions and Cooperative Societies; by this means they are enabled to come to Oxford and study the problems which they have to solve.

(b) By the Correspondence School. By means of this all who are interested in the problems of our time are enabled to study the subjects taught at Ruskin College, by home reading.[2]

In the beginning years, a student spent only one year at the college, but later on it was possible to spend several. Some scholarships were early provided by the trade unions and the co-operatives.

The first class had twenty-five members, ranging from eighteen to fifty years of age, and included a carpenter, a cycle hand, a miner, a glass-factory worker, a printer, and a newsboy.

Judging from the courses offered, the curriculum was designed judiciously to mix liberal arts and social studies, with a bias toward the latter. There were lectures in English constitutional and political history, the history of the working class, and economics. The correspondence courses covered the same ground. A check was kept on the reading of correspondence students by means of a monthly essay each returned for evaluation and critical comment. The very first year six hundred correspondence students registered. This work was the particular interest of Dr. Beard.

Both the residential and correspondence schools took firm root and still flourish, but the extension work merged into university extension and particularly into its working-class wing, the Workers' Educational Association classes.

The Workers' Educational Association—universally known simply as the WEA—was launched in 1903. It became world-famous and to most foreigners by far the best known of all the adult education undertakings in Britain. Although its story is, in a sense, self-contained, it is really a part of the story of the university-extension movement, of which the WEA has always been the section particularly concerned with serving the working-class audience. Intellectually it has been directly associated with the progress of collectivist thought in England, a trend which has deeply affected the trade unions, the Labour Party, and the whole nation. This alone would make it a major socio-political phenomenon. Contributing to its fame has been the fact that British middle-class and upper-class people have long derived intense emotional satisfaction from "doing something" for the workers—from thus expiating their "class guilt"—and talking and writing about what they have done. WEA adventitiously profited from this characteristic of its patrons.

Although many famous men and women took part in its promotion and development, WEA's "onlie true begettor" was Albert Mansbridge.

Mansbridge was born at Gloucester in 1876, the son of a carpenter; he died in retirement at Torquay, on August 22, 1952. By an accident of circumstances, he was able to continue his education beyond the tenth year and the sixth "standard"—the customary limit for working-class children of his day—to his fourteenth year and the "grammar school" level. On ability alone, his friends think he could have gone successfully through Oxford or Cambridge, but the financial hurdle was too much for him, and he had to turn to self-education to satisfy his craving for cultivation. All his life Mansbridge was deeply religious—an important part of his self-education was listening to the sermons of famous divines. The drive behind his personal educational aspirations was religious and the religio-philanthropic motivation was behind his larger educational schemes. He was thus linked to a very powerful tradition in adult education.

Mansbridge earned his living as a clerical worker. In 1897 he was in the employ of the Cooperative Wholesale Society. He took an active part in the educational work of the co-operative movement, but soon found that it was too limited in resources, scope, and aspiration to suit him. He was thus driven to search for something better. In his search he gradually evolved a formula which he presented in 1903 in three articles in the *University Extension Journal*. In these expository pieces he proposed a partnership "between enlightened scholarship and working class aspiration"—in practical terms, between university extension on the one hand and the co-operative movement and the trade unions on the other—the link to be a Workers' Educational Association. In working out the scheme, the universities were to suppy the instructors and keep up the standards, while the WEA was to supply the students.

How did Mansbridge see the working class, viewed as a source of students? He suffered few illusions. He had had experience of the actualities in his educational work for the Cooperative Whole-sale Society. He learned more from operating the WEA. After a decade of effort Mansbridge summarized his conclusions as follows (1908):

. . . artisans may be divided into three classes: those whose intention it is to become foremen, those who are filled with the spirit of combination—trade unionists before all else—and those who are satisfied simply to do their day's work. The first class will secure technical education at all costs; it is represented in our polytechnics by many keen students who study the theory of their trades. The best of the representatives of the second class are frequently to be found amongst those who study economics, industrial history and citizenship. An artisan seldom finds his interests in both of these classes; if so, it is not for long. In the third class the great body of artisans may be placed. It supplies the rank and file of the trade unions. It is the class that, even above the others, needs the influence of a wise and careful propaganda. From it, the great impression that artisans are careless of their higher educational interest has been gained. Men of this class are unwilling to submit themselves to any definite educational influences, but when they are organized they will fall into line with that modern working-class movement which is definitely and distinctly educational. This movement, clearly expressed as it is by the leaders, is to be counted upon as a factor in the future. Workpeople as a whole are seeing more and more clearly that education is the great thing and the real thing, making all things possible for the man who has it.[3]

Although in the course of time a good deal of progress was made, the general engagement of the working class in WEA was not to be achieved. Nevertheless, the WEA had an enormous impact on British working-class life, for it provided the "higher education" of so many of the *leaders* of the trade unions and the

Labour Party. In effect, WEA was a substitute for the university
education then otherwise unavailable to the working class.

Mansbridge's three articles in the *University Extension Journal*
were reprinted as a pamphlet by John Holland Rose, editor of the
Journal, later professor of naval history at Cambridge. In a brief
preface, Rose invoked the names of Arnold Toynbee and Charles
Kingsley to support Mansbridge's view. (Actually, Mansbridge's
immediate inspiration, on the religious side, came from the Anglo-
Catholic prelate, Charles Gore, but he had early been in contact
with Canon Barnett of Toynbee Hall.) Rose announced that a
constitution for the suggested organization would be fixed upon,
and officers to direct it elected, at an Extension Summer Meeting
at Oxford in August, 1903. This was done, and WEA launched
upon its career. Manbridge's proposals had come to the attention of the university people at a moment when they were, as so
often after 1850, "experiencing qualms regarding the monopoly of
culture and educational opportunity by a privileged class." [4]

Total income for the first year was £73/19/6 (about $360).
Although the budget rose to majestic heights in later years, finances
never ceased to be a major problem. Mansbridge made a virtue
of necessity by declaring that "all movements ought to be small
and poor at the commencement; they should grow from the
seed upwards."

The first national conference was held at Oxford in 1905. William Temple, "the son of an archbishop married to the grand-
daughter of an earl," at the time a fellow of Queen's College,
then became president. He continued in office for many years,
giving up the post eventually only because of the pressure of his
duties in the Church of England (later, in 1942, he became Archbishop of Canterbury). Temple not only provided the necessary
cachet of impeccable respectability, but also a dedicated, working
leadership, supported by a profound belief in the justice and value
of WEA. Mansbridge, who had been chosen honorary secretary
and treasurer in 1903, became full-time secretary in 1905, and
held the post until 1915.

In 1906 the constitution was revised and the statement of
purpose emerged as (*my italics*): "the Higher education of Working People, *primarily by the extension of University Teaching,*
also (a) by the assistance of working-class efforts of a specifically

educational character, (b) by assistance in the development of an efficient School Continuation System, (c) by the coordination of popular educational effort."

As time passed, the WEA took a very active part in the promotion of an egalitarian system of state education. It played an important role as critic of state education, as resister of relapses from virtue in the state system, ånd as propagandist for changes and advances. Specifically, it put its full power as a propaganda agency behind the most liberal versions of the educational bills of 1918 and 1944.

As early as 1904, when the first branch was established at Reading, WEA began to decentralize. The central office in London never ceased to be vitally important as the headquarters of leadership, but the day labor of the movement was done by the local branches. As early as 1908 these numbered fifty. A local group, says the historian of WEA, "promoted University Extension Courses and rounded up audiences for them; they poked and prodded their local education committees; they conducted propaganda for their local art galleries and museums; they formed clubs, libraries, discussion groups and reading circles; they organized educational excursions; they fastened upon local pundits and incited them to speak to the people. And everywhere and all the time they aimed at drawing into the orbit of educational endeavour, the keener spirits of their local trade-union branches and cooperative societies." [5]

In 1907 a notable educational invention appeared. This was the tutorial-class idea, launched on its career by Oxford University. A tutorial class was to consist of thirty students pledged to pursue a subject for at least one year, but preferably for three in sequence. The work was to be done in two-hour classes held once a week for twenty-four weeks during the winter months, plus homework consisting of extensive reading and the preparation of written reports and essays. Each class was to be under the leadership of a university tutor especially charged with keeping the work up to university standards. The two-hour class period was to be divided about equally between a lecture and a discussion period. In this fashion it was hoped to achieve "continuous and systematic student application" and avoid the shreds and patches of haphazard attendance of individual lectures and very short courses. The heart of the tutorial class was the individual relation of tutor and student, stimulated particularly by discussion. The great objective was to teach *how* to think, not *what* to think, although over the years WEA has been associated with one variety of social thought. The central assumption was incontrovertible: that there was no discoverable substitute for laborious intellectual effort in acquiring an education. None has turned up since.

The tutorial class idea was immediately adopted by WEA. In 1908 the first classes were launched at Rochdale, in connection with the co-operative, and at nearby Longton. These classes (subject: "Economic History of the Seventeenth Century") were in charge of R. H. Tawney. Tawney has been authoritatively evaluated (by Mary E. Stocks, historian of WEA) as probably "the greatest adult education tutor of all time." The first year he had 78 students, including a gardener, a plumber, a potter's thrower, a potter's decorator, a mechanic, a baker, several clerks, a librarian, a grocer, a railway agent, several insurance collectors, some elementary-school teachers. Only a minority were women. The most active students were officials of trade unions.

When Tawney undertook tutorial class work at Rochdale, he was an assistant lecturer in economics at the University of Glasgow, but as a tutor he worked under the sponsorship of his old university, Oxford. Tawney's subsequent activities in adult education, which include a period as president of WEA, were but episodes in a distinguished career as an academic economist and economic historian at the University of London. Like so many WEA people, Tawney had strong collectivist leanings and became a leading ideologist of the British labor movement, author of such "classic" works as *The Acquisitive Society* (1920), *Religion and the Rise of Capitalism* (1926), and *Equality* (1931).

The tutorial movement spread rapidly. By 1909 there were 39 classes, served by tutors from the universities of Oxford, Cambridge, London, Manchester, Liverpool, Leeds, and Sheffield. In the 1913–14 season, there were 155 classes. Classes met in schoolrooms, trade-union rooms, public libraries, and village halls. Not only were they emphasized by WEA, but they were also the focus of interest for the university-extension movement in general. This gave the most highly regarded activity in British adult education an intellectualistic character—sometimes reckoned to its credit and sometimes viewed with skepticism as excluding too many adults from possible benefits. WEA and university extension tried to cater to the less intellectual customers by single lectures and short courses, but their problems were, in general, not too perceptively handled.

In the early years there was a poverty of books adapted to the needs of the students; and also great difficulty in supplying books of any kind in the proper quantities at the proper places. From the struggle to solve this problem stemmed the WEA interest in the condition of the library system. The lack of books immediately relevant to needs was solved in time by the research and writing of such scholars as Tawney, G. D. H. Cole and the Hammonds; the supplying of books to the classes became an activity, first, of the central WEA office in collaboration with Toynbee Hall, and then, after 1916, of the National Central Library which Albert Mansbridge established. (The National Central Library was bombed out in World War II, but has since been replaced.) Tawney began by borrowing books from Oxford and the Fabian Society. The need for linking libraries and adult education could hardly be better illustrated.

By the time World War I began, the WEA had become a stable organization not readily to be displaced; the record seems to show, also, that it had assumed a pattern which has not changed very much since.

Before bringing the story of WEA to mid-century, it is necessary to retreat in time a bit and tell of an occurrence at Ruskin College in 1908–09. At the time it was a scandal of the adult education world, but today it and its sequel illustrate a difference in educational ideals of the profoundest significance to adult education— the difference between teaching *how* to think and teaching *what* to think.

In 1908 some of the advanced students at Ruskin set up a cry for courses in Marxism. They found a leader in Denis Hird, warden of the college, who, as a matter of fact, was using the Marxist approach in his sociology course. The managers of the school, however, refused "emphatically" to give official countenance to courses in Marxist thought and method. When the students formed private study groups to explore Marxism, the governing authorities asked Hird to put an end to them. At the same time, Hird was cautioned about the Marxist slant of his own course in sociology. Hird rejected the order and the advice. In April, 1909, he was asked to resign. This precipitated a student strike. In the end, Hird and a large group of students seceded from the college, migrated to London, and there founded a Central Labour College, dedicated to Marxist education. The venture was eventually supported by what was called the Plebs League.

The Marxists thus brought into the adult education world an educational enterprise dedicated to *what* to think. This was a direct challenge to the WEA and university extension, even though many WEA leaders were self-conscious about the class-angle issue, particularly in economic studies. The Plebs group argued that they alone could offer the working class instruction untainted by "bourgeois" notions. They asserted that WEA corrupted its students into passivity. Plebs prepared them for class militancy.

The idea that there is, or can be developed, a distinctively working-class culture to set off against "bourgeois" culture has a persistent and powerful apppeal in working-class circles. It was not a new idea in 1909; it is not dead today. The notion is usually strongest among Marxists, with their wish for and belief in the passing of all social power to the working class; but it has often been held by other groups, not Marxist, beset by working-class particularism. We have noted its existence, in the British context, among the customers of the Mechanics' Institutes and the Chartists, and we have seen that the reality of the idea was recognized by F. D. Maurice and the Christian Socialists. Suspicion of "class bias," moreover, not strong enough to lead to accepting Marxism, kept otherwise favorably disposed workers out of the early university-extension movement, and also out of WEA. But while the Plebs position had deep roots in British history, it never proved attractive to more than a minority of the British working class.

Nevertheless, the Plebs approach has survived to the present day, founded on a system of labor colleges and correspondence courses. The co-ordinating body is the National Council of Labour Colleges, with headquarters at Tillicoultry, Scotland. The movement supplies educational services to trade unions, conducts residence weekend and summer schools, lectures and day schools, and distributes filmstrips and publications. It reaches thousands of persons annually. In 1950 it was serving educationally 81 unions, as well as some of the co-operative societies and a variety of other organizations with working-class membership. The two unions longest favorable to the Plebs have been the National Union of Railwaymen and the Miners' Federation. Observers report that a considerable proportion of the early fierceness has gone out of the movement, but it is nevertheless quite clear that it still sustains, in some measure, the left wing of the trade unions and the Labour Party. A characteristic recent product is Aneurin Bevan, whose political base is among the Welsh miners.

It is a commonplace that World War I cut a swath across British life and, history; the total significance is much clearer now than it was to those who lived through the fateful years of 1914–18. As is almost invariably the case in periods of profound social disturbance, many British educational leaders saw in the situation a challenge to reassess and redeploy educational resources. With regard to adult education, the task was assigned to a Subcommittee of the Reconstruction Committee, appointed in July, 1917. Among the members were Albert Mansbridge 'and R. H. Tawney. The *Final Report* was published in 1919 and it soon became a landmark in British adult education history.[8] Thomas Kelley, in his *Select Bibliography of Adult Education in Great Britain* (London, 1952), characterized it as "a most valuable comprehensive survey of the history, current position, and future prospects of adult education in Great Britain, and its recommendations exerted a decisive influence on subsequent development."

This vast repository of factual information and informed thinking cannot be exhaustively analyzed here. Only what appear to be the controlling ideas can be reported. If this writer's understanding is correct, they are still valid intellectual currency in Britain to this day.

The authors—the shadow of R. H. Tawney seems to fall heavily on the thought and language—began by pointing out that the prime educational lesson of the war was the need for greater intelligence in the management of public affairs. This would necessitate that the main purpose of education should be to "fit a man for life" as a member of the community. The goal of education should be citizenship in all the connotations of the word. To reach the goal it would not be enough to fit a man for personal, domestic, and vocational duties; it would also be necessary to instruct him in the past history of the nation, in its literature, and in its position in the world of the moment, and to give him a sense of his duties toward it, including an understanding of the conditions of its economic, political, and international well-being.

To accomplish this it would be necessary that adult education, to the moment "the field of the amateur," be progressively professionalized. The professional would recognize that "education for the adult must proceed by different methods, in a different order, from those mostly used hitherto in the education of the young." Ordinarily the adult education of the individual would begin at eighteen, or after four years out of school and with that much practical working experience, but it should then continue throughout life. To reach a mind so formed, it would be necessary to "begin by answering his existing inquiries and perplexities, and go on to the satisfaction of his aspirations." The teacher should start from the immediate concrete fact to grip the student's mind and work back to the rationale of that fact. It was strongly implied, but not explicitly stated, that this could best be done, at least as far as the superior students were concerned, in tutorial classes which, therefore, were impliedly enshrined at the heart of British adult education. Alternative instrumentalities were given far less attention.

In approaching the masses of prospective students, it would have to be candidly recognized that there is a "natural aristocracy" in the population from which leaders are normally drawn, but that it would not be entirely sufficient to cultivate these people alone. Attention would have to be given to the mental cultivation of the "natural followers" as well, with a view to developing in them the "open habit of mind, clear-sighted and truth-loving, proof against sophisms, shibboleths, claptrap phrases and cant," supported by a satisfactorily large body of factual information on fundamentally important subjects. Plainly, it was the thought that the "natural aristocracy"—which, in the light of what the "natural followers" were to be, would be nothing short of a covey of geniuses—would gravitate to the tutorials, while the "natural followers" would find places in the alternative institutions. However, both groups should be freed from any social and financial handicaps which had hitherto limited their participation in adult education. As far as possible, opportunities of one kind or another should in future be open to all. In the capitals of the *Final Report* itself:

... THE NECESSARY CONCLUSION IS THAT ADULT EDUCATION MUST NOT BE REGARDED AS A LUXURY FOR A FEW EXCEPTIONAL PERSONS HERE AND THERE, NOR AS A THING WHICH CONCERNS ONLY A SHORT SPAN OF EARLY MANHOOD, BUT THAT ADULT EDUCATION IS A PERMANENT NATIONAL NECESSITY, AN INSEPARABLE ASPECT OF CITIZENSHIP, AND THEREFORE SHOULD BE BOTH UNIVERSAL AND LIFELONG.

In the WEA, the most notable organizational change that came right after World War I was the formation of the Workers' Educational Trade Union Committee, formed in 1919. It was largely engineered by G. D. H. Cole, university professor and author and, like so many WEA figures, a partisan of the labor movement and "socialism." This enlistment of the trade unions directly in an educational movement was something of a triumph, for while the movement in general had had strong educational interests for many years, the trade unions as organizations had but uncommonly shown an interest in adult education as such. The 1919 Committee sought to bring the two groups—the WEA and the unions—into the closest possible collaboration, but in the perspective of over three decades it is far from clear that it succeeded. Some trade-union financial support was brought to WEA, but there is no very convincing evidence that trade unionists appeared in sufficient numbers to change the established composition of the classes.

Indeed, as the years passed there were earnest questionings about the possibility of maintaining Mansbridge's ideal that three-quarters of the customers should be of the working class. Slowly the WEA became *middle class,* until in 1949 Roy Lewis and Angus Maude in their *The English Middle Classes* could write of the culmination of adult education in "that profoundly middle-class institution, the Workers' Educational Association." In 1947, according to statistics quoted by Professor S. J. Curtis, there were about 100,000 men and women attending WEA classes and, in that year, "twenty-one percent of students were manual workers, sixteen percent clerks, draughtsmen, travellers, foremen, teachers, civil servants, and postal workers, five percent professional and social workers, and twenty-six percent engaged in home duties and nursing. The remainder consisted of students drawn from miscellaneous occupations and those whose occupation was not declared.[7] These data would seem to show that the WEA, like the Mechanics' Institutes earlier, had begun with the idea of serving one class, but had been inexorably driven to serve another.

In her history of the WEA, Mrs. Mary Stocks emphasized that when the WEA was launched, class lines in England were still firmly drawn, nowhere more firmly than in education. Education "operated as both cause and effect of inequalities of income." Since the kind and duration of education possible was determined by the income of parents, children tended to get only such education as their parents could afford, thus perpetuating in the children the class status of the parents. A phase of the social changes in Britain in the last five decades has been the gradual equalization of educational opportunity. The WEA itself consistently campaigned for this. As a result, the WEA in its fiftieth year was faced with the fact that it had in considerable measure lost its original working-class audience, the group in search of a substitute for the unavailable state education. It was, in effect, faced with the necessity of finding a new way of appealing to the working class.

The case was admirably stated by Dr. Asa Briggs, reader in economic and social history at Oxford, in his BBC discussion of Mrs. Stocks's book. Briggs remarked (*my italics*): ". . . the role of the WEA is somewhat different in 1953 from that in 1903. *It has to supplement national educational facilities rather than to act as a substitute for them.*" He pointed out that "despite all the improvements in economic standards of working men and women in the past fifty years, we are still far from creating a lively popular culture. Preparing the way for such a culture would be a revolutionary task even in 1953." Briggs therefore proposed that

WEA find its place by continuing its emphasis on social studies, while adding as its new task the cultivation of a popular interest in music, art, and the cultural studies generally.[8]

While this evolution of WEA was going on, university extension itself continued its growth. Its favored, but not sole, instrument was also the tutorial class. The story was neither spectacular nor flashy. Rather it was a case of steady development, a never-remitted effort to reach the customers—chiefly urban at first, but then rural also—and to bring to them what they required at the highest manageable level of quality.

A few figures tell much of the story. In 1914 there were 130 three-year tutorial classes; in 1923, 282; in 1948–49, 898. Taking into account all students participating in university-extension work—short-course people as well as tutorial—sample figures were: 1938, 56,000; 1948–49, 163,000.

The government began to grant financial assistance in 1907 when it backed the then experimental three-year tutorials. In 1924 it started to help also in the financing of a variety of short courses. Under the grant regulations of 1946—based on the Education Law of 1944—the university-extension organizations were designated "responsible bodies" and allowed "both a substantial contribution from Exchequer funds toward their activities and a much greater latitude in the use of it, to allow for experiment and variety of provisions." [9]

The liberal treatment of university extension was designed to help maintain its special role in British adult education. It was considered a "core" institution of the "system." In 1950 seventeen universities or university colleges in England had extension organizations, four in Wales, four in Scotland, and one in Northern Ireland.

11

The Position Today

IT IS EXCEEDINGLY UNCOMMON to find adult education in any country at any time concentrated in one or a few well-established and firmly structured institutions, as is ordinarily the case with public-school and higher education. Rather it is at best a matter of a few "core" institutions surrounded by a miscellany of enterprises—not co-ordinated with one another or with the "core"—which can be variously described. Under the conditions of life in modern democracies, where almost any kind of voluntary educational organization is permitted, adult education enterprises are usually so numerous that they tend to confuse the observer. Thus far in this sketch of British adult education, we have deliberately concentrated on the big trees, pretty much ignoring the underbrush and the vines. The time has now come to take a look at these latter.

In 1934 W. E. Williams surveyed the British scene as it then existed.[1] It was his opinion that the big trees were far from being the only valuable parts of the forest; in fact, he argued that much of the true vitality of the forest was to be found elsewhere.

In his survey Williams was largely concerned with nonacademic, nonliterary, adult education, catering to those who did not want, or could not profit from, academic and literary studies, or to those who strongly felt a need to supplement them in various ways to achieve a better rounded personal and cultural development. Williams divided the field into eight broad groups, categories which are mostly still relevant, with specific illustrations under each. Rather than merely paraphrase Mr. Williams' survey of the situation in 1934, it is proposed here to use his categories (except for one—"Unemployed People") and draw illustrative material when relevant from more up-to-date information. In this way a freehand sketch of the current environment of the biggest tree in Britain—university extension, with its huge limb, the WEA—will be provided.

1. *Societies for the Development of Civic Values.*

a) Women's Organizations. The most conspicuous of these head up in the National Federation of Women's Institutes, the National Union of Townswomen's Guilds, the National Association of Women's Clubs, and the Women's Cooperative Guild. The first of these is devoted to the interests of farm women and in 1950 was serving 438,000 members organized in 7,281 institutes. Educationally it deals with citizenship, music, drama, etc., domestic arts and crafts, agriculture, health, and social welfare. The Townswomen's Guilds, the urban counterpart of the Federation, emphasizes citizenship and art, music and drama; the Women's Clubs concentrate on crafts and miscellaneous talks; while the Guild goes in for "causes"—peace, education, equality of the sexes, etc.

b) Social Service. The key organization here is the National Council of Social Service which includes in its ranks the National Federation of Community Associations and the Rural Community Councils, among others. Under this heading should also be placed such groups as the Central Council for Health Education and the Central Council for Physical Education, with their constituent organizations, as well as such borderline developments as the village colleges which are both social and cultural centers in rural areas.

c) General. The following may be cited illustratively: Council for Education in World Citizenship (an offshoot of the United Nations Association, itself the successor of the League of Nations Union); Association for Education in Citizenship; Bureau of

Current Affairs, servicing discussion groups; the Hansard Society; and the National Association of Citizens' Clubs.

2. *The BBC, the Cinema, etc.* Although the radio was hailed in England, as in America also, as potentially an educational instrument of immense power, optimism about it has progressively waned. The ordinary judgment is that the British radio in general has more to say for itself as an educational operation than the American and that the British Third Program (launched in 1946) is a very special illustration of what radio can achieve educationally speaking. The BBC is a major patron of the broadcastable arts. However, the BBC research people recently conducted a sample survey of the radio audience and concluded that only 2 per cent of the total were good prospects for the Third Program; 6 per cent were rated as fair prospects, 12 per cent poor, and 80 per cent very poor. Grouping the good and the fair together (8 per cent of the total audience) it was found that only twenty persons out of every hundred actually listened to the Third Program once a week or more. The other categories, numerically larger, provided smaller proportions (although numerically larger groups) as listeners. Reviewing the study, *The Economist* wrote:

> . . . the Third Programme has a far bigger market among the supposedly philistine than among the cultured. The fact that the Third Programme cannot be heard all over the country does not explain the failure to reach all the people who might be expected to listen. Fourteen per cent of the good and fair prospects said they had never even tried to hear it. The programme makes least appeal to the unmusical, since over half its broadcasting time is spent on serious music. Its talks, discussions and features are of high quality; but those who are capable of appreciating them are also those who have least lost the habit of reading, as opposed to looking and listening. Finally, the Spoken Word can be very trying when the technique of good broadcasting has been sacrificed to erudition.[2]

This appears to leave the radio in Britain, viewed as an educational instrumentality, in a rather less imposing place than is sometimes granted it; but that its place is nevertheless important need not be doubted, even though the final "meaning" of radio must be sought elsewhere.

Along with radio we can place the British Film Institute and its close ally, the Federation of Film Societies; the Federation of Scottish Film Societies; and the National Federation of Gramophone Societies (records clubs). Like the radio, these too shade off from mass entertainment and may properly be viewed as the educational upper reaches of that important but inadequately understood world.

3. *Societies for Aesthetic Training.* This category overlaps with the foregoing insofar as the radio, film, and record groups are concerned with aesthetic values, and it additionally embraces such organizations as the Arts Council of Great Britain (disburser of "collective" or state-financed patronage to music, drama, and the visual arts), the British Drama League (and the local dramatic societies it services), the Council of Industrial Design (on the side of it engaged in teaching design appreciation), the English Folk Dance and Song Society, the Rural Music Schools Association, the Society for Education in Art, the Workers' Music Association, and the Welsh Eisteddfod. All these are very active today.

4. *Care of Amenities.* With this category we are rather far afield and asked to accept as adult education enterprises official groups and private societies concerned to preserve "great houses," ancient monuments, and natural scenery of exceptional interest, as well as groups interested in country, town, and city planning, and even the nature-study organizations.

5. *Organizations of Amateurs.* This category, too, takes us a long way from our established base. We are asked to consider as adult education groups those concerned with anything from alchemy to microphotography and even more esoteric specialist hobbies.

6. *Religious Groups.* Here we are solicited to be concerned only with the obviously educational activities of the religious groups, not with their ordinary religious life. Illustratively there may be cited the YM and YWCA, the Catholic Social Guild, the Newman Association, the Central Jewish Lecture Committee, and the Church of England Adult Education Council (operating through

such church groups as the Mothers' Union, the Girls' Friendly Society and the Men's Society).

7. *The Nursery of Adult Education.* This category introduces into the purview of the adult educator organizations of boys and girls—like the Scouts—which aim to develop conscientious citizens, presumably someday to be interested in adult education.

Even Mr. Williams' valiant effort to categorize a miscellany of organizations did not wholly succeed. He had to add in the library movement as a kind of indispensable addendum. And his categories also supply no obvious place for such organizations as An Comunn Gailhealach, devoted to promoting the use of Gaelic in the Scottish Highlands, the British Association for Commercial and Industrial Education, the National Federation of Parent-Teachers Associations, or the Women's League of Health and Beauty, Ltd. He also provided no place for the correspondence schools which offer to teach writing (journalism), drawing, technical subjects, business subjects, education, and to prepare for the examinations for university degrees.[3]

The truth is that any effort to reduce adult education to neat order is reminiscent of the activities of Procrustes. Adult education always runs over any boundaries arbitrarily plotted for it. It is the activities described above rather than the "core" enterprises that tend to get offside, but it is also these which ordinarily do the pioneering in adult education and, when proved sound, exert back on the core an influence which is often decidedly creative. The proliferation of them is not, however, an invitation to dispense with the core, though some enthusiasts may from time to time appear to think so. The task is to expand the core carefully and discriminatingly to include such activities as have been proved useful to a well-rounded cultural development. This approach certainly justifies today the acceptance of music, drama, literature, and art as indispensable parts of the core-curriculum of adult education and, both on the side of demand and supply, they have been increasingly accepted as such in the last twenty years.

The British adult educators see clearly the need to escape from too exclusive concern with purely mental education on the one hand and purely manual (or vocational) education on the other, without abandoning either, but by adding the arts. The case is well put in the report of a private inquiry into adult education published in 1945 (*my italics*):

> . . . it is now becoming evident that the character of the education which has been and is being provided *appeals to only a section, and that a comparatively small section of the adult community.* It is based on school and university methods, and attracts those who are able to find satisfaction in books, lectures, and the exercise of the intellect, through study. This section of the community, though small, is important and will probably grow in numbers as primary, secondary, and further education improve. But, *in all probability, it will always remain a minority of the whole adult population.*

Today there is a growing realization that education must provide more varied opportunities than it has done in the past. In the case of children this is recognized in the proposals for different types of postprimary schools, but for adults a very much wider variety of activities will need to be contemplated unless the majority of the population are to be ignored. In the latter case, the gap between the educated and the non-educated will become wider, and the attempt to create a true democracy can never advance beyond an oligarchy of the educated minority. *Adult education should be concerned with all efforts towards the beneficial development of man's intellectual, emotional, and spiritual nature.* The most difficult task which lies ahead is to provide opportunities so varied in character and in method as to appeal to the as yet unreached majority and, at the same time, to keep in view the wider purpose of education—the beneficial development of the whole personality.

This task is the more difficult because there is little in past educational experience to serve as a guide. The variety of method which will be necessary may also easily become chaotic; and the desire to attain results may lead to mere entertainment being mistaken for education. Many types of experiment will need to be made and many will fail, but *endeavour to reach the great number of those who are not attracted by any of the present forms of education is of the*

highest importance and should receive every consideration
and encouragement. . . .[4]

The history of adult education gives small warrant for either
undue optimism or defeatist pessimism about the long-term significance of the activities being carried on at any particular time.
It is a reckless man who is sure that the key to the enigma of how
to educate adults is now in hand; and it would be equally reckless
to assume that no good methods are today in use. Certainly the
British have not in recent years been sure either way. They have
been as keen as any people about the need and necessity of adult
education and have written excellently about it, but they have not
yet been able to discover *the* answers. After about sixteen decades of unremitting effort and experimentation, they are con-
strained to admit:

> Despite all that has so far been done, it is still, however, true
> to say *that the vast majority of the adult population has as yet*
> *been unattracted by any of these movements,* which have, on
> the whole, been preaching to the converted, or the seekers,
> and have produced little impression on the indifferent and
> the uninterested. This is not in any sense to belittle what has
> been accomplished, but merely to emphasize the fact that
> adult education is still only at the beginning of its task.[5]

The distinguished men and women who were prepared to sub-
scribe to this assessment of the situation looked in two directions
for improvement: better provision for education in childhood and
adolescence, when habits of mind sustaining to adult education
should be established; and improved public knowledge of what can
rightly be demanded of adult education and of the facilities currently available.

The Education Act of 1944, a fundamental redesigning of the
state system of education, made adult education an integral part
of the system by placing large responsibilities for "further education" on the local educational authorities. The provisions of the
act governing "further education" were laid down in Sections 41
to 47. The fundamental provision (Section 41) reads in part as
follows:

. . . it shall be the duty of every local education authority to secure the provision for their area of adequate facilities for further education, that is to say:

(a) full-time and part-time education for persons over compulsory school age; and

(b) leisure-time occupation, in such organized cultural training and recreative activities as are suited to their requirements, for any persons over compulsory school age who are able and willing to profit by the facilities provided for that purpose. . . .

The local authorities were permitted to carry out their task in collaboration with established adult education enterprises—notably university extension and the WEA—when feasible, but they were expected to find ways and means also on their own initiative.

The precedents for placing heavy responsibility on the local education authorities were established by pioneering authorities during the interwar period. The London County Council showed what could be done by establishing, just after World War I, its remarkable literary institutes and its less formal men's and women's institutes. In the country, the most notable experiments were with so-called village colleges, pioneered from 1930 by the Cambridgeshire Local Education Authority, and the village halls and community centers, pioneered privately by the National Council of Social Service with funds provided by the Carnegie Trust. The latter have been officially described as "on the borderline at which adult education merges into social welfare." By the 1944 act, they became eligible for support from tax funds provided by local education authorities. Clearly the 1944 act opened the way for the local education authorities to systematize their established activities in adult education and vastly expand them. At mid-century, then, the most significant growing point of British adult education was, in terms of numbers served, local education activity.

At that time also, technical education was in an expanding phase, temporarily outrunning available facilities. Commercial education, including in it training for management, was also expanding. Art education, particularly industrial design, was in a vigorous state. Some of these developments were obviously efforts to aid the nation to meet the economic crisis in which it was involved.

The most striking postwar development in general adult education, however, was the expansion of *residential* adult education. The pioneer efforts in this field were Ruskin College, founded in 1899, and the Quaker experiment at Woodbrooke, started in 1902. The pioneers aimed to provide higher educational opportunities for those who could not find their way upward through the "structured" system. Critically viewed, they were second-class education—substitutes for the genuine thing—valid in a social situation in which many worthy people would otherwise have had no education of the kind. The Quakers were to some extent influenced by the Danish folk-school idea, but more in general than in particular because of the differences between a predominantly agricultural and a predominantly industrial society. At the outbreak of World War II there were still only eight such schools, the latest established being Newbattle Abbey College at Dalkeith in Scotland, founded in 1937. As the egalitarian principle was strengthened in British education, the need for substitutes declined —a point Mr. Briggs makes in discussing the WEA—and the ruling ideas in residential adult education changed. World War II was the turntable of the change.

The postwar schools sought to define a place, not as substitutes but as truly adult education ventures, permanently valid no matter how good the educational system might become or how far the customers had gone in it. Expansion on the new basis was rapid and in 1952 twenty-three residential colleges were in existence, sponsored by local education authorities, universities, national organizations, private groups, and even individuals. The range of purposes to be served was very wide, but there was some warrant for saying that a focal issue was the nature of the balance which should be struck between humane and "practical" studies; and this was sometimes elevated into a debate over what, at the highest ranges of seriousness, should be adult education's contribution to the survival of the nation and the individual in these difficult times.[6]

That a sketch of adult education in Britain can end on such a high note as this gives additional point to a perceptive evaluation of the record in the *Final Report* of the Ministry of Reconstruction's Adult Education Committee in 1919:

> It [adult education] has a history which can be traced at least to the end of the eighteenth century, and the efforts to which it has given birth, if in the earlier periods intermittent and unorganized, have shown sufficient continuity and power of self-renewal to entitle it to be regarded as a permanent characteristic of our society. They have not maintained a regular level or a steady advance, and they have rarely been crystallised in permanent institutions. The inquirer who traces the record of particular experiments will find that the failures have been as numerous as the successes. But failure has been the foundation of renewed effort, and when one attempt to organize adult education has collapsed, another has soon followed it, because the demand for education amongst adults has remained. The fact that throughout almost the whole nineteenth century constant efforts have been made to build up a system of higher education suited to the needs of adult men and women suggests that they are not the outcome of a merely evanescent interest or fashion, but are founded in permanent needs, which, when disappointed in one direction, seek satisfaction in another.

PART IV

THE AMERICAN STORY:

TOWARD CULTURAL DEMOCRACY?

Beginnings of Adult Education in America

ONE OF THE PILLARS on which American democracy rests is the assumption of the educability of man, that it is possible deliberately to improve and sophisticate his ability to make rational decisions on private, workaday, and public affairs. The powerful American belief in the sovereign virtue of education as a guarantor of success in life makes little sense unless this principle is understood.

The interminable arguments over education in the United States have not for many decades been over *whether* to educate, but over *how* to educate (including here both method and subject matter), and over how much education is a citizen's "right"—whether at the higher levels to concentrate self-consciously on the development of an elite group of leaders or to attempt to bring culture in all its phases to the masses of men. By and large, American education has become an experiment in mass education at all levels of its structured expression, from kindergartens to universities, the elite or leadership group being supposed to emerge by the anticipated mobility of men and women of superior talent.

American adult education has found its place within this kind of an educational environment. Professed equalitarianism in education does not automatically solve either the problems of education, organizationally or pedagogically, or the problems of cultural diffusion; but what adult education can hope to do must be considered within that general frame of reference. There is today in America practically no social acceptance of the deliberate reservation of educational opportunity to an elite group. This being the bias given to American educational endeavors after eighteen decades of experimentation, it follows naturally that all along the way the qualitative improvement of man in America through the extension of education to adults as well as children and adolescents has fascinated many minds and provoked a wide variety of experiments—some transient, some enduring.

Much that has been done to educate adult men and women in America has, of course, been done in ways and by means no longer included under the heading "adult education." In America, as in all societies, there is the distinction to be drawn between the education of adults and adult education, even though adult education covers a very great deal of ground. The education of adults is a product of the diffusion of knowledge in a society, carried on through a variety of mechanisms of which adult education, technically conceived, is but one. The American people have been peculiarly successful in the diffusion of knowledge, as many witnesses have testified. Professor Merle Curti in his *Growth of American Thought* tells us that even before the Revolution observers were noting that the wide diffusion of knowledge was an outstanding characteristic of the country.

Here is, by way of illustration, a critical comparison on this point between the United States and Germany, written by Henry Thomas Buckle about 1857. Buckle laid down the proposition that "if we wish to ascertain the conditions which regulate the progress of modern civilization, we must seek them in the history of the amount and diffusion of intellectual knowledge . . ." He then went on to survey several countries on this point, ending with a contrast between the United States and Germany:

> In America . . . We see a country, of which it has been truly said, that in no other are there so few men of great learning, and so few men of great ignorance [this paraphrases a remark

of Tocqueville's]. In Germany, the speculative classes and the practical classes are altogether disunited; in America, they are altogether fused. In Germany nearly every year brings forward new discoveries, new philosophies, new means by which the boundaries of knowledge are to be enlarged. In America, such inquiries are almost entirely neglected: since the time of Jonathan Edwards no great metaphysician has appeared; little attention has been paid to physical science; and with the single exception of jurisprudence, scarcely any thing has been done for those vast subjects on which the Germans are incessantly labouring. The stock of American knowledge is small, but it is spread through all classes; the stock of German knowledge is immense, but it is confined to one class. Which of these two forms of civilization is the more advantageous, is a question we are not now called upon to decide. It is enough for our present purpose, that in Germany, there is a serious failure in the diffusion of knowledge; and in America, a no less serious one in its accumulation. And as civilization is regulated by the accumulation and diffusion of knowledge, it is evident that no country can even approach to a complete and perfect pattern, if, cultivating one of these conditions to excess, it neglects the cultivation of the other. Indeed, from this want of balance and equilibrium between the two elements of civilization, there have arisen in America and in Germany those great but opposite evils, which, it is to be feared, will not be easily remedied; and which, until remedied, will certainly retard the progress of both countries, notwithstanding the temporary advantages which such one-sided energy does for the moment always procure.[1]

We cannot here explore what subsequently happened in Germany, but in due course, beginning within a quarter-century of the publication of Buckle's book, America began to remedy its alleged imbalance by establishing universities, interestingly enough on the German pattern, complete with the emphasis on the Ph.D. Daniel Coit Gilman of Johns Hopkins, G. Stanley Hall of Clark, and William Rainey Harper of the University of Chicago, were characteristic leaders in this. Nevertheless, the Americans did not at all diminish their very great interest in, and skill at, diffusing knowledge. (Gilman and Harper, for instance, played conspicuous roles in the history of adult education, as will appear as this story unfolds.)

This must be kept constantly in mind as we continue our sketch of the history of American adult education, for it cannot be developed in detail here.[2] Yet, if the diffusion of knowledge has been unusually successful in America, it has never been perfect, either quantitatively or qualitatively, and the education of adults has therefore never reached a pitch where experiments in adult education could be considered superfluous.

One frequently encounters the opinion that American adult education has its origin in colonial times in the New England town meeting. This is more ingenious than convincing. Aside from the fact that the town meeting is quite obviously better classified under education of adults (subhead: education by political participation) than under adult education as such, there is good reason to wonder why the town meeting has ever been considered any more important to the formation of adult minds than the theological and political sermons of the clergymen (often printed and circulated after 1740), the midweek "lectures" at the churches, the speeches and sermons delivered on "militia days," the religious and secular books which were early circulated in considerable quantities once presses were set up, the numerous newspapers issued beginning in 1704 (which by 1765 were *directly* reaching one family in five weekly) and, more indirectly, the almanacs which circulated so widely and were so carefully read and studied, or, after the Revolution, the Fourth of July Orations.

It is commonly stated that the ideas of John Locke, which were conspicuous in the political ideology of the Revolution, were first widely circulated in the political sermons of the dissenting clergy and in the almanacs. The truth is that the forces at work on the minds of adults early became surprisingly numerous, as they have been, ever increasingly, since colonial times. Professor Perry Miller points out that the early New England clergymen made no intellectual concessions to their audiences; they were not exactly popularizers when it came to dealing with the knottiest of theological conundrums; but they did use certain pedagogical devices to assist understanding, such as developing the argument under easily noticed heads and subheads, eschewing Latin quotations, and sticking to a simple style to avoid distracting attention from matter to manner.[3] In this fashion, abstruse theology and political principles were made fields of operation not only to the intelligentsia but also to the ordinary people.

All this is extremely interesting in the larger view, but from the standpoint of adult education, the most significant development in colonial times was the establishment of the precedent of tax-supported common schools to insure the basic literacy of all, an end not, of course, achieved, even with the means so clearly defined. Colonial society was too dispersed for schools to be really within the geographical reach of all, nor was it a society in which literacy was absolutely indispensable to survival. However, the endeavor was implicit recognition of the fact that literacy is basic to the education of adults and, when it arises, to adult education. But the story is not ours to tell, nor is an account of all the ups and downs of public education in America within our province, though occasionally we shall have to mention developments.

It is an interesting and significant fact, however, that the original impulse for the spreading of literacy was, in America, as in Britain of the same decades and later, religious in character; the end sought was the ability to read the Bible as a guide to salvation. This idea was brought with the settlers from their old homes, though the means seems to have been an original invention. In due course, as we know, the ideal of literacy for salvation in religious terms was replaced in great measure by the idea of literacy as a guarantee of salvation here and now in secular and even grossly materialistic terms. The two together account for the proliferation of the "structured" educational system of the country and much else, including adult education. In a society like that of early New England, in which intellectual leadership was in the hands of the clergy, the literacy gained was chiefly employed to ends the clergy approved; but literacy could be used to explore other avenues. In due course they were explored: trade knowledge, citizenship training, science. After the Revolution, indeed, citizenship training began to displace religion as the integrating idea in education. The Revolution itself dealt a heavy blow to educational institutions, teachers, and funds for education, but the idea that popular literacy was vital survived intact.

Many of the Fathers of the United States were quite clear about the proper role for education in the nation in the future, but none (except, perhaps, Thomas Jefferson) equaled Benjamin Franklin in ingenuity in promoting cultural institutions. Aside from his native genius for such enterprises, Franklin utilized a famous venture in adult education as his base of operations. Franklin, beyond all the other early American heroes, has claim to being a patron saint of adult education. He was, of course, an example par excellence of what we today call the "self-educated intellectual," a type whose significance in modern society, with its abundant opportunities for gaining education in the "structured" system, is not too widely understood. (Many Americans would undoubtedly consider Abraham Lincoln as the greatest of the self-educated leaders in American history, though some would be offended if he were called an intellectual.)

In Franklin's case, self-education added up to greatness, and it is interesting, indeed, that in addition to indefatigable private reading, study, and experiment, he resorted to a venture of a social kind further to refine his intellectual competence. He got his idea for this from, of all possible persons, the Puritan divine Cotton Mather, who in 1710 published a little book entitled *Essays to Do Good*. In this Mather emphasized one of his favorite ideas: "the importance of combined, cooperative effort," and advocated a scheme for neighborhood benefit societies attached to the churches. These societies he said should be discussion groups; to stimulate and direct the discussion, he propounded some questions which he suggested should be reviewed at each meeting. In 1727, in Philadelphia, Franklin secularized Mather's idea and set up a small society at first called the Leather Apron, but later known as the Junto, composed of his immediate associates, including a copier of deeds, a self-taught mathematician, a surveyor, a shoemaker, a joiner, a merchant's clerk, and a young gentleman of fortune. Franklin himself was at that time a working printer.

Franklin's discussion club met once a week on Friday evenings, occasionally out-of-doors in summer, and it held an annual dinner and jollification. The social side was never neglected, nor the intellectual side overplayed. In his *Autobiography,* Franklin tells us:

The rules that I drew up required that every member, in turn, should produce one or more queries on any point of Morals, Politics, or Natural Philosophy, to be discuss'd by the company; and once in three months produce and read an essay of his own writing, on any subject he pleased. Our debates were to be under the direction of a president, and to be conducted in the sincere spirit of inquiry after truth, without fondness for dispute, or desire of victory; and, to prevent warmth, all expressions of positiveness in opinions, or direct contradiction, were after some time made contraband, and prohibited under small pecuniary penalties.

This account, however, does not mention the celebrated recurring questions, the idea that came directly from Cotton Mather. Mather had suggested that his clubs discuss such questions as:

Is there any matter to be humbly moved unto the legislative power, to be enacted into a law for public benefit?

Is there any particular person whose disorderly behavior may be so scandalous and so notorious that we may do well to send unto the said person our charitable admonitions?

Does there appear any instance of oppression or fraudulence in the dealings of any sort of people that may call for our essays to get it rectified?

Can any further methods be devised that ignorance and wickedness may be chased from our people in general, and that household piety in particular may flourish among them?

Franklin's group was asked to discuss such questions as:

Have you lately observed any defect in the laws of your country of which it would be proper to move the legislature for an amendment? Or do you know of any beneficial law that is wanting?

Do you know of a fellow-citizen who has lately done a worthy action, deserving praise or imitation; or who has lately committed an error proper for us to be warned against and avoid?

Have you lately observed any encroachment on the just liberties of the people?

Have you met with anything in the author you last read, re-markable or suitable to be communicated to the Junto, par-ticularly in history, morality, poetry, physic, travels, mechanic arts, or other parts of knowledge?

What new story have you lately heard agreeable for telling in conversation?

Hath any citizen in your knowledge failed in his business lately, and what have you heard of the cause?

Have you lately heard of any citizen's thriving well, and by what means?

Have you or any of your acquaintance been lately sick or wounded? If so, what remedies were used, and what were their effects?

Hath any deserving stranger arrived in town since last meet-ing that you have heard of? And what have you heard or ob-served of his character or merits? And whether, think you, it lies in the power of the Junto to oblige him, or encourage him as he deserves?

Each question was regularly asked, discussed, and then, during a short pause before the next one was introduced, a glass of wine was drunk. The wine was Franklin's idea, not Cotton Mather's.

The Junto kept going for thirty years, a remarkable record for a rather informal organization—in today's jargon, an "auton-omous group." [4] It was limited to twelve members (so that dis-cussion would not get out of hand), and when the pressure to join exceeded the number of places available, it was suggested by Franklin that other groups similarly organized, but not linked with the Junto, be set up. Perhaps five or six came into existence.

Now too much should not be made of the "originality" of the idea of an informal discussion club, either on Mather's or Frank-lin's part. They have sprung up spontaneously many times in many places in the past and they exist to an unknown extent at this very moment wherever men of common or disparate interests congre-gate. They are one of the hardy perennials of adult education and perhaps the least likely of all its protean manifestations ever to have a formal, written history. Only when some member, perhaps of later public fame like Franklin, leaves a record of such a club, or when a biographer notes the fact of membership, does the club come to the notice of posterity.

Commonly cited, probably because it has been carefully studied as part of the history of American philosophy, is the Metaphysical Club of Cambridge, Massachusetts, of which Charles S. Peirce and William James were members and of which pragmatism was the remarkable by-product. But there are many other examples. Lately, for instance, Bertrand Russell was reminiscing over the BBC; talking about H. G. Wells, he began, "I first met H. G. Wells in 1902 at a small discussion society created by Sidney Webb, and by him christened 'The Coefficients' in the hope that we should be jointly efficient. There were about a dozen of us." Such little groups are not always at the high level of Sidney Webb's or Charles Peirce's. Mostly they are made up of ordinary folk permanently unknown to fame. Most of Franklin's associates in the Junto are remembered today only because of his mention of them in his *Autobiography*. It is hard, sometimes, to draw a line between an informal discussion "club" and an informal social group at the gatherings of which good talk is invariably to be expected, nor is the distinction too important. Plainly the "autonomous groups" exist on the wavering border line between adult education and the education of adults, and nobody really cares much precisely where they should be classified. The point about them is their profitability to their members.

An important aspect of the Junto that demands comment is that it provided a base from which Franklin proceeded to the founding of several educational organizations of a much more formal and durable character. Since the discussions at the Junto meetings were supposed to be founded in solid knowledge, and lead to true education, the reading of books on relevant subjects was required. In 1730 Franklin suggested to the members:

> . . . that, since our books were often referred to in our disquisitions upon the queries, it might be convenient to us to have them all together where we met, that upon occasion they might be consulted; and by thus clubbing our books to a common library, we should, while we liked to keep them to-

gether, have each of us the advantage of using the books of all the other members, which would be nearly as beneficial as if each owned the whole. It was liked and agreed to, and we filled one end of the room with such books as we could best spare. The number was not so great as we expected; and though they had been of great use, yet some inconvenience occurring for want of due care of them, the collection, after about a year, was separated and each took his books home again.

This scheme not having worked, Franklin immediately (in 1731) suggested another that did. It was for a subscription liberary to be formed by the Junto members and such other interested Philadelphians as cared to join with them. The new idea was duly carried into practice under the name of The Library Company, and the institution survives to the present day, symbolizing in its fashion the close bond between adult education and libraries.

Twelve years later, in 1743, Franklin outlined a proposal for what Carl Van Doren in his *Benjamin Franklin* calls "unmistakably an intercolonial Junto." This turned out to be the American Philosophical Society, actually established in Philadelphia the following year with five of its original members, including Franklin, drawn from the Junto. That same year Franklin also drew up a proposal for an academy for the education of boys of eight to sixteen to be run on fairly novel principles. It got under way in 1749 and lived to become the ancestor of the University of Pennsylvania. Of it Van Doren remarks that Franklin applied to the academy the "old method of the Junto."

Of course, not every discussion group can hope to include a Benjamin Franklin and, profiting by his exceptional inventiveness, establish so proud a record as the Junto for promoting cultural institutions. But even without a Franklin, such groups at minimum have a healthy influence on the cultural life of their members and the community, and their coming and going are a measure of the liveliness of the intellectual life of the people.

Aside from Franklin, none of the Founding Fathers seems to have thought much about how to educate adults, although almost all of them were personally distinguished by a high capacity for continuing self-education, by far the best form of adult education of all. Rather they appear to have been satisfied with the idea that the masses of the people should be given only elementary instruction at public expense as the foundation for sound citizenship. Jefferson, Jay, Madison, and Adams can be quoted to this effect, however much they differ on the proper place of the common people in society. The state of public thinking on the education question about 1787 is well illustrated by the grand but very vague stipulation written into the Ordinance of that year which organized the Northwest Territory, provided for its ultimate division into states, and safeguarded the rights of its future inhabitants: "Religion, morality, and knowledge being necessary to good government, and the happiness of mankind, schools and the means of education shall forever be *encouraged*." (*My italics*.)

Jefferson, of course, is well known to have thought carefully about an integrated system of education extending from elementary schools through the university, outlined, for example, in *Notes on Virginia*. The elementary schools would be free and open to all, rich and poor alike, and would teach reading, writing, and "common arithmetic." In Jefferson's view, however, the children of the poor could only proceed beyond the elementary level if they showed exceptional ability and were chosen to receive state-supported scholarships, but the rich could educate their children up to any level they chose. This was, in effect, to ration secondary and higher education by the purse, as was traditional, only mitigating this by state assistance to the brightest of the poor. While this comports oddly with Jefferson's political ideals, it warns us that it took a long time to apply the egalitarian outlook to educational opportunity. Jefferson accepted the necessity of an educated elite and sought ways and means of recruiting it from a broader group than was apt to be done by the purse alone. Farther than that he did not propose to go. Not until the era of Andrew Jackson did the emphasis begin to fall heavily upon raising the average cultural level of all the citizens. (The distinction between the Jeffersonian and Jacksonian approaches is given considerable emphasis in the 1945 Harvard report, *General Education in a Free Society*.)

Yet Jefferson was keenly aware that, in his own words, every citizen should be in a position "to judge for himself what will secure or endanger his freedom," and he was the author of the phrase in the Declaration of Independence about the "just powers" deriving from the "consent of the governed" who could not safely, therefore, be left in a state of ignorance. As time passed, Jefferson seems to have realized that the diffusion of the required knowledge of the masses of the citizens could not be assured by elementary schools alone. Yet he appears never to have thought through the implications of this perception, for he added little to his scheme of popular education beyond an elementary idea of libraries. Jefferson's important declaration about public libraries is contained in a letter to John Wyche, written from Monticello on May 10, 1809:

Sir,—Your favor of March 19th came to hand but a few days ago, and informs me of the establishment of the Westward Mill Library Society, of its general views and progress. I always hear with pleasure of institutions for the promotion of knowledge among my countrymen. The people of every country are only safe guardians of their own right, and are the only instruments which can be used for their destruction. And certainly they would never consent to be so used were they not deceived. To avoid this, they should be instructed to a certain degree. I have often thought that nothing would do more extensive good at small expense than the establishment of a small circulating library in every county, to consist of a few well-chosen books, to be lent to the people of the country, under such regulations as would secure their safe return in due time. These should be such as would give them a general view of other history, and particular view of that of their own country, a tolerable knowledge of Geography, the elements of Natural Philosophy, of Agriculture and Mechanics. Should your example lead to this, it will do great good. . . .[5]

But the long and short of it is that not even Jefferson worked out the educational implications of his political principles. This was left for future generations to do.

Apart from elementary schools, the Founding Fathers appear not to have gotten much beyond George Washington's counsel in his Farewell Address of 1796:

It is substantially true that virtue or morality is a necessary spring of popular government. The rule, indeed, extends with more or less force to every species of free government. Who that is a sincere friend to it can look with indifference upon attempts to shake the foundation of the fabric?

Promote, then, as an object of primary importance, institutions for the general diffusion of knowledge. In proportion as the structure of a government gives force to public opinion it is essential that public opinion should be enlightened. [*My italics.*]

Between the end of the American Revolution and the eighteen-thirties, the intellectual and social climate in the United States was not too favorable to elaborate experiments in adult education. Professor Merle Curti enumerates some of the adverse factors: the difficulties experienced in establishing the new system of government; the strength of political and social conservatism; the reluctance to tax property to support education of any kind; the conservative fear of "godless" secular schools (or, in reverse, the conservative preference for leaving education to the churches and religious charities); and the political apathy and powerlessness of the common people.[6] As noted earlier, not until the time of Jackson did the idea of raising the general cultural level begin to rule. Yet, during the first three decades of the nineteenth century, a variety of significant, if limited, experiments in adult education were made, some of which link up with major developments later on.

Mention should surely be made of the American Bible Society (1816) and the American Tract Society (1824). Both, though chiefly concerned with religious work, were definitely concerned also with the promotion of literacy and with satisfying the reading needs of the moderately literate. The American Bible Society (still in existence) distributed millions of copies of the Bible and of separate books of the Bible, and played a decisive role in making the Bible the basic—often the only—reading book in the American home. Also, by assiduously following the frontier, it was a major factor in keeping the pioneers in close touch with that Bible Christianity which for many decades was the foundation stratum of the

American mind. The American Tract Society (also still in existence) was formed as a result of a merger of the New York Religious Tract Society and the New England Tract Society (the latter an offshoot of the London Religious Tract Society whose literature it reprinted). It was designed to achieve national coverage for work hitherto conducted on a sectional basis. The Tract Society, remarks Lawrance Thompson in his sketch of its history, had a powerful educative influence "in stimulating an increased reading public, and in furnishing millions of books and pamphlets which were eagerly devoured by this increased reading public. . . ." [7] The Society issued not only what were unquestionably religious tracts (a literary genre of a very special kind) but also a kind of hybrid literature in which the religious material found its conspicuous place in the midst of "useful" secular information, as in its series of almanacs. It circulated, too, materials like the writings of Hannah More (which we encountered in sketching the British story) in which the reader was guided to piety by fiction.

It was in an intellectual atmosphere in which religious and crypto-religious literature was eagerly devoured that the early experiments in secular adult education took place. The bridge between the two cultural worlds was science. Probably this cannot be better illustrated than by citing the chapter titles in the Reverend Thomas Dick's *On the Improvement of Society by the Diffusion of Knowledge,* a book of Scottish origin first published in the United States in 1833 in Harper's "Family Library" and for years thereafter kept in print. Here are the chapter titles:

Influence of Knowledge in Dissipating Superstitions and Vain Fears.

On the Utility of Knowledge in Preventing Diseases and Fatal Accidents.

On the Influence Which a Diffusion of Knowledge Would Have on the Progress of Science.

On the Pleasures Connected with the Pursuits of Science.

On the Practical Influence of Scientific Knowledge and its Tendency to Promote the Comforts of General Society.

On the Influence of Knowledge in Promoting Enlarged Conceptions of the Character and Perfections of the Deity.

On the Beneficial Effects of Knowledge on Moral Principles
and Conduct.

On the Utility of Knowledge in Relation to a Future World.

On the Utility of General Knowledge in Reference to the
Study of Divine Revelation.

Miscellaneous Advantages of Knowledge Briefly Stated
—lead to just estimates of human character
—enable people to profit by their attendance on public
instructions
—introduce a spirit of tolerance
—vanquish the antipathies of nations
—promote the union of the Christian church

On the Importance of Connecting Science with Religion.

The upshot of the Reverend Mr. Dick's argumentation was the
conclusion, not only that science, properly taught, would support religion (the view of Brougham but not Newman, as we
have learned earlier), but also that "A knowledge of the principles of science would render manufacturers, mechanics and common laborers of all descriptions more skillful in their respective
professions and employments."

It was this latter idea that stimulated the secular adult education
ventures of the time we are discussing. Most of them were pat-
terned after the kinds of efforts which were proving useful in
England, but as throughout American history, the "introduced"
ideas usually produced different results in the very different social
ecology of America.

Lord Brougham loomed portentously over many of the earlier
experiments. A Society for the Diffusion of Knowledge was
founded in Boston in 1829 and a national society of the same
name in 1836. The Boston society had as active supporters Edward
Everett and Josiah Holbrook, men whose names will recur as this
essay goes forward, and its patron was the redoubtable Daniel
Webster. The Boston society's objective—taken over by the national society—was "To issue in a cheap form a series of works,

partly original and partly selected, in all the most important branches of learning." Most of the works issued were reprints of the British SDUK publications.

The Americans also used the Mechanics' Institute idea, but turned it into a combination of library, lecture, and vocational-training institution far more elaborate than the British model. ("Used" is the word, rather than "borrowed" in the sense of direct imitation, for not only did the Americans give the idea a twist peculiarly their own but they also had such rough precedents in their own country as the General Society of Mechanics and Tradesmen of the City of New York, organized in 1785 and incorporated by the state legislature in 1792. This organization in 1820 established a day school for mechanics' children, and a library; in 1833 it initiated a lecture series which was to last for over fifty years; and in 1858 it established an evening trades school. Today it still continues as an endowed society maintaining a technical and general library and a vocational school of high character and it still prints the words "Mechanics Institute" on the cover of its "School Information" bulletin.) The promoters, indeed, operated on two social levels: libraries and attendant services for merchants—meaning, really, mostly merchants' clerks and young, newly fledged merchants; and libraries for mechanics and apprentices. These libraries were in demand because the old subscription libraries which had hitherto met all needs—of which Benjamin Franklin's Library Company was the exemplar—had begun to weaken by the eighteen-twenties. The conspicuous promoters of the new merchants' and mechanics' libraries were John Griscom, an itinerant lecturer on science, later president of the National Lyceum, and William Wood, a liberal, reformist merchant. The first libraries on the new pattern were established in New York in 1820 when the Mercantile Library Association (which still survives) and the Apprentices' Library Association were set up. These were soon imitated in Boston and Philadelphia —the famous Franklin Institute (1824)—and so across the nation under various appellations. A Mercantile Library Association was founded in San Francisco in 1853. The libraries remained a principal resource for books for the groups served for thirty or forty years, until they fell before the rising public libraries, into which some of the collections were absorbed.

How the American effort was viewed by an English expert can be illustrated by a quotation from J. W. Hudson's *History of Adult Education* (London, 1851):

It has been correctly asserted that America seldom adopts anything useful from the Old World that she does not improve; and it is certain that in establishing and carrying out a system of public libraries, colleges, and Mechanics' Institutions, the United States have far excelled Great Britain. The perfect Mechanics' Institution can only be found in the Western World, for in no part of Europe can a Peoples' Institute be seen in which machine shops supplied with necessary mechanical tools for the accommodation of the diligent and for inventors, is accessible to all; where the laboratory is available for chemical instruction and experiments; where *free* lectures on scientific and literary subjects are systematically delivered to the working classes, and where that class alone has the management of the Institutions established for their benefit. Literary, Scientific, and Mercantile Libraries were formed, in New York and in Boston, as early as the year 1820. These societies required each subscriber to present to the library one or more volumes, either in biography, history, voyages, travels, or works relating to mercantile subjects, and chiefly by this means libraries of one thousand volumes were formed in three years. Any person engaged in mercantile pursuits, was eligible to all the privileges of the associations for a small annual fee. The management was vested solely in the class for whom the associations were designed, namely,—merchants, clerks, and persons holding subordinate mercantile offices; merchants and others engaged in non-mercantile employments were admitted members, but took no share in the direction. At the Boston Mercantile Library Association lectures were delivered as early as 1823. The establishment of Mercantile Libraries was followed by the formation of Mechanics and Apprentices' Libraries, with a degree of energy and public spirit that extended its influence across the Atlantic.

The American career of an English mechanic admirably illustrates this phase of adult education in the United States. In 1839 there was published in Boston a little book entitled *Memoir of a Mechanic, Being a Sketch of the Life of Timothy Claxton, Written by Himself, Together with Miscellaneous Papers,* which should be far better known than it is. Claxton was born near Bungay, Suffolk, about a hundred miles from London, in 1790. Like so many country-bred youngsters of his time he was apprenticed as a mechanic and in due time betook himself to London. He had a passion for self-improvement and an equal passion "to encourage my fellow-mechanics in the noble work." In London in 1815–16 he attended some popular lectures in natural philosophy given on a fee basis by a private individual and in 1817, with a few of his fellow-mechanics whom he dragooned into it, he set up what he called The Mechanical Institution, in total ignorance of Dr. Birkbeck's work in this field in Scotland. Claxton's institution had but a short and rather inglorious life. "It is astonishing, though true," Claxton reflected, "that the great mass of mechanics do not appreciate knowledge as they ought. They do not go forward themselves, and can hardly be persuaded to partake of the repast it offers, after everything is prepared for them . . ." This is a complaint that runs dirgelike through the story of adult education. In June of 1820 Claxton went to St. Petersburg, Russia, to serve as chief mechanic on an oil-gas illuminating system in the war-department building. Three years later he emigrated directly to America—to Boston.

Claxton's first American job was in a cotton mill at Methuen, Massachusetts. He found in the town the Methuen Social Society for Reading and General Inquiry. It had been founded in 1819 with forty or fifty members, but already in 1823 it was reduced to four or five active members under the leadership of a clergyman. This society Claxton proceeded to revive by adding lectures and demonstrations in mechanics, and soon it was flourishing on the new basis. In 1826, however, he moved to Boston where he remained for ten years.

By a series of those creative accidents that mark the careers of the ingenious, Claxton was eventually able to set up for himself "making and selling apparatus for illustrating the various sciences." One of his customers was Josiah Holbrook, "a gentleman much engaged in the establishment of Lyceums" (see below), whom we have already met as a promoter of the Boston SDK. When Claxton arrived in Boston, there was no mechanics' society in the city, but later in that same year a Boston Mechanics' Institution was founded. It had only a very short existence. As Claxton diagnosed the case, it failed because it was "unsocial"—because, while it offered a course of lectures, it balked at establishing a library (already otherwise available in the city, of course), a reading room, or classes. Three years later, a Boston Lyceum (à la Holbrook) was set up with Daniel Webster as president. Claxton was already sufficiently well known to be elected a "curator" of it; he lectured before it; but it was for the general public, not for mechanics alone, and did not quite meet his prescription.

When Holbrook undertook, in 1831, to promote the Boston *Mechanics'* Lyceum (evidently a cross between a Lyceum and a Mechanics' Institute), Claxton took the presidency and held it until the end of 1835. Here he was in his element and he was the life and soul of the institution. Under his guiding hand the Mechanics' Lyceum offered lectures on architecture, political economy, botany, geology, natural history, astronomy, and the biographies of practical men; and it published for four years a magazine, *The Young Mechanic,* later bound up and sold like a book. Claxton returned to England in 1836, founded a Lyceum in his home town of Bungay; met Dr. Birkbeck and wrote a valuable pamphlet (one of the "Miscellaneous Papers" in the Boston volume) entitled *Origin of Mechanics' Institutions;* and returned to the making of teaching apparatus in London, at which point he disappears from history. It was his American friends who saw to it that his work was commemorated in a book. The publisher, George W. Light, was secretary of the Boston Mechanics' Lyceum under Claxton.

From his experience, Claxton drew a pedagogical conclusion of great interest. Speaking of the members of the Mechanics' Lyceum, he wrote:

They now feel confident, that the plan of having the exercises conducted by the members alone, is not only in accordance with the true Lyceum system, but far more productive of solid improvement, than the mere attendance upon popular lectures. In the one case, the members acquire a habit of doing their own studying and speaking, and consequently of calling into exercise the faculties of their own minds, and using the means for improving their own manner of delivery, while in the other, most of the hearers of popular lectures retain little of the instruction they receive, and are too apt to go away with the impression that, because the lecturer's duty is performed, their own task is certainly completed. If the former obtain only a smattering knowledge of science—which we maintain is not the case—the latter do not obtain even that.

. . . popular lecturing ought not to be the regular exercise of any institution, the professed object of which is mutual improvement.

Such various activities must naturally have had a cumulative effect, both in impact and example. In the early eighteen-thirties there were, so it is said, "hundreds" of subscription reading rooms and libraries, debating clubs, associations to support lectures, and analogous enterprises scattered through the United States; and in the next decade Tocqueville especially remarked them in *Democracy in America* as a characteristic development of democratic society. There was unquestionably a very active interest in the diffusion and popular consumption of knowledge and a widespread and useful disagreement about how best to manage it—useful because disagreement about method encouraged experimentation.

Josiah Holbrook, the Lyceum, and Public Lectures

IT WAS against the background just sketched that an experiment that is a landmark in the history of American adult education was started. This was the Lyceum. Projected and launched in 1826, it ran a hectic course until 1839 and then subsided as a national movement to have an "after-history" lasting down to our own time, especially in small towns.

The hero of this extraordinary enterprise was Josiah Holbrook, whom we have already mentioned. Born in Derby, Connecticut, in 1788 and graduated from Yale in 1810, Holbrook began his career as a keeper of a private school in which study and farm labor were combined. He then became, after attending Professor Benjamin Silliman's scientific lectures at Yale, an itinerant lecturer on scientific subjects, particularly geology. Holbrook's interests illustrate the connection then characteristic between a concern for popularizing science and adult education in general. The Benthamite utilitarian outlook, which gave adult education such a lift in England about this time, was also influential in America. The Lyceums were largely concerned with knowledge that was "useful" but not necessarily vocational.[1]

After 1826 Holbrook was continuously associated with the Lyceums until his death, both as "onlie true begettor" and as most assiduous promoter. At first he earned his living by supplying Lyceums (and schools) with such scientific apparatus as Timothy Claxton built. From 1837 to 1842 he was either resident at or associated with the so-called Lyceum village at Berea, Ohio, where he promoted the manufacture of globes. From 1842 to 1849 he resided in New York City as manager of a bureau which supplied lecturers to Lyceums and arranged the exchange of cabinets of minerals; and for the rest of his life he lived in Washington, D.C., still promoting the Lyceum idea and serving its needs. He was accidentally drowned near Lynchburg, Virginia, in 1854 while collecting specimens for minerals cabinets. Few Americans have devoted themselves more whole-heartedly to the adult education ideal.

The full significance of this sequence will emerge as the story of the Lyceum is unfolded, but here a few words may be said about the Lyceum village—a rather surprising item in Holbrook's dossier. The enterprise, so characteristic of its age—a time when Utopian schemes of infinite variety flourished—was founded to provide a community in which social harmony was to be achieved and the people redeemed from ignorance and vice "by lectures and recitations, with scientific apparatus."

The local school was to be a training center for teachers imbued with the Lyceum ideals. But at its maximum the village had a population of only about fifty persons. Like its numerous fellows in utopian remodelling of workaday American ways, it was unable to stem the deep-running forces actually moulding American life. After five years it collapsed, but it nevertheless lasted long enough to stand as a kind of symbol of the undisciplined optimism that is forever bobbing to the surface in adult education circles. Holbrook's vaunting and unquenchable ambitions for the Lyceum undoubtedly sprang from the same root as his willingness to have a hand in the utopian experiment at Berea.

As originally conceived, the Lyceums were to operate on three fronts simultaneously: (1) they were to promote mutual improvement of the members through study and association; (2) they were to disseminate knowledge by establishing libraries and museums; and (3) they were to stimulate and support the movement for the establishment of tax-supported common schools. For the name "Lyceum," Holbrook went back to Aristotle—chiefly, apparently, Aristotle the scientist, but the philosopher and moralist not forgotten.

The mixture of purposes once more illustrates that adult education cannot be understood apart from the complex context in which it invariably operates, but in this case the complexity of the purposes boded ill for the longevity of the experiment in its original form. The evidence at hand suggests that the chief motivation of the top leadership, aside from Holbrook himself, was to back the development of the state-supported elementary schools and teacher education. Activities to these ends tended to blanket adult education. Looking back in 1864, Henry Barnard himself put the Lyceum first among the organizations that had assisted his labors for common schools. When this phase of the work passed into the hands of the professional educators, the public authorities, and the organized teachers, the Lyceum was left with its lectures and its minerals cabinets as the means of adult education. They proved insufficient to keep the enterprise at a high level, either in aims or accomplishment. The local units survived chiefly as sponsors of lectures.

The first Lyceum was organized by Holbrook himself at Millbury, Massachusetts, in November, 1826, after a lecture he had given on geology. Holbrook had published his plan in the *American Journal of Education* in the previous month, and at Millbury he was taking direct action to realize it. By 1835, when the original movement seems to have reached a peak, there were about 3,500 local Lyceums, scattered mostly over the northeastern states, numerous county organizations, perhaps sixteen state organizations, and a national organization. (When the movement became exclusively local after 1839, the individual Lyceums continued to multiply and as late as 1925 were estimated at twelve thousand.) National meetings were held annually from 1831 to 1839, when they abruptly and inexplicably ceased.

At the national level, the primary interest from the very beginning was in the elementary schools. This can perhaps be satisfactorily illustrated by noting the interests the several corresponding secretaries were supposed to cultivate: colleges and their con-

nections with common schools; books, apparatus, and branches of
study in the common schools; the qualifications of teachers; the
teaching of the natural sciences; methods of instruction and school
discipline; and—the Lyceums as adult education enterprises! Yet
this does not appear to be a case of the tail wagging the dog; this
is rather what was intended by the directing minds.

The president for six of the nine years the national organization
functioned was W. A. Duer, then president of Columbia College,
an ardent exponent of college education and the man who introduced science lectures into Columbia. He was "spelled" in 1837
by one G. W. Ridgley. The first year, the presidency was held,
appropriately, by the great Hudson River patroon Stephen Van
Rensselaer, patron of both higher and popular education (founder
of Rensselaer Polytechnic Institute); the second year by John
Griscom, a Quaker lecturer on science, promoter of libraries, reformer (interested in the relief of pauperism, the control of juvenile
delinquency, and the introduction of the reform principle into penal
practice), and a very popular lecturer on chemistry.

At the local level, where the contribution to adult education was
made, the Lyceums were organized along the lines of mutual
educational associations. Adult members were charged a fee of $2
a year, but persons under eighteen were charged $1 and not allowed
to vote. A special effort was made to bring in persons whose education was deficient, a numerous group in those days. The local
groups were encouraged to build up libraries—many local libraries
organized earlier had fallen into disuse or had been dispersed—
and collections of carefully classified geological specimens (Holbrook's abiding interest); and to assemble equipment for scientific
experiments. Meetings were held once a week in the wintertime.
Usually a discussion of a literary or scientific nature was held, led
either by a local member or a member of a nearby sister society.
The school question was frequently aired. A scientific experiment
might be performed for the instruction of the audience. But while
discussion was favored, differences of opinion were not cultivated.
As time passed, local intellectual resources tended to become exhausted—the members became weary of their own voices—and
resort was had to outside lecturers,[2] a shift of policy which was
eventually to have fateful results.

All this fitted in well with the "cult of self-improvement" of which Benjamin Franklin was the great American exemplar, but which at this very time received a new impetus from such diverse figures as George Ripley, William Ellery Channing, and Robert Dale Owen, the Unitarians, the Transcendentalists, and the social reformers—all believers in the perfectibility of man through education. Owen, for example, saw "self-improvement" transforming Tom, Dick, and Harry into Mr. Thomas, Mr. Richard, and Mr. Henry. The Lyceum drew much support from these currents of thought. Henry David Thoreau in *Walden* remarked that "This town [Concord] has spent seventeen thousand dollars on a town-house, thank fortune or politics, but probably it will not spend so much on living wit, the true meat to put into that shell, in a hundred years. The one hundred and twenty-five dollars annually subscribed for a Lyceum in the winter is better spent than any other equal sum raised in the town."

If in its immediate impact the Lyceum's great contribution was to the establishment of the elementary-school system, it also has an important record as a contributor to the establishment of other cultural institutions, in which respect it was in the tradition of Franklin's Junto. Edwin Grant Dexter was of the opinion that the Lyceum helped promote the establishment of the United States Weather Bureau, provided a precedent for library extension, stimulated the establishment of museums of natural history and scientific laboratories, and stands as a collateral ancestor of both the National Education Association and the American Association for the Advancement of Science.[3] All this may well be true, but clear and final evidence is not readily to be found.

Much clearer is the point that the Lyceum occupies an important place in the history of public lectures in America. Looking around for an ancestor for the Lyceum, Edward Everett suggested the midweek "lectures" of the old New England churches. This seems a very reasonable supposition, though we know that Holbrook was familiar with Lord Brougham's schemes in England and with their American counterparts and variants. He may have been playing upon the Mechanics' Institute theme. We know, too, that lectures were immensely popular in New England before and after the Lyceum was launched. A historian has remarked that from 1825 lectures were "epidemic" in New England and that in the winter of 1837–38 twenty-six courses (not including those of less than eight lectures) were delivered in Boston. The Lyceum was rowing with the current. But it is beyond question that the Lyceum helped spread the lecture idea beyond Boston and New England.[4] When the local Lyceums were thrown on their own, they found the promotion of lectures a sufficient excuse for being. This was not the original intent, but they thus became a major contributing stream to the vast and muddy river which is today frankly called the "lecture business" and is mostly a strictly commercial operation, save as some educational institutions dilute the waters.

The "lecture business" still awaits its historian, but a few points about the story can safely be made. The Lyceums brought the "big names" principle into play, but it seems from the available evidence that, while in the beginning the idea was to bridge the gap between the intelligentsia and the common people, a principle accepted with enthusiasm on both sides, as time passed a confusion was confounded between a "big name" based on intellectual distinction and a "big name" based on adventitious notoriety, often of a non-intellectual kind. This confusion was accepted as legitimate when another and somewhat complementary confusion became common: that between the lecture-as-instruction and the lecture-as-entertainment. The latter mixup, today pretty much taken for granted as a foundation-principle of lecturing, appears to have become established during and just after the Civil War. As "big name" entertainment (to combine the two), the lecture reached both heights of popularity and depths of absurdity—both simultaneously, sometimes—about the ultimate significance of which bitter verbal battles have been fought. That odd character, the "visiting [English (?)] lecturer," has been treated lightly as a figure of fun and also heavily as a pernicious bit of fauna worthy of nothing short of purposeful extermination. (He has broken into the popular entertainment in many ways, for example in the play, *The Man Who Came to Dinner*.)

Who is to blame for the less exhilarating aspects of the "lecture business" is hard to say. Such candid and careful studies as have been seen appear to justify an impartial, four-way distribution: to the audiences for flocking to attend the *faux bon* and bad lectures, management for putting them on, agents for offering and promoting anybody out of whom they could hope to make money, and lecturers who have proved to be not above what H. L.

Mencken used to call "boob-thumping." It is almost a habit among the serious-minded critics, however, to bear down hard on the agents for doing more than their share to commercialize lecturing. They came to the field after the Civil War—previously every lecturer was his own agent—and at once they increased prices for talent, forced managers to look more intensively for audiences if they were to make a profit (or avoid a loss), and widened the variety of talent available. Truthfully, the pristine educational emphasis seems to have gone out of lecturing before the agents appeared, but they certainly did little for it.

The evolution of the popular lecture can be illustrated by recalling the names of some of those who either brought their fame to the lecture platform or burnished it on the platforms. Up to the Civil War, when lectures still had a basically noncontroversial, cultural or educative intent, even when they turned out poorly, the great figures were such outstanding literary figures, clerics, and professors—predominantly from New England and New York —as Ralph Waldo Emerson, Henry Thoreau, Bronson Alcott (who pioneered the "conversation" or discussion method), Park Benjamin, Orestes Brownson, George William Curtis, Parke Godwin, Oliver Wendell Holmes, Theodore Parker, Henry Ward Beecher, Benjamin Silliman (who made his first great impact on the lecture-going public with his talks on science in Boston in 1835 and later traveled far and wide by popular request),[5] Wendell Phillips, Bayard Taylor (the pioneer of travel lectures), and Edwin P. Whipple. Emerson's success in the business admirably illustrates that "quality" lectures could succeed; and the fact that Emerson's written essays were developed from lectures to adult audiences assembled at random should provoke reflection in adult educators even today. It was early noticed, however, that single lectures, diverse in style and content, were not after all an ideal educational instrument—a fact constantly being rediscovered—and some attempt was made to intensify the impact by arranging lecture-series, without any great success.

When the lecture platform outgrew the political bias the Civil War gave it, the range of lecture subjects was considerably broadened and, both in intent and effect, the educational emphasis weakened. Entertainment became the watchword. A conspicuous figure in giving the lecture business its new turn was the redoubtable James Redpath (1833–1891), a journalist long associated with Greeley's *New York Tribune,* a fierce abolitionist, a Civil War correspondent, and a loud spokesman for Irish freedom. Redpath got into the business of being a lecture-agent in 1868 when he set up in Boston what he significantly called the Boston Lyceum Bureau (later Redpath's Lyceum Bureau). He began seriously enough by offering such men as Emerson (by then in his last phase), Horace Greeley, Senator Charles Sumner, Wendell Phillips, Julia Ward Howe, and Mary A. Livermore (the most successful woman lecturer of her time). He exploited P. T. Barnum on the platform and the "nineteenth wife" of Brigham Young. He put on the humorists: Josh Billings, Petroleum V. Nasby, Mark Twain. He added magicians. Finally, he offered musical soloists and even small opera companies, thus moving over into a platform field where the gradual maturation of American taste produced astonishing results.[6] Another large operator in the early days was J. B. Pond (1838–1903) whose list ranged from John B. Gough (the former-alcoholic-turned-temperance-lecturer) to Matthew Arnold, with Henry ("Dr. Livingstone, I presume") Stanley in between.

All this is very hard to interpret in satisfying generalizations. It is possible to reduce the kinds of popular lectures that have persisted over the years to the literary lecture, the philosophical (diluted, usually, to the gruel of "inspiration"), public affairs, humor, science, reform (especially moral and personal), and travel. But it must not be forgotten that while these staples go on and on, every major intellectual and social movement produces its own lectures and lecturers to our day. Some of the stock types have traditions all their own, as, for example, the travel lecture which, originating with Bayard Taylor, produced in sequence such famous practitioners as John L. Stoddard, E. M. Newman, and Burton Holmes. Inspirational lecturing, which never dies, produced such a famous phenomenon as Russell Conwell who delivered his piece "Acres of Diamonds" six thousand times and, moreover, put it into board covers as well. Science lecturing is studded with famous names from Benjamin Silliman to E. E. Slosson and beyond.

There is, obviously, a close but not invariable connection between popular lectures on the one hand and popular books on the other. A popular book has made its author into a popular lecturer; and a popular lecturer has sold thousands of books, chiefly because of his platform reputation. The audiences seem to be similar and most of the kinds of lectures that have proved popular over the years can be matched by books of the same general type perennially on the nonfiction best-seller lists. Working from one to the other and back again would tell adult educators much about the popular mind and how it works.

While popular lecturing has a strong tendency both to persist and to drift far from pastures of interest to adult educators, it is nevertheless true that the lecture method is a durable weapon in the adult education arsenal. It may not be the best, but it has its utility.

One consequence of the Lyceum movement was the establishment of endowed institutions for the support of lectures (together, often, with other education endeavors). The classic illustration of this is the Lowell Institute, endowed with a trust fund by the will of John Lowell of Boston. This was in 1836. Lowell derived his idea partly from the SDK and partly from the Lyceum. The Lowell lectures, initiated by Benjamin Silliman, have, of course, maintained a very high level of excellence throughout their history. The use of lectures over many years is also a characteristic of Cooper Union in New York (founded in 1859). Cooper Union lectures have a very complex history, including Abraham Lincoln's memorable address on February 27, 1860. As famous an experiment with the lecture method as any was the People's Institute, founded in 1897 by Charles Sprague Smith and directed for many years by Everett Dean Martin. It ended its career in 1934 and was succeeded by the Department of Social Philosophy which still carries on some of the same kind of work. Moreover, the promotion of lectures of serious intent is occasionally stimulated by such developments as the Chautauqua. Many persons who attended a session of the Chautauqua returned to their home towns and set up local lecture courses. Public schools, colleges, and universities have long promoted lectures on a community service basis, maintaining a reasonably high level of seriousness over lengthy periods. In fact, the idea that lectures can play a creative role in adult life is never apt to die out.

In recent times the serious discussion of public affairs using the lecture method has been associated with the forum idea. The forum —or sometimes the *open* forum to indicate that it is a vehicle for the untrammeled flow of ideas—has a history running back perhaps a hundred years. Unfortunately, the history is rather discontinuous. Before World War I the open forums of Ford Hall in Boston were imitated across the country; Open Forum National Council, under the leadership of George Coleman of Ford Hall, had at once time an institutional membership of two hundred. However, a study of forums made in 1937 showed that "with a few notable exceptions all of the forums which had been established prior to 1917 discontinued" during World War I. Although the forums revived after the war, it was not until the early years of the Great Depression that they experienced something like a boom (illustrating that adults [7] seek knowledge most actively in troubled times). In the 1936 edition of the *Handbook of Adult Education,* the forum idea was discussed quite enthusiastically, but in the 1948 edition it was not separately considered, though it was indicated that its legatees were the *film* forums and discussion groups. World War II disrupted the forums as completely as World War I. Although numerous forums exist today, especially in connection with public-school adult education programs, they are not at this time looked upon with particular enthusiasm by adult educators, whose attention, for the moment at least, is directed elsewhere. They tend to assess rather low the educative value of the lecture and to promote discussion groups instead.

The great boom in forums after 1929, which petered out during World War II, was in considerable part a spontaneous response to the social disorder of the Depression, but it was given leadership by John W. Studebaker who, with Lyman Bryson, had pioneered a particularly successful forum, or rather group of forums, in Des Moines, Iowa, where he was superintendent of schools. For the first five years of their existence, the Des Moines forums were supported by grants from the Carnegie Corporation. Studebaker wrote an enthusiastic book about his experience, *The American Way: Democracy at Work in the Des Moines Forums* (New York, 1935). In 1934 Studebaker became United States Commissioner of Education and in 1936, with an allocation of $330,000 from Federal emergency relief funds to the Office of Education, he started out to spread the Des Moines system across the nation and to stimulate and strengthen forums wherever, and in whatever form, they were to be found. Closely associated with Studebaker in this work were Chester S. Williams and Paul H. Sheats. In all, nineteen demonstration centers were set up coast-to-coast, from Manchester, New Hampshire, and Atlanta, Georgia, in the East to Seattle, Washington, and Santa Ana, California, in the West. At that time, moreover, no less than seven hundred forums were in existence, sponsored by public-school systems, universities, colleges, religious organizations, citizens' committees, civic and educational organizations, public libraries, political organizations, and individuals. What was learned about forums under the Studebaker program was reported in *Choosing Our Way: A Study of America's Forums* (Washington, 1938). Regrettably, the study failed to explain why forum history is so remarkably discontinuous.

Chautauqua: The Cultural Striving of Small Towns

AN ADULT EDUCATION MOVEMENT called Chautauqua, which was to make a tremendous impression on the American mind and imagination, was launched in 1874. Let us glance at the men who founded Chautauqua and especially at what they had in mind.

Chautauqua stemmed from religion, like so much adult education, and its best adventures in "culture" were deeply colored by religious presuppositions. Specifically, it was a project of the Methodist Episcopal Church, but it was never run as a strictly denominational venture, and from its earliest days it solicited and won the co-operation of all the Protestant sects. In original form, it was *a substitute* for the old camp-meetings, those "terrific saturnalia" which flourished on the frontier for many years after the first one of record was held in Logan County, Kentucky, in July of 1800 by the Methodists and Presbyterians in collaboration.

By the time of Chautauqua the camp-meetings had become infinitely more decorous than they had been in their heyday. One such decorous meeting had been held by the Methodists at Fair Point on Lake Chautauqua in western New York State, beginning in 1871. (The name Fair Point was not officially changed to

166

Chautauqua until 1877.) In 1873 it was visited by two Methodist leaders, Rev. John Heyl Vincent, subsequently a bishop, and Lewis Miller, a wealthy layman. Both were keen on education, but Vincent was the educator, Miller the organizer. Vincent, born in Tuscaloosa, Alabama, was educated for the ministry in the North and in 1866 had become general agent of the Methodist Sunday School Union, a position he held for twenty years. He had a lively interest in the pedagogical side of Sunday-school work and was something of an innovator in it. Miller was an inventor and manufacturer of agricultural machinery from Ohio. When he visited Fair Point with Vincent, he was already a college trustee and had served as member of a state government board on the assignment of land-grant funds in his state. Vincent and Miller had decided that the day of the camp-meeting was about over. After studying the situation at Fair Point, they proposed to build upon the foundation it provided a new kind of institution, described later by Vincent as "a school, a Bible school, a normal school, a Sunday-school institute . . ." to be called The Sunday-school Teachers' Assembly—a direct imitation, in fact, of the normal schools for public-school teachers. The idea was proposed to the board of managers of the Sunday School Union and accepted by them in October, 1873. Miller was designated president and Vincent superintendent of instruction. They immediately invited the participation of the Baptists and Presbyterians.

The first Assembly opened at Fair Point on Tuesday evening, August 4, 1874, and closed on Tuesday morning, August 18. The keynote of the venture was struck by the reading of Zechariah 4:1-6, of which the sixth verse is the key passage (*my italics*):

> Then he answered and spake unto me, saying, This is the word of the LORD unto Zerubbabel, saying, *Not by might, nor by power, but by my spirit,* saith the LORD of hosts.

At the first Assembly, the teaching emphasis fell upon the problems and methods of organizing, administering, and teaching Sunday schools—strictly normal-school matters in a religious atmosphere for religious purposes.

The professors, almost all active clergymen, taught by lecturing; and one of the lessons the managers learned was that "More emphasis should be placed upon the conversational [i.e., discussion]

method" in the classes. Unfortunately the lesson was but imperfectly learned, as subsequent history shows. Another thing early
learned, though whether at the very first Assembly or not is not
clear, was that, in addition to a knowledge of the Bible, denominational literature, and pedagogical method, the teachers could also
effectively use secular knowledge as "illustrations by which [they]
may set forth the mysteries of the spiritual kingdom," as indeed
religious leaders were even then doing in their war on the rising
secularism. It was on this latter discovery that the managers of
Chautauqua built a turntable which switched the Assembly from an
affair of concern only to Sunday-school teachers to one at which
the laity outnumbered them.

By 1886, when his invaluable book, *The Chautauqua Movement,* was published at Boston, Vincent had gotten his ideas about
Chautauqua as clear as he ever got them. He was not a notably
clear and logical writer and his book, shot through with fervent
sincerity, strikes one today as made up of chapter-sermons rather
than simply chapters. Nevertheless, it must stand as a classic of
American adult education literature. Carefully sifted and sorted, the
ideas put forward in it are mostly still basic to the thinking in
adult education down to our own day, except for the rooting of the
movement in religion.

Vincent argued that the true basis of education is religion; all
knowledge, religious and secular, is sacred to the religious person.
He saw life itself as an educative process from birth to death, of
which the self-conscious search for "education" in the specialized
sense was but a part, though a supremely valuable part. He argued
that education must be lifelong. In an essay of 1891 he got this
point very clear indeed: "The principle now so generally accepted,
that education is the privilege of all, young and old, rich and poor,
that mental development is only begun in school and college, *and
should be continued through all of life,* underlies the Chautauqua
system . . ." (*My italics.*) He believed that "In mature life, beyond
the limits of the usual school period, the intellect is at its best for
purposes of reading, reflection, and production," a view cohering
very well with Aristotle's. He entered a "protest against the sus-
pension of intellectual effort when the compulsory regime of the
recitation room has been remitted,—a fault so common and so
pernicious that college men themselves frequently bring into dis-

repute the college system." He felt that formal preparation should weigh less heavily with adult educators than the "exaltation of [culture's] value and desirability, and a craving for its possession." The underlying motive of the students might be self-improvement, as it had been in the Lyceum, but the Chautauqua aimed to encourage not so much isolated adventures in self-education, as group efforts under competent direction. The wish to achieve, Vincent argued, could best be satisfied with the guidance of good teachers; and Chautauqua was much concerned with how to bring good teachers into contact with the students. He assumed without discussion that there was a very large public able to profit from the courses offered; he placed no niggardly evaluation on the intelligence of the people at large; and he thought education of the Chautauqua variety ought to be and could be universal.

The education Vincent had in mind was "liberal education," not vocational, but he was not blind to the value of recreative cultural activities. The gravest fault that Vincent recognized in Chautauqua was superficiality. He argued, however, that only if the activities criticized were treated either by the students or the critics as sufficient ends in themselves could they correctly be called superficial. He himself did not look upon them that way, but as what he called "intellectual quickening." Having been "quickened" by experiences the truly learned could only regard as superficial, the beneficiaries would be inspired to move on to the mastery of the complex realities the truly learned were talking about. The Chautauqua, Vincent said, "exalts the college"—apparently the liberal-arts denominational college as it was in the mid-eighties (and which Vincent all his life regretted he had not himself attended). The end sought by Chautauqua was the universalization of liberal-arts college breeding, surely not a mean educational ideal. Vincent was "content and grateful to have been permitted by a gracious Providence to engage in the good cause with the worthy workers who have helped to found and build it up."

To describe adequately in a few words the machinery which was erected to realize Chautauqua's ends is difficult, not only because it became exceedingly complex, but also because it is impossible to sort it into a strictly logical pattern. After the first Assembly in 1874, which was, so to speak, a residential summer normal school,

Chautauqua grew in a variety of directions until at one stage it was capped by a degree-granting university. It then began to shrink up again until it was mostly a kind of popular adult summer school and vacation resort on the lakeside—the Chautauqua as we see it today.

To the Sunday-school teachers' normal school (later called the Assembly Normal Union) was added in 1879 the Chautauqua Teachers' Retreat for public-school teachers, a short summer school in pedagogy. An offshoot of this was a Chautauqua Teacher's Reading Union (founded 1884), a year-round book club. The Assembly Normal Union was supported by a so-called Intermediate Class in the Bible, a kind of preparatory stage for the Union itself, or a scheme for recruiting candidates for fullfledging as Sunday-school teachers.

The religio-theological interests took on their own life and were institutionalized in a Chautauqua School of Languages (Greek, Latin, Hebrew, etc.—the traditional languages of the ministry), founded in 1878; a School of Theology (worked by correspondence) founded in 1881; a Missionary (home and foreign) Institute; and a Chautauqua Church School of Church Work, offering training in "practical" theology.

In August, 1878, there was launched the still-surviving Chautauqua Literary and Scientific Circle, designed to offer an opportunity for the summer visitors to the lakeside to study by correspondence during the whole year. This was the core of Chautauqua's work in serious adult education and will be discussed more fully below. A Book-a-Month Reading Circle supplied worthwhile reading to those not disposed to close study in such fields as history, biography, travel, popular science, the essay and the novel (often historical), all in a planned three-year cycle. A Young Folks' Reading Union was also established. Special adult interests were catered for by a Society of Fine Arts, a Musical Reading Circle, and a Town and Country Club, concerned with nature study, gardening, and farm practice, worked in each case mostly by correspondence.

On the Chautauqua grounds each summer were numerous more or less *ad hoc* organizations like the Boys' and Girls' Bible Class; the Temperance Classmates (based on the traditional churchly and adult education enmity to drink); the Sunday afternoon Society of Christian Ethics; and the Chautauqua Cadets and the Calisthenics Corps, the one offering physical training for boys, the other for girls.

To serve the needs of the organiaztion, a Chautauqua Press was set up to print materials for the courses (instruction sheets, examination forms, books, etc.), and a magazine—also linked with the courses, but having a general appeal—which reached a circulation of fifty thousand a month and loomed up as an equal of *Harper's, The Atlantic,* and *The Century.*

The summer Assembly, later simply "the Chautauqua," in time became in part not only an occasion for numerous religious exercises—they set the tone of the affair, Lewis Miller in the mid-eighties declaring that they preserved the camp-meeting spirit of prayer and praise—but also for secular lectures, educational in character, in politics, economics, industry, literature, and science. Some seasons as many as 180 lectures were delivered in various series, 50 concerts were given, and 40-odd formal social and athletic events, not to mention the activities of the special clubs and the unscheduled fun and games. A daily newspaper was required to keep the visitors posted on what was going on.

Around 1900, the religious emphasis began to moderate (though it was never to disappear) and a shift was made to an emphasis on psychology and the humanities, later still to citizenship, finally to holiday-making with strong educational overtones.[1] After 1880, music, both vocal and instrumental, occupied a more and more conspicuous place, working up to the symphonic performances that began after World War I. After World War I, also, the drama was strongly emphasized. It was the platform activities that brought celebrities of high and low degree into direct contact with Chautauqua audiences. The roster included Presidents from Grant (who had been a member of Vincent's congregation at Galena, Illinois, before the Civil War) to Theodore Roosevelt. Those performers who drew large audiences helped pay for those who drew small.

The whole vast structure was financed by fees for courses, gate receipts at the lakeside grounds, and profits from the hotels, stores, and concessions that grew up to serve the multitudes who attended the summer events. The sessions themselves grew in length from two weeks to seven. The structure was capped by the Chautauqua

University and its College, chartered by the State of New York as a degree-granting institution in 1883.

The Chautauqua organization was erected primarily to serve adults. It was designed to make it possible for adults to educate themselves from the level of casual but worth-while reading, plus attendance at the summer lectures, to that of university training. In Vincent's mind, the college was to be the center of the structure; it was to set the tone of the whole. It did not turn out that way. The title "University" was dropped in 1892, the power to grant degrees in 1898. The Chautauqua Literary and Scientific Circle, of which Vincent was the inventor and prime mover, became the core-institution of the whole setup as far as serious adult education was concerned. Its members were, said Vincent, "advanced Chautauquans"; and its motto, characteristically, was "WE STUDY THE WORD AND THE WORKS OF GOD." It was "a school at home, a school after school, a 'college' for one's own house." Its aim, in Vincent's own words was:

> . . . to promote habits of reading and study in nature, art, science, and in secular and sacred literature, in connection with the routine of daily life (especially among those whose educational advantages have been limited), so as to secure to them the college student's general outlook upon the world and life, and to develop the habit of close, connected, persistent thinking. It encourages individual study in lines and by textbooks which shall be indicated; by local circles for mutual help and encouragement in such studies; by summer courses of lectures and "students'" sessions at Chautauqua; and by written reports and examinations.

In actual practice, the work of the CLSC was done basically by correspondence. What was accomplished in the local circles is very hard to say since no evaluatory survey of them seems ever to have been made. Attendance at the summer Chautauquas was often just not possible for the enrollees. At one stage, Chautauqua experimented with the university-extension lecture approach, having been convinced of its merits by its famous American exponent, Herbert Baxter Adams (see below), and having its interest reinforced by a visit of a delegation of extension workers from Oxford, Cambridge, Edinburgh, and Glasgow in 1888. Launched in 1889, it reached its peak three years later with 168 lectures and then faded away. Insofar as solid work was done over the years in CLSC, it was done by individual initiative and correspondence. Those who did the required reading, prepared the answers to "recitation papers," wrote the required essays, and took the final examinations really collected the profits of the system and were rewarded with seals and diplomas and the kudos of honorific attention when they turned up at the summer Chautauquas.

Since correspondence [2] was the heart of the matter, we are fortunate to have a careful analysis of it as a teaching method by William Rainey Harper, later president of the University of Chicago, who joined Chautauqua in 1883 as professor of Greek and Latin in the School of Languages.

Writing of the correspondence problem as it faced the Chautauqua, Harper asked four questions:

1. What *is* the correspondence system of teaching?
2. What are its disadvantages as compared to oral teaching?
3. What are its advantages?
4. What results are accomplished? [3]

The system, said Harper, had three indispensable pedagogical tools: the instruction sheet telling the student what he was to do; the examination paper designed to ferret out what the student had learned; and the recitation paper in which the student gave his answers to the questions asked on the examination paper and in his turn asked of the instructor any questions which may have occurred to him. The student, of course, had obtained the required books for his course as well as *The Chautauquan* magazine, which contained up to 50 per cent of the whole body of material to be studied. What he missed, as compared to the student in the classroom, was the personal "magnetism" of the teacher, the incidental help offered by the teacher under classroom conditions, the advantages of the greater frequency of oral recitations, and the ease of reciting by voice rather than in writing. However, Harper went on, some of these alleged advantages of classroom work were very dubious. The magnetic teacher, he realistically observed, was fairly uncommon; orally presented lessons were ordinarily far less carefully planned than written ones; the incidental help offered students

was often capriciously distributed; frequent attendance at oral recitations was advantageous only to those called on regularly—ordinarily not all the members of the class—and a single written recitation was therefore often equivalent to three or four oral classes;
writing out answers, instead of reciting them orally, cultivated the
habit of exact statement, demanded greater precision of knowledge, required the student to "recite" all of every lesson, and thus
required more study. Nevertheless, while plainly putting a firm
finger on all the positive values he could discover, Harper still
had to concede that correspondence was but a substitute for classroom study—that the face-to-face relationship was best after all.
Using italics, he wrote:

> Only those persons are encouraged to study by correspond-
> ence, or, indeed, admitted to such study, who because of age,
> poverty, occupation, situation, or some other good reason,
> cannot avail themselves of oral instruction.

Despite the concessions, Harper made a large claim for correspondence instruction. "The day is coming," he wrote in 1884
(?), "when the work done by correspondence will be greater in
amount than that done in the classrooms of our academies and
colleges; when the students who shall recite by correspondence will
far outnumber those who make oral recitations." Harper, rather
oddly, failed to foresee that the colleges were in good time to become institutions for mass education as the common schools alone
were at the time he wrote. As here, much of the Chautauqua planning seems to have been based upon a very limited idea of what
changes were to take place in educational opportunity in the
America of the future.

What did the CLSC students study? The courses were organized
on the basis of four years of linked work. After some experiment,
the instructors settled down to the habit of prescribing four or five
books per year as required reading. Each year the courses offered
had a theme drawn from broad areas of persistent interest: English,
American, Continental European, Classical. Within these areas
almost any special theme might turn up—the variations possible
were infinite and curbed only by student response. In the mid-
eighties Lewis Miller specified some of the subjects in which the
Chautauqua audience should be interested: the rights of property,

labor, trade, money, women's rights. The record shows that it soon overswept these boundaries. The CLSC students tackled history, economics, political science, sociology, literature. But it is impossible to state with any precision what ideas about any of these matters were inserted into their minds. To do so with any show of reasonableness would require not only a knowledge of the books they read—a not inconsiderable effort in exploring the out-of-date—but also a valid yardstick for measuring pedagogical success.

Fragmentary indications are available, however. Take the subject of economics. The famous economist Richard T. Ely, who held that economics was a subdivision of ethics, and who was something of a Christian Socialist of the F. D. Maurice persuasion (therefore not a Marxist), lectured at Chautauqua for seven seasons, 1884–91. His books, *Introduction to Political Economy, Outlines of Economics, Strength and Weakness of Socialism,* and *Studies in the Evolution of Industrial Society* were used in the CLSC courses. The *Outlines,* originally written for CLSC, reached a circulation of 200,000 copies. In his autobiography Ely wrote: "It was largely through Chautauqua that I was able to exercise my greatest influence. No one can understand the history of this country and the forces which have been shaping it for the last half century without some comprehension of the important work of that splendid institution . . ." [4] CLSC was, then, among other things, one vehicle for the spread of liberal ideas on social, economic, and political policy —of the kind of thinking that supported the careers of Presidents like Theodore Roosevelt, Woodrow Wilson, and Franklin Roosevelt. The whole question, however, is one that demands far closer analysis than anyone has yet chosen to give it.

Chautauqua was chiefly a small-town phenomenon; it flourished most mightily in the decades when the small town had its heyday, before the great urban conurbations really began to develop. Whether it is a question of who attended the lakeside summer sessions, or who enrolled in the CLSC, the small town was the source of support. Between 1874 and 1894, it is reported, 10,000 local study circles were established, 75 per cent of them in towns of less than 3,500 population. The summer sessions ran up the numbers who in some degree responded to the Chautauqua appeal;

those who joined the CLSC, numerically a much smaller group, put themselves in the way of being influenced intensively. Between 1874 and 1918 perhaps 300,000 individuals enrolled in the CLSC. Of these perhaps 45,000 to 50,000 actually did the required reading for four years, took the examinations, and were granted the appropriate rewards.

The ratio seems, at least, to follow from the precise figures given by Vincent for the first CLSC class—that which began work in 1878 and finished in 1882. The original registration for this class was 8,246. The graduating class had 1,694 members. The original registrants were distributed by age as follows:

Under 20	881
20-30	3,805
30-40	2,346
Over 40	1,214
Total	8,246

The graduates were distributed thus:

Under 20	27
20-30	628
30-40	567
Over 40	472
Total	1,694

Vincent adds that there were five women for every three men among the original registrants and three women to one man among the graduates. About 25 per cent of the women and 14 per cent of the men actually went through with the program. These figures clearly show that the CLSC had its greatest impact on women of college age or older, and that once the plunge was taken, the resolution to complete the work was firmer among the more mature, and firmer among women than men. The heavy wastage can be variously explained—lack of time, inadequate preparation, even the stiffness of the standards Vincent insisted be maintained; but the figures in any case illustrate the point that in adult education, as in all education, a large allowance must be made for "dropouts" if the education attempted is serious in nature and exactingly administered.

Now few people who severely criticized Chautauqua—as "entertainment" or on other grounds—in its flourishing days seem to have examined material like this; and indeed the writer found no evidence that it has ever been carefully studied *in extenso* to this day. If the critics had really burrowed into the workings of Chautauqua, they might have rendered different judgments and even have offered some constructive ideas, which were needed, about how to teach adults and keep them at their lessons. Rather, attention was directed chiefly at the lakeside summer sessions and they, it must be admitted, were vulnerable. Of necessity the lectures were uneven in quality, the better to serve all levels of intellectual competence, and discontinuous in the subject matter. Moreover, the public lecture, as has so often been discovered, is not an ideal pedagogical form, especially if unsupported by any other intellectual or academic discipline. It may "quicken" some of the auditors, but it mostly beguiles, or entertains, or creates a false illusion of intellectual employment. The summer sessions at the lake tended to be genteel merry-go-rounds, as Professor George Herbert Palmer noted in 1892: the student "there . . . attends the swiftly successive Round Tables upon Milton, Temperance, Geology, the American Constitution, the Relations of Science and Religion, and the Doctrine of Rent; perhaps assists at the Cooking School, the Prayer Meeting, the Concert and the Gymnastic Drill; or wanders under the trees . . ." [5] But perhaps the most vivid and complex reaction to the summer Chautauqua was that of William James who gave the substance of his famous *Talks to Teachers* at the Chautauqua of 1892. His first reactions are recorded for us in his *Letters* and his mature reflections in the printed version of his *Talks* which came out in 1899. Here they are in all their brilliant rightness and wrongness:

A few summers ago I spent a happy week at the famous Assembly Grounds on the borders of Chautauqua Lake. The moment one treads that sacred enclosure, one feels one's self in an atmosphere of success. Sobriety and industry, intelligence and goodness, orderliness and ideality, prosperity and cheerfulness, pervade the air. It is a serious and studious picnic on a gigantic scale. . . . You have culture, you have kindness, you have cheapness, you have equality, you have the best fruits of what mankind has fought and bled and

striven for under the name of civilization for centuries. You
have, in short, a foretaste of what human society might be,
were it all in the light, and no suffering and no dark cor-
ners. . . .

   . . . This order is too tame, this culture too second-rate,
this goodness too uninspiring. This human drama without a
villain or a pang; this community so refined that ice-cream
soda-water is the utmost offering it can make to the brute
animal in man; this city simmering in the tepid lakeside sun;
this atrocious harmlessness of all things,—I cannot abide
with them. Let me take my chances again in the big outside
wordly wilderness with all its sins and sufferings. There are
the heights and depths, the precipices and the steep ideals,
the gleams of the awful and the infinite; and there is more
hope and help a thousand times than in this dead level and
quintessence of every mediocrity. . . .[7]

Up to this point we have kept attention firmly fixed on the
"original" Chautauqua, but to complete the picture some attention
must be given to its progeny, legitimate and illegitimate. Of its
legitimate progeny little need be said beyond the observation that
they were summer assemblies, usually on lakesides like the "original," on a slightly lower intellectual plane. They began to appear
within two years of the establishment of the "original" and within
a decade had been set up in Iowa, Ohio, New York, Indiana,
Minnesota, California, Kansas, Massachusetts, Wisconsin, Tennessee, Maryland, Nebraska, New Jersey, Maine, Arkansas, Ore-
gon, Florida, Michigan, Pennsylvania, Illinois, Washington, and
Texas—sometimes several in a single state—to a total of fifty.
In the long run six of them achieved more than transient fame:
Winona Lake, Indiana; Lakeside, Ohio; Boulder, Colorado; Bay
View, Michigan; Franklin, Ohio; and Ocean Grove, New Jersey.
All these were "legitimate" in the sense that they were loosely
linked to the "original," accepted its ideals, and the participants
were registered, in some proportion, in the CLSC. Since these
assemblies made much of lectures, the custom grew up for the
popular speakers to itinerate among them in the season, thus providing a kind of link between the "legitimate" Chautauquas and the
illegitimate. They also went in for music, another link.

The "illegitimate" progeny were the tent-show Chautauquas which, by one of those odd mischances of history, are what most people today think of when they hear the word "Chautauqua." The tent shows succeeded in giving the word an aura of disreputableness so that anything plastered with the epithets "chautauqua" or "chautauquan" (lower-case *c*) is thereby and without further elaboration presumed to be expelled from sophisticated society. The tent-show Chautauquas were strictly commercial ventures, not linked with the "original" in any way, except for the overlapping of the performing personnel. They did not come into existence until 1903, when Chautauqua was already almost thirty years old, and they ran a hectic course for three decades, reaching a peak in the early nineteen-twenties when about thirty million persons attended them in a season in twelve thousand small towns from coast to coast in sessions lasting from three to seven days. Rarely did they appear in towns of over ten thousand; and they could, in their best years, make money in towns of five hundred, if there was a good supporting countryside. Yet if they rose to stupendous numerical heights, they disappeared with surprising rapidity. Between the early twenties and the early thirties they lost around 90 per cent of their audience and shortly they faded away.

The entrepreneurs who thought up the tent Chautauquas were two gentlemen named J. Roy Ellison and Keith Vawter, both lecture agents. They got the idea of selling talent to the "original" and "legitimate" Chautauquas so that they, and their clients, could make something during the slack summer season, but they quickly perceived that more money was to be made by establishing their own Chautauquas. Between them they contrived a cross between the Chautauqua on a permanent site and the tent-show technique uséd by medicine shows and circuses, thus making it possible to send both the "artists" and their housing in a package on circuit. To diminish the risk to the vanishing point, they developed a contract that put the financial responsibility on the merchants of the towns in which they proposed to appear. The merchants underwrote the figure set for the show by the entrepreneurs and recouped the guarantee by an intensive ticket-selling campaign, finding additional profit in any increase in store sales that might result from the visit of the "attraction" to town.

As there was no patent on the scheme, traveling tent-show

Chautauquas, good and bad, mushroomed all over the country, but operated with greatest success in the Middle West. The South was considered the poorest country for the Chautauqua gambit. When the great shakedown came late in the twenties, three organizations dominated the dying field: the Redpath (the pioneer, named for the old lecture bureau which Vawter controlled), the Swarthmore, and the Community. Of these the historians consider the Swarthmore to have been quite the best. It was named after Swarthmore College, but had no official connection with it, and was run by Paul M. Pearson, father of Drew Pearson, the newspaper columnist and radio personality.

A very large and difficult question about the tent Chautauquas is whether what they offered by way of instruction and entertainment was better or worse than what was otherwise available to adults in small towns. The intellectual climate of small towns as portrayed in novels from Ed Howe's *The Story of a Country Town* (1883) to Sinclair Lewis's *Main Street* (1920) is not such as to inspire much enthusiasm. It is difficult to see how the Chautauquas could have worsened the situation. At their best, it is pretty clear that they improved it, and when they were poor, they rather conformed to the ruling tone than lowered it. For years the tents throve on the allegation that they offered the only truly free platforms in America. They promoted the lambasting of "Wall Street" along Populist lines, an "act" still popular in the grass-roots areas. Later on they "plugged" prohibition, pacifism, the abolition of poverty, better citizenship, good roads—all "sure-fire" in the rural districts.

Not all the speakers who handled these large and complex subjects are remembered today, but a few still are: Charles Zueblin is still recalled as a municipal reformer, George Norris and Robert M. La Follette as liberal political leaders, Eugene Debs as the exemplar of the grass-roots American Socialist. (La Follette is alleged to have used Chautauqua to build up his Progressive Party, just as he is also alleged to have used university extension to the same end.) The tent Chautauquas also sent on circuit men and women of the quality of Vilhjalmur Stefansson, Sir Hubert Wilkins, Dr. Wilfred Grenfell, Ida Tarbell, Jane Addams, Lorado Taft, Judge Ben Lindsey, Herbert Hoover, Edna Ferber, Brand Whitlock, and Glenn Frank.

It was at the time the fashion for city-dwellers to look down on the tent Chautauquas as offering "thin pap for yokels," but they seem never to have noticed that many of those who performed in tents in summer also served as the "star attractions" in lecture series to which the city-dwellers flocked during the winter! Rather than the figures both rural and urban audiences found very satisfactory, the toplofty urbanites were thinking of the mother-home-and-heaven orators who really packed them into the tents, men like Russell Conwell and, above all, William Jennings Bryan. Bryan made a stupendous appeal to the Chautauquans at all levels— his political strength was always rural after his failure to win the Presidency in 1896—but he came to be identified with the tents, and by some curious magic, the tents came to be identified with Bryanism, even though Bryan himself was only one "attraction" among many.[8] The secret probably is that Bryan was the "cultural lag" personified; he epitomized the rural mind of his time. But this is to underestimate his immense shrewdness. If Bryan was hardly an Aristotle from the prairies, he was also hardly an intellectual vacuum.

Speech-making, moreover, was not the whole of the tent shows. Music was extremely important. It has, indeed, been said that "Chautauqua means music." [9] There is plenty of evidence that the music offered improved in quality as the years passed, reaching highly respectable heights in the later years. The Swiss yodelers may have toured, but the tents also popularized Beethoven. Bands were popular, but so were small orchestras. And if jazz infiltrated the tents in the end, it hardly did so in advance of its conquest of the urban masses. Drama, too, was made respectable to country people by the tents. One drama, originally a Broadway "hit," became a kind of classic of the tents: Winchell Smith's *Turn to the Right*.

The tents, in fact, offered a surprising range of thought and entertainment, but they failed to cut very deeply. Here superficiality was rampant and, worse still, a superficiality that led almost, but not quite, nowhere. "Not quite," because every so often a person, usually a young person, caught a glimpse of something beyond the usual small-town horizon and followed the gleam in later life; talk to men and women who were young small-towners in the 1910's and 1920's to confirm this. Many boys and girls, later to get to college, first had their eyes raised above the local limits in Chautauqua tents; and the Chautauqua at this and its other levels played an unknown but probably large role in preparing the way for the great migration into college in the succeeding generations. Finally, a learned historian of the American mind has ventured the opinion that "Chautauqua culture" was far superior to the "radio culture" by which it was in large measure succeeded.[10]

Why, after spreading so far, if not so deep, and establishing a claim to being a pioneering venture in mass adult education, did Chautauqua in the end shrink back to the lakeside summer assembly from which it had issued?

It shrank back, if the analysts are right, because the movies and the radio took over the audience, the automobile made better cultural facilities more readily accessible, the public-school system expanded to include high schools, public libraries and museums became more common, and college got within the reach of more and more young people. It shrank, too, because it failed to find a dynamic *secular* principle to sustain in an increasingly secular world a movement which was based upon a religious impulse and throve with the support of religious-minded people. Chautauqua failed to meet at all adequately the challenges implicit in the growth of cultural institutions, the elaboration of mass communications, and the spread of secularism. It failed to adapt to a changing world.

Such adaptability as Chautauqua showed was greater on the side of thinning the cultural brew than on the side of thickening and enriching it, a fault it shared with American education in general. The tent Chautauquas were a kind of ultimate thinning, the CLSC about as rich as the brew got. The culture of the tent shows disappeared into "mass communications" culture, the vigor of the lakeside Chautauquas into academic summer schools (which were suggested by the Chautauquas), the university and private correspondence schools, and university extension. A solid, enduring, mass-based popular cultural movement was not really established in spite of many hopeful signs that it was going to put down firm roots. The whole adventure cries out for a more intensive analysis than anyone has yet given it. If the leaders could find today a dynamic principle suited to our complex age, Chautauqua might flame across the nation once again.

15

Higher Educational Institutions and Adult Education

HILE CHAUTAUQUA was still very active in the 1890's, an experiment in bringing the cultural resources of the universities to the people was launched. This was called "university extension." [1] The basic idea behind it was that knowledge should be diffused through society and that the universities should, in addition to conserving and extending knowledge within their campuses, also participate largely in the diffusion of it to the people. In an effort to provide an impressive background for the activity, some writers have cited as precedents practically every adventure in adult education since the late eighteenth century in England or, in the United States—everything back to Franklin's Junto, with "university extension" as the culminating development. This seems to me quite unjustifiable. University extension is not really the culmination of all prior adult education efforts, nor has it had, since its establishment, any true claim to being more than one of many valid enterprises in what of necessity must be a complex and diversified field.

The roots of a rationale for university extension are to be found in the rationale of the place of a university in a democratic society. We have already seen how this question was given an answer in

England. In the United States we must again refer to the Jacksonian as opposed to the Jeffersonian approach to educational problems. In proportion as thinking about the place of the university in American society has been dominated by the elite principle of Jefferson, there has been little likelihood that university extension could flourish. But when the Jacksonian yeast has begun to work, university extension in some form or other has become a likely prospect.

It is not accidental, then, that the rationale for university extension has been provided by the writings of university leaders like Daniel Coit Gilman of Johns Hopkins, C. R. Van Hise of Wisconsin, George Vincent of Minnesota, David Starr Jordan of California—all of whom in one way or another were concerned with establishing the closest possible relations between the university and the people at large, either in the immediate vicinity or in a whole state. It is probably a historical accident that two of the six university presidents conspicuously identified with university extension in its early years—George Vincent and William Rainey Harper—had experience in Chautauqua; but it is a significant accident, in that no other prior adult education enterprise had so much to teach.

Chautauqua, as we noted, aimed to operate at the college level and even tried to build a university. The idea was to build upward to the university from adult education. University extension reversed this approach and aimed to "extend" the university downward through adult education. This proved the better approach, but to all who paid heed the Chautauqua unquestionably demonstrated that significant educational work was to be done among the people at large if the resources could be assembled and a satisfactory machinery for their distribution worked out. A university *had* the requisite resources. The problem was to find the machinery, the personnel, the pedagogical procedures, which would at once supply and also create a demand for them. University extension appeared to be such a machinery. After some fumbling, it caught on and is today an integral element of the American university system, even though the most optimistic evaluators must doubt after six decades of work that the task of diffusion has much more than begun. There is infinitely more valid knowledge stored up in the universities than extension has ever yet been able to diffuse to the people for individual and social use, and infinitely more people in dire need of it than extension has thus far been able to reach.

University extension was borrowed from England. The decade of transplantation was 1880 to 1890. But it was the form given the idea that was novel, not the idea itself. American college teachers had been making their knowledge available directly to the people at large, chiefly in the form of single lectures, for a long time before they heard of university extension. As early as 1816, a professor at what is now Rutgers in New Jersey had offered lectures in science; the popular-science lectures of Silliman of Yale, beginning in the 1830's, have been referred to earlier in another connection; and Columbia in the 1830's, Harvard as early as 1840, Michigan State in 1855, Kansas State in 1868, Minnesota in 1881, and Wisconsin in 1885 had begun experiments along the same general lines, not always with much success. In 1876, President Daniel Coit Gilman made planned lecture series for the "educated public," including specifically art students, teachers, lawyers, physicians, clergymen, bankers, and businessmen, an integral part of the system of instruction at Johns Hopkins.

With this variegated background it is altogether odd that the earliest attempts to naturalize the idea of extension in its English form were not made by the universities but by private organizations and public libraries. This is even more remarkable when it is realized that the pioneer exponent of university extension in America was a professor at Johns Hopkins, Herbert Baxter Adams, a historian distinguished in his generation and still well remembered by the practitioners of his art. Adams began to talk and write about the university extension he had observed in England in the middle eighteen-eighties and put on what can only be described as a sales campaign for it. What Adams saw in university extension was an escape from the fragmentariness and discontinuity of subject-matter inherent in any scheme of single lectures unaccompanied by any other discipline than voluntary attendance. University extension provided for lectures in series on a single subject-matter and gave opportunity to impose disciplines like occasional essays and reports and final examinations. Adams first found support for the idea in two places: the public libraries and Chautauqua.

As we have already noted, it was taken up enthusiastically at Chautauqua, had distinguished backing, but did not last. Similarly it made a strong appeal to librarians, but it had but a short life among them. To the librarians Professor Adams said in 1887:

> The thought of higher education for the people through libraries, which are the highest of high schools, is in the air and sooner or later will find lodgment in all our great towns and cities. It is not enough to connect public libraries with the work of the public schools. You must connect your institutions with the educational wants of the people. There should be in every great community organized instruction, through public libraries, for the graduates of public schools, for persons past the school age, for mechanics and working classes in general. Desultory reading and individual use of the public library are not sufficient. There must be methodic and continuous work under proper guidance. There must be concentration of energy on the part of both readers and managers in our public libraries.[2]

Buffalo, Chicago, and St. Louis libraries took up the challenge without success. Even when Melvil Dewey brought his immense prestige as leader of librarians to the support of the idea, success eluded those who experimented with it.

The proper place for university extension proved, not illogically, to be the universities. But before we look at what happened there, we must examine an organization called the American Society for the Extension of University Teaching, which attempted to draw upon the universities for teaching personnel, but aimed to carry out the actual teaching as a highly decentralized private enterprise. The ASEUT lasted about twenty-six years, from 1890 to 1916, being strongest from 1890 to 1900. It originated in Philadelphia, drew its leadership from the citizens of that city, and conducted most of the classes in the city, eastern Pennsylvania, and in New Jersey across the Delaware River, though it had offshoots farther afield.[3] It was set up as a direct result of news of the English university-extension system and a first-hand study of the English system made by the first secretary of the organization. It drew Englishmen into its work as lecturers.

When the ASEUT was established, Philadelphia already had a service called the University Lecture Association, established in 1887, which arranged for afternoon lectures by the teaching personnel of the University of Pennsylvania. Although it continued for at least five years after the ASEUT was launched, a motive for establishing the latter was dissatisfaction with the ULA. In the end, the ASEUT absorbed the work of the ULA. The ULA system was criticized as isolated lectures, no matter what their quality individually, are always criticized by those concerned with thorough teaching. These faults the ASEUT aimed to escape by giving the lectures in integrated series and relating the series one to another, thus aiming to achieve intensity of impact. In doing this, the over-riding aim was "To attempt to solve the problem of how much of what the Universities do for their own students can be done for people unable to go to universities." The system was "meant for those for whom religion is intended; for those for whom life, liberty, and the pursuit of happiness is intended. It is meant to help the ignorant who desire knowledge that they may learn wisely; to reveal to the half-educated the insufficiency of their knowledge; to rouse intellectual sluggards; to stimulate those who are in the right way; to bring questioning to the hearts of the self-satisfied." [4]

The central organization in Philadelphia provided the general management of the undertaking, lined up the instructors and dealt with the basic finances; but it depended upon locally sponsored and organized classes actually to reach the people. The local classes were sponsored by libraries, YMCA's, clubs (including church clubs), and *ad hoc* organizations of interested citizens. The local organizations collected the student fees. Only as local classes came into being could the scheme work, but it is not quite clear what steps were taken to stimulate their appearance, although reference is made to the missionary work of Richard Green Moulton, an Englishman with university-extension experience brought over by the central organization and described not only as an enthusiast but also—significantly, perhaps—as "the descendant of four generations of itinerant Methodist ministers." (Later Moulton went to the University of Chicago.) In the first ten, and the best, years an average of 18,000 persons a year were served at a cost of about $33,000 annually, met as follows: student fees, 55 per cent, provided by local centers, 17 per cent, contributed by interested philanthropists, 28 per cent.

During the same decade the numbers of lectures in the broad categories of favored subject-matter were:

> 378 literature
> 272 history and biography
> 143 civics, economics, finance, sociology
> 67 music
> 67 science
> 16 religion, ethics, philosophy
> 11 painting and architecture

Whether this represents demand or supply, or some subtle combination of the two, is far from clear, but the emphasis on the liberal studies and the then burgeoning social sciences is exceedingly interesting. Above all, the ASEUT did not cater to vocational interests.

Equally interesting is the roll of lecturers, which shows that at that stage university extension could command the services of men then of great distinction, or later to achieve distinction, in many cases far beyond the academic average. On the list of occasional lecturers we find such American names as those of Charles M. Andrews, James H. Breasted, Edwin G. Conklin, Franklin H. Giddings, John Bach McMaster, James Harvey Robinson, and Paul Shorey; and such distinguished English names as Halford J. Mackinder, Michael E. Sadler, and Graham Wallas. It was the staff-lecturers, however, who carried the bulk of the teaching load. Most of these were Americans: Edward T. Devine, Henry W. Rolfe, Lyman P. Powell, William C. Lawton, Stockton Axson, Albert A. Bird, Fred H. Sykes, William H. Mace, Edward H. Griggs, and Cecil F. Lavell. To these may be added the names of the English staff-lecturers: R. G. Moulton, W. Hudson Shaw, and—very interesting, this—Hilaire Belloc.

At the same time that the ASEUT was having its best years—i.e., the 1890's—the universities were also beginning experiments with the idea of university extension, although, of course, a few were already in the field, as noted earlier. No less than twelve began university extension work in the nineties:

State University of Iowa	1890
University of Wyoming	1890
University of Kansas	1891
University of California	1891
University of Oklahoma	1892
University of Chicago	1892
University of Nebraska	1892
Oregon System of Higher Education	1893
Pennsylvania State College	1893
University of New Hampshire	1894
Indiana University	1895
University of Kentucky	1899

But during the ten years following, 1900 to 1909, there were but four newcomers:

Columbia University	1904
Georgia Institute of Technology	1908
New York University	1908
University of Texas	1909

Then in the years 1910 to 1919 came the greatest expansion of any decade out of the six of university extension's history:

University of Washington	1910
University of Virginia	1910
University of North Dakota	1910
Purdue University	1910
University of Michigan	1911
University of Arkansas	1912
University of North Carolina	1912
Iowa State College	1913
University of South Carolina	1915
West Virginia University	1916

University of Alabama	1917
Ohio University	1917
Syracuse University	1918
General Extension Division of Florida	1919
Louisiana State University	1919
University of Illinois	1919

Since 1920 every decade has seen a few more institutions enter the field, but while progress has been steady, it has never been as spectacular again as in the 1890's and the 1910's.

The dates cited, however, refer uniformly to the year in which the institutions began work in the field, usually informally. There is frequently a very wide gap between the date and the "official establishment" of the service, or its formal acceptance as part of the university system. Rutgers is credited with first offering extension lectures in 1816, but it did not officially establish its university-extension system until 1925; Harvard in 1840, but official establishment did not come until 1910; Michigan State 1855 and 1948; Kansas State 1868 and 1905; and so on. The precedent for granting university extension full university recognition is usually said to have been established at Chicago by William Rainey Harper in 1892; then, in his basic plan for the institution, he gave extension equal status with the four other university divisions he envisaged. But Gilman of Johns Hopkins certainly adumbrated the idea in 1879, as noted earlier. Most of the official establishments, however, came in the twenty-year span from 1905 to 1925. Those systems added in the last quarter-century have mostly been "officially established" from their initiation. A National Association of University Extension first met at Madison, Wisconsin, in 1915 with twenty-two members.[5]

The facts and figures cited above suggest that, succeeding the great outburst of energy in the eighteen-nineties, there was a period of doubt and hesitation. This is the historical fact. By 1900 it seemed as though university extension had failed to take root and was about to fade away. As so often happens in adult education, the crop which had come up so vigorously suffered a blight. It looked for a time as though it would doom this particular variety of academic cultivation. Even at Chicago, where the Chautauqua experience was fresh in Harper's mind and where the director was the same R. G. Moulton who had helped establish the ASEUT, the blight was at work. The causes of it are indefinite, if precision of identification is wanted, but Herbert Baxter Adams was prepared to cite at least five specific adverse influences at work: the exceedingly limited number of lecturers able to deal successfully with adults; lack of money; lack of time and energy on the part of the university people who had to put campus duties first; administrative subordination of extension to campus activities; and the competition of cheaper educational opportunities. One has a suspicion, however, that without dismissing any of Adams' causes, one should put heavy emphasis on some remarks made by Harry Pratt Judson (later president of the University of Chicago) at a National Conference on University Extension held at Philadelphia in 1891:

> . . . the English experience really counts for little, so far as we are concerned. The conditions in the two countries are radically different. A vast deal that passes in England under the head of "university extension" is nothing but the work of Chautauqua circles here. A vast deal more is merely the ordinary work of our American high schools, and is "university extension" only in the sense that all study leading to the university is an extension of the university downward. It must be remembered that the free high school does not exist in England . . . there is no intention of depreciating what our English friends have done, but there is danger in indiscriminating imitation.

In short, the import required acclimatization before it could hope finally to succeed; as with many plants, it almost died out before it really took hold. Even Harper failed to allow enough for acclimatization. He had put his extension service in charge of R. G. Moulton whose university extension was English university extension. It was not until the latter years of the first decade of the twentieth century that it was at all certain that university extension could be successfully acclimatized in America. When the job really began to move toward completion, it was apparent that what Englishmen and Americans called "university extension" was as different in the two countries as the birds they both call "robin." The difference arose from the differing conceptions of a university and the differing intellectual climates of the two nations.

The reorientation of university extension in America was carried out in the state universities which, it was strongly felt, had an obligation to take the diffusion of knowledge to the people with especial seriousness. This of necessity led them to emphasize practical, or vocational, knowledge. What the people needed and wanted, it was assumed, was help in dealing with the problems they met in their daily lives as workers on farms and in factories, and as citizens. It was the University of Wisconsin that led the way. Wisconsin had had university extension since 1885 and had experimented widely with ways and means of reaching the people —institutes for farmers, short courses, a summer school, lecture series, correspondence instruction, mechanics' institutes. When the geologist Charles R. Van Hise became president in 1903 (he had been on the staff since 1879), he emphasized service to the state in his inaugural address. What he had in mind was not university extension but rather research into and advice on state problems in the large. Today, this kind of activity is often closely linked with university extension, but then it was not.

Van Hise who, after all, had been an extension professor at the University of Chicago from 1892 to 1903 while also on the Wisconsin faculty, was finally brought around to the support of university extension in Wisconsin by pressure from three men from outside the university community: Frank A. Hutchins, Henry E. Legler, and Charles McCarthy. Hutchins is chiefly remembered today as the "imaginative founder of libraries in Wisconsin" and was then on the Free Library Commission. McCarthy is recalled as the inventor of the Legislative Reference Service, later adopted by the federal government as well as many states. Legler succeeded Hutchins on the Library Commission. Van Hise was not at all a willing convert and he was to an extent confirmed in his caution by the professors at the university who held to the elite, or Jeffersonian, conception of university education. As McCarthy once put it in discussing a director for the extension service: "Frankly, I think, President Van Hise, that the professors in the University have, as a body, opposed this whole work and a man who would be acceptable to them would in my opinion be of no value to this movement." [6]

The appointment finally went to Louis E. Reber in 1907 and his view of the task was:

> Right or wrong, you find here a type of University Extension that does not disdain the simplest forms of service. Literally carrying the University to the homes of the people, it attempts to give them what they need—be it the last word in expert advice; courses of study carrying university credit; or easy lessons in cooking and sewing. University Extension in Wisconsin endeavors to interpret the phraseology of the expert and offers the benefits of research to the household and the workshop, as well as to municipalities and the state.

Thirty-odd years later Lincoln Steffens assessed the University's role in Wisconsin:

> The University of Wisconsin is as close to the intelligent farmer as his pig pen or his tool house. The University laboratories are a part of the alert manufacturer's plant. To the worker the University is drawing nearer than the school around the corner and is as much his as his union is his. Creeping into the minds of his children with pure seeds; into the debates of youth with pure facts; into the opinions of voters with impersonal, expert knowledge, the State University is a part of the citizen's own mind.[7]

(It should be made clear, however, that Wisconsin and most of the other universities with elaborate extension services were sooner or later relieved, in part at least, of two major tasks: the extension service of the United States Department of Agriculture took over a considerable part of the job of dealing with the problems of farming; and at least elementary education in the mechanic arts was otherwise provided for.)

In his search for a satisfying rationale for university extension, President Van Hise found what he wanted in the writings of Lester F. Ward, today a neglected philosopher of adult education. After ten years of experience with extension, Van Hise wrote:

> . . . utilizing the opportunity to carry out knowledge to the people will be an advantage rather than a disadvantage to the growth of a university along other lines. But this should not be

its purpose. This idea was fully clarified in my mind when Ward's *Applied Sociology* [1906] appeared. Ward there proved that the greatest loss which we as a nation suffer is loss of talent. Talent is not the heritage of the rich, but is equally the heritage of the poor.[8]

Ward, who ranks with Comte and Spencer as one of the founders of sociology, emphasized the importance of what he called the psychic factors in social evolution, or the various knowledges which enable man to control and transform his environment. He regarded barriers to the attainment of knowledge as among the worst obstacles to progress, and since he did not believe that intellectual capacity was distributed on a race, sex, or class basis, he argued that providing equality of opportunity to gain knowledge is indispensable to orderly progress. The problem as he saw it was to systematize and erect into "true arts" the origination and distribution of knowledge. Even in this brief and superficial statement of Ward's position, it is to be perceived readily that from his writings a very powerful rationale of education at any and all levels, including adult education, could be drawn; and President Van Hise was surely not alone in noticing it.

Wisconsin, then, set the pattern of university extension. It included the following elements: university-extension classes; home-study or correspondence; institutes and short courses; library bureaus that circulated packets of books and clippings; a bureau of visual aid (originally stereopticon slides, later moving pictures); bureaus for lectures; and miscellaneous specialized services to individuals and groups. In the early 1950's it was possible to set out extension activities under eleven heads:

1. Correspondence teaching
2. Lecture services
3. Summer-school programs
4. Extension classes
5. Press and publication services
6. Evening-school and resident-center activities
7. Library lending services
8. Film and visual-aid services
9. Conference, institute, and short-course activities.

10. Broadcasting services
11. Special services for communities, institutions, and other
     interest and professional groups [8]

Some of these are controlled apart from university extension in some institutions; and to trace out the origin and development of each would require a disproportionate amount of space in this generalized discussion; but some of them have already been referred to and others will find their place later on. Rather, it may be emphasized here that by the 1940's university extension had shaken down into something like a fixed pattern of activities. As Professor W. S. Bittner, secretary of the NUEA put it, by then university extension had a "traditional pattern showing little evidence of reshaping. There are, of course, some changes. One of them, curiously enough, is presumably a kind of reversion to academic strictness by the adoption of such names as University College or Evening School in place of University Extension and the practice of designating by fiat certain extension centers as 'residence' centers for degree-credit purposes. Such changes are superficial variations of an old pattern." [9]

Examples of the changes Professor Bittner cited may be more precisely identified as such developments as Cleveland College of Western Reserve University, founded in 1925; the University of Minnesota's Center for Continuation Study founded in 1936; the Adult Education Center of Washington University, St. Louis, founded in 1939; and such off-campus adult education centers as those maintained by Wisconsin at Milwaukee (home campus, Madison); the University of Alabama's centers at Birmingham and Mobile (home campus, Tuscaloosa); and the schools of the University of Chicago and Northwestern in downtown Chicago.

There are also some other innovations of which Bittner's remarks do not take clear notice which it is not too grossly imperialistic to claim for adult education. Conspicuous among these are such developments as the Nieman Fellowships in Journalism at Harvard, dating from 1937, the refresher courses offered practicing doctors and lawyers, and the courses requiring temporary college residence offered to business executives and trade unionists at various universities. Even citing all these, no notice has been taken of the rapidly growing practice of in-service training at all levels and in all branches of American commerce and industry, from banks to factories, often today including liberal studies as well as vocational, usually designed and taught with university assistance at some or all stages.[10]

CHAPTER

16

Teaching Adults Agriculture and the Mechanic Arts

ALTHOUGH it was not until 1920 that the urban population of the United States exceeded the rural, the history of adult education shows that it has always been easier to reach city and town dwellers than residents of the open country. One might risk the generalization that adult education is an urban phenomenon which has occasionally reached into farming areas, were it not for the fact that one of the largest and most spectacularly successful ventures in American history has been the Co-operative Agricultural and Home Economics Extension Service. This, "a nation-wide, tax-supported organization for rural adult education,"[1] is based upon a three-way collaboration of private organizations of farmers, of which the Farm Bureau is the most conspicuous but not the sole example,[2] the state land-grant colleges of agriculture, and a special unit of the United States Department of Agriculture. Popularly known as Agricultural Extension, it came into existence under the federal Smith-Lever Act, named for Senator Hoke Smith of Georgia and Representative Asbury F. Lever of South Carolina, passed by Congress, and signed by President Woodrow Wilson in 1914. There was thus provided a sound legislative framework to forward

197

the movement toward a scientific basis for agriculture which had its origin in colonial days.

Paradoxically, the development came at a time when the proportion of American workers directly engaged in agriculture had entered upon a long-term decline. It insured, however, that the productivity of those who continued in agriculture would increase as the gap between scientific knowledge and farm practice was narrowed (but never completely closed). It has been, therefore, a very important passage in the complex story of American agriculture during the last forty years, a story to be fully understood only by exploring the economics and politics of farming, which cannot be done here.[3]

It will be sufficient for our purposes to sketch the story of rural adult education on the vocational side from its beginnings to 1914, illustrating how it is necessary to have a body of valid information, a sound method of instruction, and an idea of how to stimulate and satisfy a widespread demand before success can be achieved on a mass basis. Thus far, this fortunate conjunction of circumstances has been more common in vocational education than with regard to the social sciences, the arts, and the humanities.

While it is possible to trace adult vocational education in agriculture back to colonial times, it is the opinion of the specialists that it was not until around 1880 that any considerable body of scientifically verified knowledge which could be successfully diffused among the working farmers began to be developed. Since *circa* 1880 such knowledge has grown at an accelerating pace, until today the problem is to get all that is available into use on the farms within the politico-economic framework enclosing agriculture.

Although farming in America had to be learned by trial and error (with some teaching by the Indians thrown in), it soon settled into a routine strongly fortified by ancient lore which was the farmers' version of the wisdom of the ages. By Benjamin Franklin's day, the farmers were "set" in their ways; and Franklin remarked to a correspondent, "If the farmers in your neighborhood are as unwilling to leave the beaten road of their ancestors as they are near me, it will be difficult to persuade them to attempt any improvement." [4] Nevertheless, Franklin and other distinguished contemporaries did what they could to persuade them to improve. Franklin

himself was very little the working farmer—he was an urban man
with a liking for rural employments; but Thomas Jefferson, with
his firm belief in the sovereign virtues of small free-holding farmers, not only took a keen interest in farming methods, but also
gathered and circulated presumably useful information on practices
and even added something experimentally, as by his invention of
the mold board for the all-metal plow. John Adams, who sprang
from the New England soil, proposed to the Continental Congress
in 1775 (with no result) that it encourage the establishment of an
agricultural society in every state. A Society for Promoting Agriculture was actually set up in Philadelphia in 1785 with Benjamin
Franklin and George Washington as members; in the same year
a State Agricultural Society was launched in South Carolina; and
agricultural societies were set up in New York in 1791 and Massachusetts in 1792. However, the dirt farmers paid small heed to
such activities. They continued with time-hallowed methods and
were satisfied if land policy was "right"—if there was easy access
to land on reasonable terms—and, if when they were on the frontier, they got federal help against the Indians.

Between 1800 and the Civil War various tentative moves to improve farm practices by education were made. A famous invention
in the field was the agricultural fair, for which credit is given to
Elkanah Watson of Pittsfield, Massachusetts, who did not take up
farming until he was fifty and had retired from business as a promoter of canals. In 1810 Watson began to hold public exhibitions
of livestock, one of the earliest of which centered around his own
merino sheep, then unique in his neigborhood. To back the livestock shows, he promoted the formation of the Berkshire Agricultural Society on a county-wide basis and became its first president.
He then carried on a vigorous propaganda for fairs and societies,
both of which spread far and wide in the following decades and in
some states won financial support from the state governments.
Watson's idea, as stated by his son, was:

. . . to address the interests and sentiments of the people. The
public exhibition of choice animals, while it made them familiar to the farming community, attracted their attention to their
beauty and value, and to the importance of their introduction.
It aroused the emulation of the farmers and by the brilliant

display of premiums excited their self-interest. Competition in crops awakened scientific investigations, and their practicable application. The management and the appliances by which the fortunate competition had secured success, were described and widely adopted. Domestic industry was fostered, and its labors accelerated. Farmers at the fairs and business meetings of the Society were brought into intercourse, and were led to act in concert, and to appreciate the dignity and importance of their vocation.[5]

This covers almost all the ground that has ever been covered by rural adult vocational education.

In addition to the county societies, state-wide societies were also commonly founded and these often took the lead in promoting state aid to agriculture, permanent offices of agriculture in state governments, and (in due time) agricultural schools. By 1852 it was possible for twelve state societies to join together in establishing the United States Agricultural Society. It eventually included the societies of twenty-three states and territories. The state societies, and the national society, were pressure groups for agriculture and drew active politicians into their membership. The county societies were closer to the dirt farmers and their problems. Education focused in them and in the fairs.

The year 1862 saw three dramatic events with far-reaching influence on the course of American agriculture. One was in the field of land policy, one in education, one in federal government organization. The first was the Homestead Act, the second the Morrill Act "for the Endowment, Support and Maintenance of Colleges of Agriculture and Mechanic Arts," [6] and the third the establishment of the Department of Agriculture (not raised to cabinet rank, however, until 1889). All three were signed into law by President Abraham Lincoln.

Looking back, it is of course obvious that adult education in agriculture could hardly hope to succeed in a major way until scientific knowledge relevant to agriculture was systematized. The first professorship of agriculture was established as early as 1823 at the Gardiner (Maine) Lyceum, but most of the pioneer work was done by the professors of chemistry in the academic colleges, under the stimulus of the example of the German, Justus von Liebig, founder of agricultural chemistry. With chemistry leading the way, the other sciences which were relevant were enlisted and gradually specialization provided the basis for intensive advance in many directions. This was not accomplished "all of a sudden," or in accordance with anybody's plan.

Only one enduring college of agriculture had been established before the Morrill Act was passed, Michigan State in 1855, so it alone was available to give the land-grant people a possible pattern to follow. The first quarter-century of land-grant college history was one of toil and struggle, complicated by uncertainty of direction and unclear ideas about what and how to teach the students drawn to the colleges, and how to make the cumulating knowledge available to the dirt farmers.

After the founding of the colleges, the next great forward step came in 1887 when President Grover Cleveland signed the Hatch Act making federal money available for the agricultural-experiment stations, a move advocated by the agricultural leaders since 1871. The experiment stations not only purposefully extended the knowledge of agriculture, but by publishing their findings freely, also provided a *literature* of scientific agriculture, something up to that time simply not in existence. From this point, the final step was obvious, though it took a good while to make it: to find a sound way to carry the knowledge to the dirt farmer. In the end this was provided by Agricultural Extension.

Let us now retreat for a casual look at certain efforts to diffuse agricultural knowledge undertaken between the Civil War and World War I. Initiated in Massachusetts in 1863, farmers' institutes spread to every state by the end of the century and continued to be popular right up to World War I. These were two- to five-day affairs, with lectures at morning and afternoon sessions and entertainment in the evenings. They suffered from the limitations inherent in the lecture method and had too little impact on farm practices to be truly effective. They were something like agricultural Chautauquas, and Chautauqua actually had much influence on them.

A different tack was taken by the Patrons of Husbandry, or The Grange, a secret fraternal society launched in 1867 which really grew in the 1870's and which has continued to the present day. The Grange was a prophetic combination of elements, of which education through discussion was but one, and of which political action proved to be historically the most significant. It provided a precedent for the political organization designed to advance the special interests of farmers as an economic group which has been characteristic since farming became a commercial enterprise. What influence it, or its progeny, had on farm practice is a moot question.

The land-grant colleges began to feel their way toward an extension system in the early eighteen-nineties, when in 1892 Pennsylvania State College, and soon after Cornell and Illinois, tried adaptations of the Chautauqua techniques to reach the farmers. In 1906 Iowa State College made a somewhat more carefully-thought-out attack on the problem by offering short courses throughout the state in growing field crops, fruits, and stock; in dairying and land-drainage; and in domestic science. "Take the College to the people," wrote Director Perry G. Holden. "Go the people and help them where they are, as they are, under their own conditions, with their own problems. . . . See that knowledge is translated into actual life, and living, by the people of the state." [7] Holden got wide, though often thin, coverage in Iowa.

By 1907 at least thirty-nine of the colleges were doing *something* in the way of extension, but there was no common form of organization and no generally used method. The idea was there, but how really to make it do its work was not clearly known. Purdue University's program of about this time well illustrates the variety of forms the work could take at a single institution:

Lecturing at farmers' institutes; holding normal-institute schools for institute lectures; providing short courses in agriculture; equipping and accompanying railway specials; assisting at teachers' institutes; providing courses in corn and stock judging in district centers; holding summer schools for teachers; sending out field specialists to give advice to farmers; providing courses of study for agricultural high schools [which began to appear in 1888]; preparing and sending out bulletins, reports, and circulars; preparing articles for the public press [which Cornell had pioneered]; conducting and publishing an agricultural journal [an intrusion on well-established private enterprise!]; conducting co-operative experiments in agriculture; providing educational exhibits at fairs [thus returning to join hands with Elkanah Watson]; organizing excursions to the college by agricultural associations and individual farmers; conducting experiments and demonstration tests on county poor farms; and organizing farmers' clubs, women's clubs, and boys' and girls' clubs.

It is no wonder that the Association of American Agricultural Colleges and Experiment Stations in 1908 warned its members to get clear in the minds of the farmers that extension meant teaching, not advertising the college or trapping students for the college!

At this point it is necessary to shift the focus to the career and ideas of one man, Seaman Asahel Knapp.[8] This remarkable man was born on a farm at Schroon Lake, New York, on December 16, 1833, and educated at Union College, Schenectady, where he was in the class of 1856. He married and turned to school teaching, but a playground accident crippled him and for some years, and until he regained the use of his legs, he preached and acted as superintendent of a school for the blind at Vinton, Iowa. It was during these years that Knapp became actively interested in agriculture and made a wide survey of the available literature. When able to resume an active life, he set up a pig farm, specializing in fine breeding stock. His efforts to improve methods of handling pigs led him into farm journalism to pass on what he had learned. He preached "cultivation rotation, diversification, tested seed, improved stock, account keeping and careful farm management practices." In 1879 he was appointed professor of practical and experimental agriculture at Iowa State Agricultural College at Ames, where he combined a passionate interest in teaching what he knew with an equally passionate interest in extending the boundaries of knowledge. But he was allowed at maximum only $750 a year for experimentation; he could get no more from the Iowa legislators; so he turned to the idea of federal subvention. He first advocated the idea in 1882 and his propaganda led straight to the Hatch Act of 1887. However, on March 1, 1887, his resignation at Ames took effect. He had turned at fifty-three to a quite different line of work. His experiences at Ames had convinced him, nevertheless, that the great task in American agriculture was to take the available knowl-

edge to the working farmers—that adult education was the really
crying need.

Knapp approached the goal circuitously. From his professorship
he went to Louisiana and engaged in the promotion of the sale and
settlement of a tract of virgin land as large as Delaware. Because
it proved harder than expected to sell the property and establish
people on it, Knapp tentatively returned to the educational side
by setting up demonstration farms to prove what could be done.
After two years of this he left the land company that had brought
him to Louisiana and set up in business for himself as a kind of
banker-agent for English developmental capital and set out to
build a fortune in rice-growing. This led him to make two trips to
Japan to observe rice-growing methods and gather hardy plant
strains. Thus his commercial activities were complemented by his
never-lost interest in good farm practices and the spreading of the
news about them. He actually laid firm foundations for rice-growing in the United States.

By 1902, as well known for his agricultural teaching as for his
commercial astuteness, he was asked to join forces with two Department of Agriculture men—both famous in Departmental history, B. T. Galloway, specialist in grass and forage, and W. J.
Spillman, specialist in demonstration farms and farm management
—in doing something about the slack farming methods of the
South. Knapp was given the title of Special Agent for Promoting
Agriculture and a salary of $1,000 a year. Naturally he kept up his
business ventures as well. It was quickly apparent to these men that
the nub of the problem was how to diffuse the knowledge they had
or could readily develop.

Knapp stumbled on the solution. Oddly enough, he did so in
seeking to avoid too heavy a load of work. To meet a demand for
a demonstration farm at Terrell, Texas, Knapp contrived a contract
under which the farmer supplying the land and labor, but scrupu-
lously following the instructions of the government agent, could
keep the profits of the enterprise. This relieved Knapp of the burden
of managing a demonstration farm as a completely government-
operated enterprise. It turned out that farmers were quicker to
imitate methods used successfully by one of their own number on
his own place than they were to experiment with methods used on
a government-operated demonstration farm. The latter they per-

sisted in regarding as only succeeding because of "government backing"—which allowed the free spending of money—not because the methods followed were of a kind useful to dirt farmers. This mental hurdle was eliminated in Knapp's new scheme.

The rapid spread of the new kind of demonstration technique was facilitated by the need to fight the boll weevil in cotton. The scientific data for dealing with the boll weevil was in hand when, in 1903, the Texas cotton growers took panic and began to abandon their farms in droves. After some experimentation, it was found that the way to get the farmers to use scientifically valid methods to combat the weevil was the kind of demonstration project Knapp had devised for general purposes at Terrell. The Knapp idea was put into practice on a big scale beginning in January, 1904.

It was in spreading his scheme far and wide that Knapp discovered the vital importance of the agent chosen to guide the work and to collaborate with the farmers. He himself chose successful farmers who were also blessed with a missionary's zeal to do good.[9] In time the Knappian "missionary" became the professionalized County Agent, the key figure in adult agricultural vocational education. What they have taught has always been scientifically valid methods in their practical application, not the scientific agriculture of the books.

The experience in the campaign against the boll weevil showed clearly that Knapp had really hit upon the way to reach the dirt farmer, hitherto considered a rugged individualist pretty much impervious to the blandishments of the government experts and also of private philanthropists seeking to ameliorate the farmer's lot by making him a better farmer. The opportunity to make it conclusively clear that the approach was right in all kinds of circumstances, not merely under emergency conditions, was provided by the General Education Board (one of John D. Rockefeller's philanthropies), which was seeking ways to improve education in the South. The necessary underpinning was higher agricultural incomes. The way to achieve these was Knapp's way. The Board and Knapp linked fortunes in 1906.[10] In that year the Board pledged one million dollars to the Department of Agriculture to extend the Knapp scheme throughout the South, but the full sum had not been spent by 1914, when the arrangement ended. Knapp and his people worked in areas where the government was not at the moment active. At the same time W. J. Spillman was spreading his own version of the Knapp idea in the North and West. Thus by the time the discussions leading to the Smith-Lever Act began, the Knapp approach had had wide use and had gained many firmly partisan admirers.

Nevertheless the campaign to establish Agricultural Extension involved the Knapp followers in fierce arguments with exponents of other schemes for adult education among farmers, but by the accidents of circumstance, the Knapp approach was written into the act as a basic methodological requirement. It was but poetic justice that the sponsors of the Act were both Southerners, Smith of Georgia and Lever of South Carolina. The utility of the act in meeting the agricultural demands during World War I insured that Extension put down firm roots immediately; and it has thrived ever since. Thirty years after its inception, M. L. Wilson summarized the education principles underlying the work as follows:

(1) *Participation.* Interesting farmers or members of their families in acting either as project demonstrators or co-operators, or as local or neighborhood leaders.

(2) *Democratic Use of Applied Science.* Translation of scientific research and experimental findings in such a way that farm people can adapt them or reject them, according to their own wishes and needs.

(3) *Co-operation.* Co-operating educationally and otherwise with the three levels of government—Federal, State, and county—and with local groups and organizations.

(4) *Grass-roots organization.* Sponsorship of local programs by local groups of rural people in co-operation with the resident agent representing the Extension Service. Extension work reaches into the community, neighborhood, and family, with projects for every member including boys and girls 10 years old or over.

(5) *Variation of methods according to needs of groups.* Development of a variety of teaching methods with which to reach different groups in a community.[11]

Knapp's influence was still visible at that time.

While the emphasis of Agricultural Extension work to this day is on the spread of scientific knowledge to the working farmers, and must of necessity remain so, the tendency in recent years has been to include as legitimate elaboration of the fundamental idea work designed to stimulate an interest in the discussion of public affairs—a trend initiated by the Great Depression—and the aesthetic aspects of home and community life. This is in accordance with the change in emphasis in adult education from the strictly utilitarian, narrowly defined, to the struggle to create a viable general culture, traced and supported in this book. Under Extension, such interests usually find their way into programs through "recreation" and "community affairs," and include such various activities as art; textiles; pottery; basketry; beautifying highways, school grounds, and parks; and building playgrounds. In 1946 a federal report on the scope of Extension put the point this way:

> *Delineation of field.*—Scientific principles of cultural development and change; man's relationship to his family, his community, and society as a whole; recreation and wise use of one's leisure time; growth and well-being of children; adjustment and development of youth; appraisal, interpretation, and development of cultural values; development of an appreciation for the significance and beauty of rural life; aid in developing gracious social customs and manners; the place of an attractive home, in family and community development; expression of personality through related cultural arts; guidance and development of handicraft activities.[12]

These developments within Extension have been complemented and re-enforced by the coming of other adult education activities to rural areas through the mass media, the public schools, public libraries, churches, and colleges and universities. However, Charles P. Loomis has stated, on the basis of a thorough study, that "the more rural the area, the more disadvantaged it will be in nonvocational adult education facilities.[13]

John Milton Mackie, writer of biographies and travel books and teacher at Brown University, was in St. Louis in 1856 on one of his trips in search of material. Reflecting on the men he saw about his hotel, he wrote (*my italics*):

The genius of this new country is necessarily mechanical. Our greatest thinkers are not in the library, nor the capitol, but in the machine shops. The American people is intent on studying, not the hieroglyphic monuments of ancient genius, but how best to subdue and till the soil of it boundless territories; how to build roads and ships; how to apply the powers of nature to the work of manufacturing its rich materials into forms of utility and enjoyment. The youth of this country are learning the sciences, not as theories, but with reference to their application to the arts. Our education is no genial culture of letters, *but simply learning the use of tools*. Even literature is cultivated for its jobs; and the fine arts are followed as a trade. The prayer of this young country is, "Give us this day our daily bread"; and for the other petitions of the Pater Noster it has no time. *So must it be for the present*.[14]

The concentration on "learning the use of tools" had begun long before 1856 and it has continued long after. As was remarked earlier, by far the great part of adult education, measured in opportunities available and numbers responding, still remains in any reasonably accurate sense simply "learning the use of tools," whether it is called trade and industrial education, agricultural education, business education, home economics, or arts and crafts.

Why has this concentration of interest continued so long in America; why does it show few signs of abating? In 1856 it was to be explained by the need to build up the country—on the frontier, from scratch. Knowledge of tools enabled those engaged in the work to get on with the job, and as individuals to "get on." When the land frontier disappeared about 1890, the same impulses continued to rule even though the task was no longer to push the frontier over the next horizon, but to build more intensively within the area already staked out. Deeply ingrained in the American mind was a belief in the "cash value" of personal efficiency, and one of the ways of increasing efficiency was to add systematically to one's knowledge of one's job, whether by trial-and-error brute experience, purposeful observation of the already efficient, or schooling.

Americans long leaned heavily on the acquisition of skills by self-teaching and the imitation of the already taught; hence the high approval of the self-made man (even when he showed the effects of unskilled labor). The reward for personal efficiency, or skill, has always been the expectation of higher money earnings, the objective measure of success in America. The effort to acquire skill has also had, it should not be overlooked, a social ramification. What was done for the individual's private benefit worked out to the good of the group of which he was a member. The skilled individual contributed his personal bit to increasing national productivity and the annual income. The American interest in learning to use tools is fundamentally related to any explanation of how the United States has come to possess the largest and most productive economy in the world and why it is still the American aim to make it larger and more productive in the future. Until this collective ambition, which has so long been part of the air every American breathes, dies down, there is little likelihood that the interest in "learning the use of tools" will greatly diminish, however much the numbers of individuals interested in other kinds of learning may multiply.

All this being reasonably obvious, it is odd how late in the day it was before "learning the use of tools" was matched by a comparable interest and skill in *teaching* the use of tools and by opportunities to learn and be taught in a systematic fashion in schools. One consequence of this, our industrial historians tell us, was that in many of the highly skilled trades the United States long lived upon the skills brought with them by incoming immigrants. The great shift of emphasis in the history of vocational education occurred at the time of World War I and the end of mass immigration.

In colonial times what we now call vocational education was covered by home training and "domestic apprenticeship," and these sufficed until the end of the eighteenth century. As the techniques of production changed in the nineteenth century, the domestic apprenticeship system declined in importance; and as the home ceased to be something like a self-contained economic unit, its teaching functions narrowed. Yet the need for vocational training continued and ways to provide it were devised. We have already noticed one famous effort, the mechanic's institutes, and have cited especially the career of Timothy Claxton to illustrate the situation at that time. As we know, the institutes did not provide the final answer; vocational education in that form did not work out successfully. There proved to be no direct and easy road to the "institutionalizing" of vocational training. Rather the way was circuitous.[15] A viable substitute for the old apprenticeship system was hard to find and when found failed to provide all the answers so that apprenticeship had to be revived and modernized.

The complete story would bring in many of the greatest names in educational theory from Pestalozzi to John Dewey. To recount the story in detail would require us to look at philanthropic efforts to deal with the problems of orphans, neglected poor children, and other socially disadvantaged persons whom their protectors usually sought to feed back into society as trained workers. It would also involve taking a look at the early experiments in combining labor and academic study in so-called manual-labor schools (of which a modern example is Antioch College) which were made in this country in the eighteen-thirties and forties. There was once a Society for Promoting Manual Labor in Literary Institutions, founded in 1831 in New York City, but it was short-lived.

It will be recalled that Josiah Holbrook experimented with the labor-and-study school both before he launched the Lyceum and while the so-called Lyceum village was being tried. That is not the only way the Lyceum ties in here. Mention was made earlier of the fact that the first known professorship of agriculture was established at the Gardiner (Maine) Lyceum which was opened in 1823. This institution was less a Holbrook-type Lyceum than a manual-labor school which was evolving toward a full-time scientific and technical school. It pioneered higher education in applied science, and while it did not live to reap the fruits of its experiments, its educational influence was nevertheless very great.

More enduringly successful was Stephen Van Rensselaer's venture in this field which evolved into what we know as Rensselaer Polytechnic Institute. Van Rensselaer, it will be recalled, was first president of the National Lyceum. He was chosen because it was known that he had had the idea of supplying scientific information to farmers and had hired the geologist Amos Eaton to go about giving lectures. Eaton so impressed Van Rensselaer that in 1824 he set up a school to train others to do similar adult education work, with Eaton in charge. Out of this school grew R. P. I. It pioneered engineering, graduating its first class in civil engineering —the first also in America—in 1835.

The Gardiner Lyceum and the Rensselaer Institute were the forerunners of the scientific course at Union College (started in 1845 by that amazing educational leader, Eliphalet Nott), Sheffield Scientific School at Yale, and the Chandler Scientific School at Dartmouth (founded 1852). Massachusetts Institute of Technology, later to gain such high prestige, was founded in 1862. When the land-grant colleges came along after the Civil War with the double charge to offer work in "agriculture and mechanic arts," they mostly met the latter duty, after first dealing with agriculture, by establishing schools of engineering.

To make something of vocational education of "less than college grade," the problem was to discover a pedagogically sound way to organize shopwork. The pioneer here was the Worcester County (Massachusetts) Free Institute of Industrial Science, originally designed to serve the needs of all comers. Out of it eventually grew Worcester Polytechnic Institute. The Free Institute was founded in 1868 as a philanthropy. What was done in the Worcester institution set the ball rolling and made pedagogically feasible the founding of such famous and enduring schools at Pratt Institute in Brooklyn, New York, (founded 1887) and Drexel Institute in Philadelphia (founded 1891).

Success at this level did not immediately solve the problem of what to do in the public schools. The progress there was, roughly, from manual training, to the manual arts, to the industrial arts, the changed terminology indicating a change of emphasis and scope. Of great stimulation to American educators seeking ways to teach manual vocations was the system of instruction of the Russian Imperial Technical School at Moscow, shown at the Centennial Exposition at Philadelphia in 1876. This suggested "manual training," the name for which was supplied by J. D. Runkle, president of M.I.T.; its "great American champion," however, was Calvin Milton Woodward (1837–1914), Massachusetts-born and Harvard-educated, who made his career in St. Louis, Missouri. The first manual training offered in the public schools was offered at Montclair, New Jersey, in 1882. The great period of its diffusion was from 1880 to 1900.

About 1894, however, Charles A. Bennett, teacher of vocational

arts, teacher of teachers at Teachers College, Columbia, administrator of vocational schools, and eventually historian of the movement, shifted the emphasis from mastery of the basic operations
of trades with no concern for the production of finished articles, to
precisely a concentration on the production of well-designed, finished articles. This he called manual *arts*. The "sloyd" idea, im-
ported from Sweden, was a contributing idea here.

Another shift in emphasis began, around 1906, this time to what
was called "industrial arts," under the leadership of men like Professor Charles R. Richards of Teachers College, Columbia (who
also began the infiltration of the field with John Dewey's educational philosophy to provide it with a theoretical base) and Professor Frederick G. Bonser, also of Teachers College, and also a
Dewey man. Dewey's *School and Society* had appeared in 1899.
Both the term "industrial arts" and the Dewey philosophy are
dominant in the field to this day.

Arts and crafts, now often, but by no means always, taught in
close association with industrial arts, took shape as a movement
about 1897 when The Society of Arts and Crafts was founded in
Boston. The principles of handicraft the Society enunciated were
generally accepted in the schools, for they were close to the ideas
behind industrial arts.

Business education in America began in urban evening schools
in pre-Revolutionary times. In its modern phase it dates from
about 1853 when Bryant and Stratton tried to develop a chain of
private business schools with uniform texts, standards and, presumably, results. This failed, but only because competitors entered
what promised to be a rich field. With the coming of the typewriter, precursor of "business machines," the business school really
took hold. This was in the 1870's. Combined with stenography, of
which American business had made little use before the arrival of
the typewriter, typing became a staple of the business schools.
Business education began to invade the high schools as early as
1850 (in Boston, Philadelphia, and St. Louis), but not until the
nineties did rapid growth begin. At the college level, the Wharton
School of Finance and Economy of the University of Pennsylvania,
founded 1881, was the pioneer. It had no fellow until 1898 when
the universities of Chicago and California entered the field.

The same pattern of development—private enterprise to the

high schools to the colleges with, incidentally, no vacating of any field as it ascended the ladder—characterizes home economics. This began in the 1870's with private cooking schools for adults (which also taught sewing and dressmaking), pushed into the high schools in the decade of 1880 to 1890 along with manual training, and moved up to the college level through the land-grant agricultural colleges, notably Iowa, Kansas, and Illinois.

By 1906 sentiment favorable to the principle that vocational education of all kinds at less than college grade should be widely supplied at public expense was rapidly developing. The idea was focused by the reports of a Massachusetts committee on industrial education appointed by Governor W. L. Douglas (the maker of the widely-known brand of shoes bearing his name), and headed by Carroll D. Wright (who had been the first United States commissioner of labor, but was then the first president of Clark College, Worcester, Massachusetts). It was taken up and made the basis of a national campaign by the National Society for the Promotion of Industrial Education, formed at a meeting at Cooper Union in New York City on November 16, 1906. Prominent among the founders were Professor C. R. Richards and Henry S. Pritchett, who that year had shifted from the presidency of M.I.T. to the presidency of the Carnegie Foundation for the Advancement of Teaching; while among the supporters in the public-at-large were President Theodore Roosevelt, Andrew Carnegie, President Charles W. Eliot, of Harvard, and Jacob Riis, the journalist and social worker. On this Society fell the burden of getting the needed state and federal laws passed.

Massachusetts passed the first significant law in the field in 1906, followed by Connecticut in 1907, New Jersey in 1909, New York in 1910, and Wisconsin with an especially notable law in 1911. Work for a federal law making funds available to the states began in 1908. One, not entirely approved by the Society, almost passed at the time the Smith-Lever Act for agricultural extension was put on the books in 1914, but it was shunted aside until a Federal Commission on National Aid to Vocational Education could report. This was headed by Senator Hoke Smith of Georgia. Out of the Commission's studies and consultations came the Smith-Hughes Act, signed by President Woodrow Wilson in 1917. Congressman Hughes had added home economics to the legislation. Since Senator

Hoke Smith put his name on both the law for agricultural extension and that for federal support of industrial arts, he should be
something of a hero to the partisans of vocational education, but
the writer has found no very heartfelt recognition of him in the
literature.

The Smith-Hughes Act remains the basic federal law in the field
of vocational education to the present day. The administration of
it is the responsibility of the Division of Vocational Education,
Office of Education, Federal Security Agency. In 1920 vocational
rehabilitation was provided for by law, a service greatly expanded
in 1943. It is administered by the Office of Vocational Rehabilitation, Federal Security Agency. Vocational guidance has grown up
in close association with vocational education. As this is written,
the federal role in vocational education is under intensive review
by a committee of experts.

About the time of World War I also, for reasons suggested
earlier, there was a revival of interest in apprenticeship. The first
state to pass a law on the subject along modern lines was Wisconsin
in 1915. This law placed apprenticeship under the jurisdiction of
the state industrial commission. During the 1920's a campaign for
a uniform national system was carried on, resulting in 1934 in the
establishment by the Secretary of Labor of an interdepartmental
committee to advise on apprentice training. In 1937 the Fitzgerald
Act, a national apprenticeship act, was passed "to extend the application of such standards [i.e., labor standards] by encouraging the
inclusion thereof in contracts of apprenticeship, to bring together
employers and labor for the formulation of programs of apprenticeship, to cooperate with State agencies in the formulation of standards of apprenticeship." The administration is by the Bureau of
Apprenticeship in the Department of Labor.

Now this great structure of vocational education, supplemented
by YMCA-sponsored schools, the two hundred private correspondence schools which are so very important in this area of adult
education,[16] schools maintained by corporations (often but not always for the exclusive use of employees and their children), a
variety of private schools of less than college grade both free and
profit-making, and special institutional developments stemming
from public-school systems (notably the so-called opportunity
schools), is not entirely or exclusively at the disposal of adult

education. It nevertheless constitutes the basic resource of adult vocational education. It far surpasses in richness and variety what is as yet available to those interested in the humanities, the social sciences, and the arts. As a rule, adult vocational education makes use of the resource *evenings*. That large segment of the resource which is found in the public schools provides the basis for much that the public schools do in adult education.

Vocational education is described in an official bulletin of the Office of Education as "giving vocational training to individuals to the end that they may be effectively prepared to enter or advance in *profitable employment*" (*my italics*). The purpose is "to assist persons in securing the abilities, information, attitudes and understandings which will enable them to enter employment in a given occupation of field of work, or to make advancement in that occupation after they have entered it." It is obvious to the most casual observer of vocational adult education that the principles implied are very liberally (even fantastically) interpreted by adult educators, and not least when the arts and crafts enter the picture. The bulletin goes on:

> There is full recognition of the need of all workers for instruction in other phases of education—those which train for citizenship, leisure time activities, health and physical development, and all other essentials of a complete education. Each one of these is necessary and no one of them should be considered as a substitute for any other. Although vocational education funds [of federal government origin] may not be used as reimbursement for any part of the cost of providing instruction in nonvocational subjects, there should be close cooperation among all educational workers so that the instruction given in vocational courses may be rounded by properly integrated nonvocational instruction.

This passage raises a profoundly important question which is now plaguing all vocational educationalists whether they are working in schools of less than college grade or in colleges or universities: How can "nonvocational instruction" be improperly integrated with vocational instruction? How can the "other essentials of a complete education" best be defined and how can they best be promoted to the attention of adult vocational students when their attendance of classes is in any case purely voluntary? Important as the question is, adult vocational education people appear today to give it less attention than their fellows of the college and university level. This is a misfortune for the future well-being of adult education as a movement.[17]

The Public Schools Serve Adults

P UBLIC-SCHOOL ADULT EDUCATION is so ubiquitous that it is a fair
assumption that most people form at least their first impression of
the field of adult education from observing this phase. Although
government researchers complain that "meaningful statistics" about
it "are hard to get," they nevertheless estimated in 1947–48 that
three-fourths of all school districts with populations of over 2,500
offered some kind of adult education. While programs were not
quite so common in rural areas, they were still remarkably frequent,
especially in consolidated school districts. In both urban and rural
areas a powerful upward trend was then operating. By 1951 there
may have been four million adults participating in public-school
programs, perhaps three million in urban and one million in rural
areas. If numbers really lend splendor to adult education, then the
public-school programs must be reckoned as indeed splendid.[1]

To a very great extent the programs are carried out evenings in
school buildings planned for and used by children during the day;
the leadership and teaching are largely in the hands of men and
women who by training and occupation are teachers of children.[2]

In short, public-school adult education is in essence a scheme
for the use of public-school personnel and teaching resources for
the benefit of such adult wayfarers as find their way to it. Although

217

there is a long tradition supporting this use of public-school resources, it has, throughout its considerable history, been a marginal
activity of the system, and so remains to this day. The leaders of
public-school adult education would like to see it placed on an
equal footing with the formally established activities of the public
schools, but thus far they have not succeeded.

The background of public-school adult education is to be found
in the story of evening schools in America and the field is still
dominated by the evening-school pattern. Even before the public-
school systems were established, evening schools were a feature of
American urban life. Curti tells us in *The Growth of American
Thought* that they taught "mathematics, accounting, modern languages, and other subjects useful to those seeking to climb in the
ranks of commerce." In colonial and early post-Revolutionary
times they were private ventures. The private evening schools undoubtedly suggested the use of the public schools for evening instruction, but since the public schools have always been a local
responsibility, looking for the date at which the first public school
opened its doors evenings to adults is something like looking for
the proverbial needle in a haystack.

The earliest date found by the writer was 1834, when Boston,
Massachusetts, and Louisville, Kentucky, offered evening classes.
In New York City the Board of Education authorized evening
schools for boys and men in 1847 and six schools were actually
opened in November of that year. The following year schools for
girls and women were started. Cleveland, Ohio, began its evening
schools in 1849, and Springfield, Massachusetts, in 1851. And so
on. These ventures were, of course, at the elementary-school level.
The first public high school opened evenings appears to have been
that at Cincinnati, Ohio, in 1856. It was ten years later that New
York City first offered high-school work evenings.

The earliest state law authorizing evening schools, apparently
permissive, was that of Ohio, passed in 1839. In 1883 Massachusetts passed a law making it mandatory for towns of 10,000 population and over to provide evening classes. Around 1870 labor leaders began to campaign for the opening of schools for evening classes
and the United States Commissioner of Education supported the
proposal in his reports. This helped spread the practice. The tradi-

tion of evening public schools is, therefore, something like a century and a quarter old.

In the early years, the students appear to have been a very mixed bag of adolescent boys and girls already working, immigrants seeking to learn English, and a miscellany of adults for one reason or another seeking to "make up" work they had missed earlier in life. The words for the work were "continuation" and "remedial." For many years—up to the 1920's—the public evening schools chiefly served those who were, to use an old phrase, "deficient in the rudiments."

With exceptions, the courses were directly imitated from those served out daytimes to children and adolescents. On the average the standards of instruction and acceptable student performance were lower than what was demanded in the same schools in the daytime. Only uncommonly was anything in the way of *adult* education offered, even when adults took the courses. Usually truly adult offerings were public lectures, the classic example being the New York City system of public lectures offered by the school authorities from 1889 to 1928, especially as it operated under the direction of Henry M. Leipziger. The Leipziger experiment is worth special notice.

The fame of Henry M. Leipziger burned bright for the three decades he was superintendent of the New York Free Lecture System. This adventure in adult education which provoked admiring articles in the serious magazines of the time was under the control of the New York City Board of Education and immediately in charge of the Committee on Evening Schools. In 1887 the *New York World* had advocated free evening lectures on science and history for working men and women and the idea caught on. It was given legislative sanction in 1888 and a $15,000 appropriation was arranged for the first lectures in the spring of 1889. Six public schools in thickly settled areas were selected as sites and between January and April 186 lectures with a cumulative attendance of 22,000 persons were given. The subjects were physiology, hygiene, physics, travel, history, and political science. The following season, however, attendance dropped off. At that point Leipziger was put in charge. He believed in popular education. It was his flaming energy that made the system a success.

Leipziger was born in England in 1853, brought to New York as a boy of eleven, and educated at the City College of New York, graduating in 1873. Two years later he took his LL.B. at Columbia. His interest in the law appears not to have been very keen, for he turned to teaching in the evening schools and the daytime grammar schools, interesting himself also in the YMHA and Jewish intellectual and social activities generally, and in libraries. In 1881 he took charge of the Hebrew Technical Institute [3] and he was the dominant figure in the Aguilar Free Library Society, eventually absorbed into the New York Public Library. A very popular lecturer, he became an influential person in Jewish circles. In 1888 he took a Ph.D. in education at Columbia. He was poor, his health was uncertain, he never married, but he was moved by a fierce idealism about education both for its own sake and as a means of acculturating the immigrant masses.

It was Leipziger's idea that the lecture system should be designed to satisfy the cultural needs of the working people, not merely to fill in their time pleasantly. He aimed to create a kind of people's university, an ideal which perennially appears in adult education, and to cross this with the idea of the schoolhouse as a community center. In 1914 he said:

Never before in the history of the [New York] lecture system has there been such evidence of goodwill on the part of the people themselves. A movement is now being started for the adoption of what are called "community centers" as part of our educational life. Let it not be forgotten that this idea has been broached time and time again by the Supervisor of Lectures, for seventeen years ago the hope was expressed that each schoolhouse would become a neighborhood house where all questions of a civic, political, and cultural nature would be discussed; and five years ago it was repeated. . . . In this form may we hope that soon each schoolhouse shall become a neighborhood center in which the social, intellectual, moral and political life of the residents of such a neighborhood shall be developed; that there shall be ample provisions for scientific illustration; that in rooms properly decorated men and women should not alone be permitted to listen to the words of the lecturer but a discussion should be freely had by them;

and civic clubs formed to encourage neighborhood interest so that through the medium of this chain of people's forums and houses of instruction extending through the city, there may be developed a higher type of citizenship without which no city or republic can endure.[4]

Now of course Leipziger never realized his ideal, but he did nevertheless bring his lecture system to a high pitch of success. In 1916 Nicholas Murray Butler, president of Columbia University, published a flattering evaluation of it in his influential *Educational Review*, founding his comment on the proposition that "Public education is not solely a matter of the schools."

What Leipziger was able to do was to apply relevant pedagogical disciplines to the lecture, and while not in the least lessening its attractiveness to the casual customer, make it educative for the serious-minded. He got his audiences in the first place by employing the arts of publicity, advertising heavily, circulating pocket-handbooks of the lectures, and so on. Insisting on a quality product, he gave much attention to getting the best lecturers he could— something of a problem, for at the height of his success he needed to employ at least five hundred a season. Even though he could pay a fee of only $10 per lecture, he was able to induce men like Theodore Roosevelt, Woodrow Wilson, G. Stanley Hall, and Melvil Dewey to give talks on aspects of American history, James T. Shotwell to discuss the French Revolution, and generally to draw in men of stature whatever the subject. He could communicate his belief in popular education to others. Every lecture was carefully scrutinized in advance for its probable comprehensibility and appeal to the audience. Stereopticon slides were used as visual aids wherever possible. In the science courses, experiments were performed on the platform (as at the old Lyceum lectures). Reading lists were distributed; relevant library books were handed out at the close of the lecture; and when the lectures were planned in a linked series, as they were in biology, physics, and engineering subjects, written examinations could be taken. The resources of Cooper Union and the Metropolitan Museum of Art were brought into play. The language barrier was hurdled by offering lectures in foreign tongues: Italian, Yiddish, and German. And of course Leipziger himself knew exactly what the lecture should be. He himself lectured indefatigably, specializing in biographies of great Americans of humble origin who rose to high positions but did not fail to serve the people. He knew intimately the problems of using the lecture to instruct.

The result was that in his first year in charge Leipziger increased attendance by 50,000 over the year before, and in 1900–01 (the last season before the five boroughs of New York were consolidated under a single city government) drew an audience of over half a million. By that time the scheme had been imitated in Boston, Chicago, and Philadelphia. Extending the system to the entire city, attendance was about doubled, reaching a peak of 1,295,907 in 1914–15. The number of lectures given rose from 186 in the first season to 5,715 in 1908–09, the year of the maximum appropriation for support: $168,700. Yet with all his success, Leipziger had to argue fiercely for his money each year. In 1915 he "took a beating" and had severely to cut back his program. The system never quite recovered and by 1918 both attendance and appropriation had shrunk by half from their respective peaks. Ten years later, in 1928, no appropriation at all was made and the system ignominiously perished.

What happened? *The New York Times,* in announcing the death of the "old institution," wrote: ". . . Appropriations were cut progressively every year until now, when the last request, for only $7,500, has been refused. . . . The chief factor in causing the enthusiasm for lectures to wane seems to have been the growing popularity of moving pictures. As for the radio, its advent came after the appropriations for fees to lecturers began to go down." But other forces also seem to have been at work. The principle that a public-school system should make a contribution to adult education was not then generally accepted. Leipziger had the requisite enthusiasm to build up a successful program, but he did not succeed in establishing the point that it should be a permanent fixture. In 1917 he died, and thereafter it was obviously doomed. Moreover the prospective audience changed markedly between 1888 and 1928. Those forty years saw the tide of immigration reach its high-water mark and recede to the low point of the twenties. As the children of the immigration got an American public school education, and sometimes a college education as well, the audience for Leipziger's enculturative lectures shrank. An entirely new kind of program was needed, but there is no evidence that thought was given to evolving one. What works in one social situation will not necessarily work in a quite different one.

When the Leipziger program was faltering to its end, adult education in the public schools was actually looking up, though it was not achieving the security of assured continuity. The upward movement was supported in large part by the activities of the schools in the movement to Americanize the immigrant during World War I. In this famous undertaking, the public schools participated chiefly by supplying the facilities and teachers for instructing immigrants in English and imparting information in history and civics useful in meeting the requirements for naturalization. Although this was, in actuality, a relatively inconspicuous phase of the total movement, it was, in retrospect, perhaps the most constructive. In any case, it is beyond question that it played a strategic role in establishing adult education as a legitimate activity of the public schools. A sketch of the Americanization movement will illustrate this and the contingent point, that an entirely adventitious influence worked very favorably on adult education.

The social and personal adjustment of the immigrant to the American environment was in essence an educative process, but it was "slow and organic" and could not readily be "isolated from the totality of the immigrant's experiences and relationships in the United States." Least of all could the essential elements be abstracted and taught. The direct contribution of adult education to the process was, therefore, in any proper perspective, very small, whether it is called assimilation, acculturation, or Americanization. Assimilative elements—even assimilative intent—can be pointed out in such activities as Henry Leipziger's New York Free Lecture System, but in the pattern of an immigrant's total history, attendance at lectures was but an episode in a very complex story. For that reason, apparently, much of the self-conscious, and most of the useful, work of assisting the immigrant to assimilate was carried on by social workers—among whom Jane Addams and Jacob Riis are especially well remembered—on the one hand, and patriotic societies on the other.

The classic case of an intensive effort to speed up assimilation on

a mass scale was the so-called Americanization Crusade. This
rather famous affair started quietly enough in efforts to "do something" constructive about the so-called "new immigration" of the
period 1880–1914, largely made up of people from Russia,
Austria-Hungary, the Balkans, and Italy—all non-English-speaking—totaling upwards of ten million, chiefly congregated as unskilled laborers in industrial centers. The evening schools of New
York City began to attend to the special needs of these people
about 1900 and similar efforts started in other great immigrant
centers a little later.

Various private groups also began to tackle the problem both
earlier and later. Two such efforts survive to this day. The first was
the Educational Alliance, formed in New York City in 1890
through the collaborative efforts of the Hebrew Free School Association, the Aguilar Free Library, and the YMHA, to work among
the immigrant Jews on the East Side. The rather differently oriented American International College of Springfield, Massachusetts, was established by Dr. R. DeW. Mallary to train in American
culture and ideals immigrant "leaders, teachers, members of the
professions, and men in industrial and commercial fields" of any
and all nationalities and religions. To reach the foreign-language
workers isloated on construction jobs, a teacher and social worker
named Sarah W. Moore pioneered the scheme of establishing evening schools in the camps themselves.

Among the patriotic societies, which used pamphlets, classes,
and lectures, the Colonial Dames were the pioneers, with the Sons
of the American Revolution following closely after. The YMCA
began to deal with non-English-speaking people in 1907. In that
year it called a conference of interested persons from which
emerged the North American Civic League for Immigrants, called
by George Hartmann, historian of the Americanization movement,
"the first of the active Americanization groups." [5] Out of it grew
in 1914 the Committee for Immigrants in America, the second
significant group.

These early efforts to deal sympathetically with the immigrants
and their problems did a great deal of good and useful work, not
only on their own but also by inducing the states and the federal
government to take notice in a practical way of the problems with
which immigrants were confronted. The approach was that of social

work; educationally they rose little above pamphlet distribution. They did not succeed in dramatizing the problem for the general public. Little popular notice was taken of their work until the coming of the first World War transformed the situation. Fear of the "unassimilated" immigrant then grew apace; the patriotic felt a need to achieve national unity. Out of this mixture of fear and patriotism there was generated enough steam to transform a quiet movement, aimed at doing something helpful for the immigrant laboring slowly through the tedious process of assimilation, into a tremendous crusade—with banners and speeches and brass bands —to Americanize the same immigrant immediately.

The consequences of this change of tempo were astonishing, as Hartmann's careful account makes abundantly clear, but the non-educational aspects almost swallowed up the educational. The teaching job was left chiefly to the evening schools. Little new was added at the point of crucial interest to adult educators.[6] The net result as far as adult education was concerned was to help establish adult education as a legitimate activity of the public-school systems, including those of four states—North Dakota, Minnesota, Iowa, and New Mexico—in which up to 1917 it was *prohibited by law* to use public funds for the education of adults. The Crusade in the postwar period got entangled with the "red scare"—immigrants were alleged to be especially vulnerable to Bolshevism— with the Ku Klux Klan, and with the campaign for highly restrictive immigration laws. It collapsed in the depression of 1921.

After World War I wayfarers found their way to the public-school adult education programs in considerable numbers. These were not only recently "Americanized" immigrants seeking to use their newly acquired English for additional education, but many others as well. This favorable development had but a short life. Looking back in the early years of World War II, Hendrickson found that the number of cities reporting programs reached a peak in 1928, and the numbers enrolled and the expenditures attained their peaks in 1930.[7] Unluckily, it seems, the public schools were not yet ready just after World War I to serve adults as adults evidently expected to be served. A new generation of customers had arrived. It has been pointed out that at that time many evening schools had "drop-out" records of 50 to 75 per cent. The public schools failed to meet the problem of dealing creatively with adults. The practices sufficient for continuation and remedial education in the rudiments were inadequate to the new task. A new audience required new methods. The public-school people were slow about reorienting themselves.

Nevertheless, forces were at work between the wars which helped to stabilize public-school participation in adult education and to establish its characteristic shape.

For one thing, those working in public-school adult education were brought into communication with one another through an organization, thus circulating whatever thinking was going on and, by contagion, spreading patterns of action. In 1921 the National Education Association, the organization of the public-school people, began to give special attention to adult education. On July 8 of that year the Representative Assembly authorized what it called the Department of Immigrant Education (an echo of the Americanization campaign then fading away). In 1924 it changed the name to the Department of Adult Education, though only "to include the native illiteracy problem in the South." By 1927, however, the outlook had broadened sufficiently to allow the Department to declare that its objective was to "include in a coordinated field of adult education all those educators who instruct adults from beginning English classes to evening high school and general evening classes in special subjects, all under public auspices. . . ." Within this framework, all subsequent growth took place.

In the dictionary of the National Education Association a *Department* is an independent, autonomous membership association which has its own constitution, officers, staff, dues, and publications, designed to serve the needs of a specific group of educators. The Department of Adult Education drew its membership chiefly from the directing and supervising workers in public-school adult education. Its fortunes, therefore, directly reflected the growth of adult education in the public schools.[8] Preceding the American Association for Adult Education, founded 1926 (see Chapter 21), the department continued to 1951, always an independent organization—sometimes friendly to AAAE, sometimes not. When in 1951 a new, national organization in the field of adult education was formed, both the Department and the AAAE, now for some years looked upon as rivals, agreed to sink their identities and merge into the new group, the Adult Education Association of the United States of America.

In 1945 the National Education Association had formed a *Division* of Adult Education Service. This was an administrative arm of the NEA, not an autonomous association, and was charged with serving the adult education needs wherever they turned up in public-school education, including the area represented by the Department. Dr. Leland Bradford was appointed Director of the Division, responsible administratively to the Executive Secretary of NEA. The Division naturally continued after AEA entered the field. However, the inherent impulse toward fragmentation in adult education is such that active groups with special interests and orientations always seek to express them organizationally. The public-school people, therefore, in October, 1951 established a new organization of their own called the National Association of Public School Adult Educators. This organization affiliated with the AEA in 1952 and the NEA in 1953.

For another thing, developments in vocational education under the Smith-Hughes Act of 1917 (discussed in the preceding chapter) provided resources which were usable in public-school adult education. That use caused it to assume the shape characteristic to the present day, lopsided in favor of vocational training. Many public-school adult programs, now offering work in a variety of fields, had their origin in strictly vocational training. But there are critics who feel strongly that the fact that funds were available for vocational education, while none of comparable size were available for humanistic studies, distorted adult education in the public schools almost irremediably.

This rather overlooks the nature of the demand side of the equation. The public schools responded to a persistent demand, vocational in emphasis. The same demand, complemented by an educational outlook responsive to it, helped give the public schools themselves a vocational bias only a little less pronounced than that observable in public-school adult education. Adult educators, it must always be kept in mind, have long been influenced by their own version of "give the public what it wants": "take the people as they are, where they are." The results are plain for all to see. But as little in this world is absolutely inevitable, it is probable that if the administrators of public-school adult education had been interested in developing an adult education oriented toward the liberal studies, and had had the luck to acquire funds to support their effort, they would have found a responsive audience. The experiment was never very vigorously tried; and instead it became something of a dogma that wayfarers were responsive only to studies having a visible cash value. Thus a dogma—in essence a rationalization of the situation in which public-school adult education found itself—became an obstacle to the experimentation required to redress the lopsidedness so widely criticized. The shape given the public-school programs in the twenties and thirties survived to be still characteristic after World War II.

Looking over the statistical and other material on public-school adult education as it presented itself in the late nineteen-forties and early nineteen-fifties, one is struck, first, by the wide range of courses offered,[9] and then by the fact that this "richness" was but uncommonly available in any single public-school system. Rather the range commonly offered was narrow. Only 1 per cent of the cities covered in the NEA-DAES study offered the complete range. The common offerings were general academic education, Americanization and elementary education, commercial and distributive education, homemaking education, vocational and technical education (other than agriculture), and practical arts and crafts. These formed the core of public-school adult education.

Fully to convey the flavor, or perhaps better, the *appearance* of public-school adult education, it is necessary briefly to note the results of the powerful disposition to encrust the core with an elaborate collection of jewels (real and paste), barnacles, and educational nonsuches. There seemed to be no theoretical limit to what could be done in a public-school adult education program, given the disposition, the customers, and the money. Some of the odder manifestations of the willingness of the public schools to be helpful to all and sundry were to be found under "recreational skills" and "practical arts and crafts." On the other hand, it was in this same general area of annexes and additions that one would have to look for creative developments, probably to be found under "fine arts" and "civic and public affairs." As it stood in the early fifties, the true and final significance of public-school adult education was exceedingly difficult to estimate.

The Great Depression, which dealt harshly with teachers and the public educational system, had a stimulating effect on public-school adult education. When the Federal Emergency Relief Administration came into existence early in 1933, officials found forty thousand teachers on the relief rolls. On August 19, 1933 the Administrator, Harry L. Hopkins, authorized the use of relief funds to pay allowances to teachers for *rural* schools that otherwise would not open in the fall and to teachers to be employed in instructing illiterates in reading and writing. The latter program was to be directed by Dr. L. R. Alderman, Specialist in Adult Education, in the Office of Education. (It was estimated at the time that there were four million illiterates in the United States.) Gradually other uses of relief funds and teachers on relief were devised and authorized, including the establishment of nursery schools in conjunction with public-school systems, the promotion of vocational training and vocational rehabilitations, the development of workers' education (described below), and in supplying training in "general subjects" to unemployed adults and others. Additionally there were experiments like the Studebaker project in forums (described earlier) and the educational activities in the Civilian Conservation Corps.

The effect of all this activity, discontinuous though it was and hedged about by the restrictions customary in relief administration, was to introduce thousands of people to adult education for the first time, spreading the idea to groups of people and to geographical areas that hitherto had never been able to experience it and judge its utility. While *ex post facto* the experts have taken a rather critical view of the *quality* of the adult education offered under the relief program, there has been very little skepticism expressed about its value as advertising, whether the projects were conducted in, or in connection with, the public schools, or elsewhere by public-school teachers.

Yet, while everything appeared to conspire to keep public-school adult education securely in being, no force appeared which was sufficiently strong to move it beyond the periphery of the public-school system. If Hendrickson's figures (cited above) are to be relied upon, there were actually fewer city adult education programs at the end of the between-wars era than in 1928 and they catered to fewer people and had less money to spend than in 1930.

In any case, the coverage on a national basis was spotty, a characteristic which has persistently obtained. Looking at the situation by states, the pioneer in terms of accomplishment, within the limits defined, was Wisconsin. Wisconsin took a strong lead around 1911. In the middle nineteen-twenties California and Pennsylvania became outstanding.

World War II and its aftermath had a stimulating effect on all adult education—a point discussed in Chapter 22—and by 1947–48 the ten top states by percentage of the population enrolled in adult education courses were (in descending order) California, Wisconsin, New York, Iowa, Utah, Colorado, Washington, Delaware, Michigan, and Arizona. But this way of ranking the states places an excessive emphasis on mere numbers. As a matter of fact, by 1946 the states with the most liberal provision of state aid and leadership (both regarded by the public-school people as indispensable to success) were California, New York, Pennsylvania, Wisconsin, Connecticut, and Michigan. Moreover, improved legislation had lately been put on the books in Maryland, Virginia, Florida, Georgia, and Nevada. High-ranking states from the point of view of constructive leadership were California, Michigan, New York, Connecticut, and North Carolina. By far the most elaborate public-school adult education system at that time was California's, which had about a million clients, approximately one-fourth of the national estimate. What effect all this had had on the quality of life in the several states is not for us to say.

Professional adult educators were doing some hard thinking about how successfully to handle this growth. Since in most states and communities public-school adult education was still a stepchild of the school system, the first hope (in words employed by Reeves, Houle, and Fansler in their 1938 report on the New York State situation) was that adult education would "be placed on a parity with the fields of elementary, secondary, and higher education as far as administrative structure and functions are concerned." [10] This alone, it was thought, would improve the chances that guidance and control would be forthcoming; but just what guidance and just what control to just what end would not thereby be made certain. To the answer to that vital question, Howard Y. McClusky's attempt to "formulate a statement of consensus of professional workers in the field" was a useful index (*my italics*): public-school adult education should aim "(*a*) to provide such educational facilities and services as it can offer *more effectively than other agencies,* (*b*) to cooperate with and assist nonschool agencies with an educational function to increase the value of *their* educational services [but not to absorb them], and (*c*) to take, *or see that some other agency takes,* chief responsibility for the coordination of the nonschool educational activities of the community, unless some other agency is effectively carrying on such leadership." [11]

The Libraries as Adult Education Institutions

IT HAS BEEN so often emphasized that libraries and adult education have, in theory, what the biologists call a symbiotical relation that it may seem totally necessary to elaborate the role libraries play in adult education. It should, however, be self-evident that libraries do not exhaust their contribution to adult education by supplying books either to students in adult education classes or to readers-at-large, including those who can reasonably be said to be engaged in informal self-education. Though most libraries to this day remain satisfied with circulating books and making them available for consultation in their quarters, with no particular self-consciousness about the educative nature of the operations, there is, or should be, more to it than that. Historically there often has been a larger intent. Yet the libraries of the United States have been rather inconstant in their devotion to adult education, though they were started on the assumption that adult education was a primary function and from time to time powerful voices have asked that they resume or recover it. The demands of their custodial and circulating activities upon the available time, energy, and money have made it difficult to do so.

232

What was in the minds of the founders of the American public libraries cannot be reduced to a simple formula, for the principle of multiple causation operates as obviously in this field as in adult education. But it is rather important that in Massachusetts, where there was an early and unusually vigorous discussion prior to the establishment of the Boston Public Library in 1851, such statements as that by Edward Everett—whom we earlier encountered in connection with the SDK—were made:

The sons of the wealthy alone have access to well-stored libraries; while those whose means do not allow them to purchase books are too often debarred from them at the moment when they would be most useful. We give them an elementary education, impart to them a taste and inspire them with an earnest desire for further attainment, which united in making books a necessity of intellectual life, and then make no provision for supplying them.[1]

This locates the public library precisely at the point where we have also found adult educators persuaded they must take an active interest in providing reading matter: the point where, literacy assured, the question of what the literates were to read inevitably arose. In Everett's mind the public library was to be a public provision of proper reading matter for those made literate in the common schools. Educators like Henry Barnard and William Torrey Harris agreed: they saw public libraries as providers of the books for post-school self-education. And George Ticknor, the great historian of Spanish literature, followed the logic of the situation even more rigorously and argued that *public* libraries should pay attention to supplying in adequate numbers current books in popular demand, even at the expense of scholarly materials which the librarians as custodians of the printed cultural heritage might be inclined to favor. The outlook of the Massachusetts group was brilliantly summarized in a suggested preamble to the legislative act enabling the establishment of libraries. Unfortunately it was not used.

Whereas, a universal diffusion of knowledge among the people must be highly conducive to the preservation of their freedom, a greater equalization of social advantages, their industrial success, and their physical, intellectual and moral advancement and elevation: and

Whereas, it is requisite to such a diffusion of knowledge, that while sufficient means of a good early education shall be furnished to all the children in the Common Schools, ample and increasing sources of useful and interesting information should be provided for the whole people in the subsequent and much more capable periods of life: and

Whereas, there is no way in which this can be done so effectively, conveniently and economically as by the formation of Public Libraries, in the several cities and towns of this Commonwealth, for the use and benefit of all their respective inhabitants . . .[2]

This stated the case very succinctly and the adult education purpose was quite explicit. It was, nevertheless, a formulation which stopped short of suggesting that the public library form classes or discussion groups, as had been done by the merchants' and mechanics' libraries of an earlier day. This outlook eventually made it possible for the librarians to concentrate on book accumulation, conservation, and circulation, without feeling that they were in any way slighting their work. In fact, they could feel a sense of accomplishment when they built up libraries from scratch, or when the only predecessor was a reference library that did not provide for the free circulation of books.

By the time the American Library Association was established in 1876 and librarianship had begun to be professionalized, there were people who, while not abating at all their interest in the technical sides of the job, were keen on increasing the social impact of public libraries. Notable among these was Melvil Dewey (1851–1926), inventor of the Dewey decimal classification system, pioneer of the library-training school, and reformer-at-large (simplified spelling, temperance, anti-smoking, the metric system) who as early as 1888 in advising on the management of the New York State Library at Albany wrote:

People's University. This oft quoted phrase should be made a fact in your library. To every citizen of the state this splendid collection in its splendid home, all paid for by the state, should be the real university "where any person may find information on any subject." This requires practically nothing but the disposition on the part of the management. Books, rooms, and facilities are already provided. . . .[3]

Today it is easy to see that Dewey's proposal was hardly enough to make the library an active participant in adult education and Dewey himself came to recognize the point, for later on he tried to apply Herbert Baxter Adams' university-extension idea in the library situation. This, too, was not the answer. The hard fact was that the job of getting the libraries established and properly maintained was task enough in itself and to our own day it has not yet been completed.[4]

It should be noted, moreover, that when Carnegie money was available for libraries after 1881, it was chiefly for buildings. Carnegie saw libraries as collections of books freely available for the education of those who chose to use them—defined by him as the "swimming tenth."

Being locally controlled and administered, American libraries have always differed freely on policy, so generalizations about what they have and have not done are made with a risk. But it seems reasonably certain that in general they did not recommit themselves to an active role in adult education until the 1920's. In 1924 the American Library Association, stimulated directly by the Carnegie Corporation's activities in adult education, appointed a commission to study the role of the library in adult education. The commission reported in 1926 and suggested two lines of approach: (1) to improve the opportunities for the individual to use the books for self-education; and (2) to co-operate actively with the adult education programs of *other agencies*. This resulted chiefly in the spreading of the idea of Readers' Advisory Service to libraries that hitherto had not adopted it,[5] the multiplication of planned book lists, and the freer use of library facilities (like auditoriums and other meeting rooms) as quarters for adult education sponsored by "other agencies." This was progress, but it was far from satisfying the demands of those who saw the public library as potentially a "people's university."

This was Dewey's phrase in 1888; it was also Alvin Johnson's

phrase five decades later. Johnson used it in 1938 as a subtitle for
a survey of the public libraries and adult education, made for the
American Association for Adult Education. He was discreet and
diplomatic, but it was perfectly clear that he felt, rather strongly,
that the potentialities of the libraries had not been imaginatively
apprehended, let alone realized. His evaluation of the situation in
the late 1930's was:

> The adult educational undertakings of the public libraries are
> in the aggregate impressive. Many interesting leads have been
> opened; hundreds of thousands of persons have been helped
> to improve their cultural status and the efficiency of their lives.
> All will agree, however, that the work is only in its initial
> state. No library has come anywhere near developing the pos-
> sibilities within its easy reach. No library, indeed, has even
> worked out a clear program. Most librarians exhibit decided
> reluctance to throw themselves wholeheartedly into the adult
> educational movement. They have been educated to regard
> themselves as custodians and administrators of books, books
> in general, whether or not educational and educationally em-
> ployed. If adult educational work will increase the circulation
> of books, at the same time raising the quality of circulation, all
> libraries will regard this as their proper function. But if adult
> education should involve changes in operation that resulted
> in a reduced circulation, most librarians would regard this
> with misgivings.

His prescription for the future was (*my italics*):

> . . . *develop the public library into a permanent center of
> adult education, informally, a people's university.*

> The public library has, as a first requisite of leadership in the
> adult education field, control of the supply of books. And
> books, I may repeat, contain the better part of the essentials
> of adult education. The public library has built up its scheme
> of behavior in relation to a public which, unlike the school
> population, refuses to submit to compulsion. Adult education
> can deal only with volunteers. The public library, north of
> Mason and Dixon's line, is remarkably free from censorship,
> and the real adult despises censorship, doubts that any honest

conclusions can be reached where one side is suppressed. The public library, with its numerous branches, is in a position to reach a larger proportion of the population of a city than any other institution except the public schools.[6]

Having said this, Johnson looked at the obstacles: lack of time, trained personnel, and money to do the job. He quoted John Cotton Dana (1856–1929), one of the greatest and most original of American librarians, for 27 years in charge of the Newark (New Jersey) Public Library:

In common with many others we librarians have been much concerned over a new phrase, "Adult Education." I regret to say that we have been moved to worship the phrase, and to speak of it almost with bated breath. In our quasi-religious frenzy we imagine that in the world with us is now a vast multitude of young men and women, limited in the formal education of the schools; but, awakened now to the verities of life, yearning to become "educated," and not knowing how to go about it. . . . We librarians have been moved by a phrase to think of education as a process which can go on only with the aid of teachers and courses of study; and that, consequently, we can help adults to become educated only by personal contact with them. No library has a staff large enough to spare more than a few minutes each day to the special demands of each of a few inquirers. To do what the shibboleth "Adult Education," as we are now interpreting it, asks us to do, that is, to act as guide and teacher to all the adults we can persuade to come and ask us what they should read, and how, and to quiz them on their progress and advise them from day to day—all that is quite impossible. Libraries have not now and never will have an income which will suffice to do it.[7]

Johnson, however, tended to minimize the obstacles to his program, or to evade them, by saying, quite truly, that the libraries should be more liberally financed, and suggesting that by redefining their cultural role they could escape some of their current costly burdens. For example, he came down hard on the fetish of circulation—the measurement of the library's success by the annual circulation figures, a fetish which, he implied, led the librarians to prefer trashy popular books which moved around rapidly to sound books that moved slowly. Johnson asked that the libraries say good-by to all that and become instead people's universities.

Although the libraries did not accept Johnson's proposal, they have retained an affection for the phrase, "people's universities" to the present day. It occurs with surprising frequency in discussions of adult education in libraries, actual and suggested. By the beginning of the nineteen-fifties, therefore, the pattern of adult education activities in the libraries was much more comprehensive in its coverage than anything Johnson saw in the late thirties. While no single library could be presumed, without special inspection, to be engaged in all the activities which could be illustrated from the libraries of the nation, a brief tour along the frontier of library work turned up the following items: the Readers' Advisory Service continued with greater expertness; the libraries commonly stocked and circulated and showed moving pictures; they stocked and circulated records and gave record concerts; they effected ingenious tie-ups between radio and TV and books; they held institutes —that is, short instructional programs—on current problems; they assisted in planning education programs for other agencies; they ran forums on public affairs; conducted reading-discussion programs based on current magazine articles; and they strongly favored book-centered discussion programs of their own local devising, or ALA-sponsored—(like the "American Heritage" program, first offered to the public in New York City in October, 1951), or sponsored by an outside agency (like "Great Books"). Basically they aspired to be "learning materials" centers and they made the stimulation of purposive reading their fundamental adult education function—which is undoubtedly as it should be in a country not notably devoted to book reading.[9]

Adult Education in the Labor Movement

W HAT IS CALLED workers' education, union education, or labor
education has never been resoundingly successful in the United
States, even though immense of amounts of time and energy have
been put into it. In 1951 Professor I. L. H. Kerrison of Rutgers
wrote that "Today workers' education is in much the same position as elementary education a hundred and twenty years ago." If
so, it was not for lack of trying.

Not only is it the case that a universally acceptable definition of
what workers' education is, or should be, has never been evolved,
but it is also the case that a completely satisfactory relationship
between workers' education (whatever in a particular instance it
may be) and the resources of education in general (including both
teaching personnel and subject-matter knowledge) has never yet
been worked out. Professor Selig Perlman once defined workers'
education by writing that it "seeks to help the worker solve his
problems not as an individual but as a member of his social class." [1]
We have already seen what *that* has meant in England at various
times. In America it has usually meant an emphasis on the so-called
"tool" subjects, such as the techniques of collective bargaining,
public speaking, parliamentary procedure, and "officer training"
(or leadership training), together with a little work in economics

239

and labor history. Some unions still get along without education even of this limited kind; some which attempt it feel they can manage it themselves; while others seek outside help in doing the limited job and sometimes tentatively explore the possibility of doing more.

A recurring fear among unionists is that if too much emphasis is placed on general education, only to be given with outside help, those attracted to it may be drawn out of the union, or at least in some disagreeable measure out of the union's field of intellectual force—that loyalty to the union will suffer. But a trade union or labor movement institutionalizes but part of the interests and needs of the members, and if the education offered only serves that part and no other, then it is a constrictive and not a liberating force. The most generally interesting dilemma of workers' education is, then, that concealed in the never-ending struggle between a kind of education designed only to strengthen and extend the movement and the kind which opens the way to full participation in the nation's cultural inheritance, even if along a labor avenue. History throws some useful light on the dilemma, even if it fails to help much in resolving it, since the resolution in large part must wait upon the discovery by the workers themselves of their wider needs.

The beginnings of workers' education in the United States must be sought in the apprenticeship system established in colonial times. It is more usual to use this as the background only of education in the "mechanics arts," or vocational education, but general education of a limited kind went along with it. As time passed, the general education elements, together with some vocational education elements also, were institutionalized in such forms as the mechanics' and apprentices' libraries, the Mechanics' Institutes, the Lyceums, and the publication-distribution activities of the societies for diffusing knowledge. We have also seen that the public schools and public libraries were both originally conceived of as serving the educational needs of the workers—not of course as members of a "movement," but as citizens.

The workers, organized and unorganized, have an excellent record for supporting these developments, particularly the public schools, both day and evening. But quite early the suspicion found expression that education, at least that above the reading, writing, and arithmetic level, might have a "class bias" and that hence the workers should tend to their own education. Professor Merle Curti mentions a New England farmer named William Manning who, before the end of the eighteenth century, "with keen insight . . . demanded not only education for the masses but also their control over newspapers and other agencies of cultural life in order that the common people might be able to protect their interests from the learned aristocracy." [2] Later on William H. Sylvis (1825–1869), the first great post-Civil War labor leader, definitely felt that the workers should found and control their own reading rooms and libraries. But as trade unionism itself developed only slowly in the United States, so such expressions of opinion were uncommon. Labor in general was not sufficiently class-conscious to draw any impressive radical inferences about education. The most it did was to develop an acute suspicion and distrust of intellectuals who approached it bearing educational gifts. The "bread-and-butter" craft unionism developed by Samuel Gompers beginning in the eighteen-eighties, which dominated the scene for fifty years, did not appear to need any elaborate special educational support. When in 1901 Walter Vrooman offered to help the AF of L establish in America something like the Ruskin College he had founded in England, the offer was spurned.

Before the unions began to develop an interest in workers' education, several experiments in the field were made, two of which appear to be worth particular notice.

The first was undertaken by Johns Hopkins University, that fertile source of educational experiment. We have already noticed under university extension President Gilman's plan to serve the white-collar and professional workers. He also provided a scheme to reach the manual workers. This was the Workingman's Institute, set up at Canton, Maryland, an industrial town near Baltimore, seat of Johns Hopkins. This was done in 1879. Gilman himself opened the institution and explained that the university would maintain the reading room and circulating library, offer courses of lectures, and give evening instruction in vocational subjects. The venture was a cross between what was to become university extension and a mechanics' institute. It was rather a case of working *on* the workers than working *with* them.

A fuller analysis must be given of an experiment initiated in New York City in 1898 by Thomas Davidson, described by William

James as "A Knight-Errant of the Intellectual Life," and "a man
of character extraordinarily and intensely human, in spite of the
fact that he was classed by obituary articles in England among the
twelve most learned men of his time." [3]

Davidson was born in Scotland in 1840, but spent many years
of his adult life in America, largely as a free lance, lecturing, writing, and teaching private classes. After 1882 his base, and principal
source of income, was his "Summer School of the Culture Sciences" for adults, held at his place in the Keene Valley of the
Adirondack Mountains (lovingly described by James in his essay
on Davidson). In the fall of 1898 Davidson gave a lecture at the
Educational Alliance in New York in which he argued that "It
should be possible for every individual to share in the inheritance
of the ages, in all, that is, that the ages have produced that is of
real soul-satisfying worth, in the highest culture of the time. . . . It
should be the duty and privilege of every more favored individual
to labor without ceasing in order that he may help his fellowmen
into their inheritance . . . such help consists not merely in giving
them knowledge and culture and helping them rightly to distribute
values,[4] BUT ALSO in helping to make them more efficient and
competent craftsmen." That was a staggeringly high ideal of adult
education and it so appeared to the audience, but during the discussion that followed Davidson offered to give a weekly class to
realize it. The offer was taken up and the relationship continued
until Davidson's death in September, 1900.[5]

As Davidson saw it, "the chief educational problem which the
nineteenth century passes on to the twentieth is, By what means
shall every citizen in the nation receive such a training for body
and soul as shall enable him to enjoy all the treasures of culture
won by past generations, and to take part in all the activities of
life with intelligence, energy, and beneficence?" This, he felt, could
be accomplished for the wage earners by the establishment of
"Breadwinners' Colleges" or "People's Universities" of two parts:
(1) a college for culture, and (2) a polytechnic for vocational
training. He referred to the English and French experiments of
the time, but rejected the American version of university extension,
not because it was blighted, but because it merely "extended" the
defective education offered by the universities, on a reduced scale,
into a somewhat wider circle. "It is a thing of shreds and patches,

without a coherent plan or any idea of rounded culture." Extension of the universities could therefore well await upon the reform of the universities. Davidson, however, in spite of his cultural emphasis, was far from being a snobbish and canting culture-monger. He knew workers had to earn a living—hence the polytechnics. Hence, too, his concern for "body culture—health, strength, grace, dexterity." He aimed to build whole men. He knew, moreover, that the workers had problems which weighed heavily upon them and that pat schemes for solving them had an immense appeal. He rejected them in favor of an uncompromising individualism. He preached self-reform to the workers, not social reform; and he approached education from that angle.

Davidson did not propose to serve culture predigested on a platter—silver or otherwise—nor to spoon-feed the customers. He did not, either, "wish to do at second-hand the work of the periodical press." He proposed to make his people work for what they got. "As Froebel never tired of telling us," he wrote, "all true education comes through self-activity. The teacher who does least himself, and makes his pupils do most, is the best teacher." "The sooner a teacher makes himself useless the better." His disciple and friend, Charles M. Bakewell, stated the problem in its context in his preface to *The Education of Wage Earners:*

> The agitator and the demagogue, and to some extent even the social reformer, carry their audiences by means of flattery, by appealing to prejudice, and by dealing in vague and ambiguous, if high-sounding phrases. These are the means by which the unenlightened mind is most easily swayed. *We cannot hope to stem the tide of error, which these modern sophists cause, by persuading sober-minded scholars to give occasional lectures to the workingmen.* The scholar scorns the sophist's methods, and so he cannot strike home until much preliminary work has been done to lead the workingmen to that habit of mind that puts calm, clearsighted and unprejudiced reason at the helm. Even with those who have had the advantage of a good common-school education, with trained students in the colleges, nothing worth while can be accomplished by lectures *unless the student follows them up with hard and persistent intellectual effort of his own.* Is it not absurd to suppose that those who lack such

training can gain truth more easily, can dispense with the hard and slow and painful intellectual discipline that is the condition of all clear thinking? Must we not either frankly confess that the great body of workingmen must remain simply the "masses," shut out from the light of truth, doomed to walk in the darkness of confusion and prejudice, swayed by caprice and blind feeling; or else face the stern fact that there is no royal road to learning for them any more than for others—and then do our duty by supplying a sound education that shall be within the reach of all who are capable and willing to put forth the effort necessary to win it? [6]

To do the job, Davidson thought in terms of a course lasting three to four years. He arranged that instruction be given by others in Latin, Greek, algebra, geometry, history, comparative religion, the natural sciences, stenography, freehand drawing, and elocution (to correct bad pronunciation of English). Davidson himself undertook the "cultural courses." It was his habit to select a particular book as a way into a subject, as for example, *Faust;* to insist on the investigation of works of related kind and merit, e.g., Book of Job, *Orestes,* or *The Divine Comedy,* for light on the focal work; and to assign for special investigation topics which either arose out of the study or were plainly related to it. He directed his students to the libraries and the museums, which some had never ventured even to visit before joining his class, to find answers. The answers were worked up into essays, and the essays were read and discussed in the classes. The aim, said Davidson, was "to make my pupils self-directing at the earliest moment." The hope was that they would be able to go forward, either as a group or as individuals, even if he were no longer there to lead. It proved a false hope.

When Davidson died, the whole scheme had to be rearranged. The chairman of the reorganization committee was Morris Raphael Cohen, then a newly graduated A.B. from the College of the City of New York, who had arrived in America as an immigrant from Russia eight years before, and was eventually to become a distinguished philosopher of his generation (author of *Reason and Nature,* etc.). The committee designed a scheme based on progression from an elementary course of English, arithmetic, geography, and United States history, to an academic high school, and finally to the "cultural classes," or Davidson's Breadwinners' College. In spite of some excellent assistance—as from David Saville Muzzey, later identified with the Ethical Culture Society, itself a base for adult education [7]—it was precisely the "culture classes" which were the weakest part of the structure. The troubles were shortage of money, poor housing, and above all weakness of *leadership,* once again proving that adult education is peculiarly dependent upon strong leadership.

Davidson aimed at self-reform, but the exponents of social reform were, of course, early active in adult education for workers. There is, in fact, a fairly long tradition of educational activity on the "left" where social reform gets badly mixed up with ideological particularism. This kind of educational enterprise is at best an effort to offer radical ideas in the market place and at worst shameless indoctrination of the self-selected customers. It is rarely concerned with education as such. Since the leftist ideologists have always had a primary interest in reaching the workers, this is perhaps the proper place to take notice of their activities.

A full story of this phase would no doubt include references to the spreading of the doctrines of Fourier and Robert Owen and especially Edward Bellamy, whose *Looking Backward* (1888) stimulated the establishment of about 160 clubs to support and propagate his doctrines. But the really lush period for the maintenance of leftist schools for adults was the years from about 1900 to 1940. A few famous and accurately illustrative names may be mentioned.

The Rand School was established in New York in 1906 by the Socialists and its fortunes have reflected their fortunes to the present day. While the school survives and still offers courses annually, it is hardly socialist at all in the particularist sense any more, but rather left-liberal and not always even that.[8] In its great days it appears to have made its strongest impact on the needle-trades workers of the city, then busily organizing their subsequently powerful unions; but it also drew students from all over the country. For their part, the syndicalists of the IWW had for a time a residential school near Duluth, Minnesota, beginning in 1908. It had an especially powerful influence on Finnish workers of the area. The anarchists in New York established a school for both

children and adults in 1911 and named it for the Spanish anarchist
Francisco Ferrer. In 1915 it moved to the country in New Jersey
and evolved into a "progressive" school for children only.

After World War I the adult schools established by the far left
were mostly under Communist domination, either of the Party itself
or of a dissident group, like the Lovestoneites. The Party schools
were at first called Workers' Schools, but during the "patriotic
period" of World War II were renamed for Founding Fathers like
Jefferson and John Adams. After the war they were declared sub-
versive for they were, and always had been, simply "transmission
belts" for Communist propaganda, though they claimed to be
Marxist "schools."

It cannot be shown that these schools in themselves had much
direct influence on the unions, except on an occasional local. In
most instances the groups supporting them had quite other means
of infiltrating the unions. The schools rather served to indoctrinate
more intensively those already influenced by other means and thus
served the fringe groups in the labor movement, rather than the
main mass of the movement.

The true-blue trade unions got into workers' education but
slowly. Selig Perlman has pointed to the Women's Trade Union
League (founded 1903) as the pioneer. The locals of the League
were early encouraged to support lectures and classes for their
members if they had the funds. To meet the need for women or-
ganizers to deal with organizable women and girls, the headquarters
at Chicago in 1914 gave "several months training to three trade-
union girls" in co-operation with—this is highly significant—the
University of Chicago and Northwestern. However, this seems not
to have led to a permanent program for the purpose, for in *The
Trade Union Woman* (New York, 1917), Alice Henry,[9] a conspicuous figure in the WTUL for many years, wrote:

> The need for a training-school is attested by the constant de-
> mands for women organizers at the headquarters of the
> League from central labor bodies and men's unions, and by
> the example of the thorough training given to young women
> taking up work in other fields somewhat analogous. Such a
> school for women might very well prove in this country the
> nucleus of university extension work in the labor movement

for both men and women, similar to that which has been so successfully inaugurated in Great Britain, and which is making headway in Canada and Australia. [Reference is to WEA, established in Australia in 1913.]

Actually the pioneer workers' education effort which has had a continuous history down to the present day is that of the International Ladies' Garment Workers' Union in New York City. The educational activities were started in 1916 under the leadership of Fannia M. Cohn and since 1935 have been directed by Mark Starr.

The history of workers' education in the four decades of its active and continuous history is a very choppy sea on which various craft have been navigated, three of the most conspicuous being the union enterprises, the efforts of independent bodies, and the university programs. The intercommunications of these further complicate the scene.

In 1921 a Workers' Education Bureau was launched in New York by a group of interested persons under the leadership of Charles A. Beard, whom we met earlier as one of the founding group of Ruskin College in England.[10] From its founding until 1942 it was directed by Spencer Miller, Jr. The Bureau aimed to co-ordinate, give direction to, and stimulate the development of workers' education. It was accepted as a collaborator by the AF of L, this development in itself representing a significant change of attitude on the part of that body. This fact also, however, defined the intellectual climate within which the Bureau had to work educationally. The Bureau's first president was James H. Maurer, president of the Pennsylvania Federation of Labor. From 1924 the AF of L contributed to the support of the organization. When the CIO was founded in 1935, the Bureau's close indentification with the AF of L prevented it from even trying to become a central organization serving all American unions. Instead, it became the educational office of the AF of L, which it is today, while the educational work of the CIO is handled in some phases by its Department of Education and Research and in others by its Community Services Committee.

As to other developments within the unions, the elusiveness of data makes it necessary simply to note that, while in 1951 the following "international" unions had educational programs, it is not possible to say when they were launched (mostly, however, in the last two decades):

United Automobile, Aircraft and Agricultural Implement Workers, CIO

United Automobile Workers, AF of L

Building Service Employees, AF of L

Chemical Workers, AF of L

Amalgamated Clothing Workers, CIO

International Brotherhood of Electrical Workers, AF of L

Communication Workers, CIO

International Ladies' Garment Workers, AF of L

International Association of Machinists, AF of L

American Newspaper Guild, CIO

Oil Workers, CIO

Packinghouse Workers, CIO

Pulp, Sulphite and Paper Mill Workers, AF of L

International Brotherhood of Paper Makers, AFof L

Brotherhood of Railroad Trainmen, Independent

Rubber, Cork, Linoleum and Plastic Workers, CIO

American Federation of State, County and Municipal Employees, AF of L

United Steelworkers of America, CIO

Textile Workers of America, AF of L

United Textile Workers Union, CIO

The programs differ in aim and scope, ranging from what is simply publicity for the union point of view to gestures toward education of the "whole man," with a heavy emphasis on study of union problems, training for union service, and the study of labor history. The most highly developed programs are those of the United Automobile Workers (CIO), the ILGWU (AF of L), United Steelworkers of America (CIO), and the Textile Workers Union (CIO). Similar work to that of the international unions is also done by state labor bodies, as in California, Kentucky, Massachusetts, Minnesota, and Wisconsin by the AF of L; and in Michigan, New Jersey, and Wisconsin by the CIO. Local unions sometimes develop important programs while the "international" to which they belong does not.[11]

Shifting now to the contributions of the colleges and universities during the last forty years, the earliest connection with workers' education was apparently that of Chicago and Northwestern with the WTUL in 1914. However, it was university extension that provided the first wide-open avenue of approach in either direction. In 1920 a director of workers' education was appointed in the University of California's Extension Division and this development led to classes jointly controlled by university extension and the State Federation of Labor (AF of L). In 1937 Professor Leon J. Richardson, who had initiated the work, made a devastatingly realistic assessment of it:

> Men in America have not yet got to the point where workers are willing to give large blocks of time and long sustained effort as we find in countries across the Atlantic. The men among us show an uprising surge of a will to power. They seek to gain it, less by education, than by organization.[12]

The California precedent, however, was followed by Syracuse in 1922 and about the same time or a little later by Harvard, Massachusetts Institute of Technology, Tufts, Amherst, the University of Cincinnati, and the University of Oklahoma. By 1923, the University Extension Association was able to set up a standing committee on workers' education which has had a continuous existence ever since.

On a different basis, the Bryn Mawr Summer School for Women Workers in Industry was launched in 1921, with advice from the WTUL, and directed for thirteen seasons by Hilda W. Smith.[13] This pioneer venture operated at Bryn Mawr until 1939, when it was more or less transferred to another site as the Hudson Shore Labor School at West Park, New York. In turn, the latter was taken over by Rutgers University. Along the same lines, a Summer School for Workers was operated at Barnard College in New York City from 1927 to 1933. These schools served both union and nonunion workers.

Other schools for workers were established during the twenties in Wisconsin, Virginia, and on the Pacific Coast. The Wisconsin school, dating from 1925, has had a particularly interesting history, both from the standpoint of the experimental character of its teaching and its relations with the legislature, from which it draws its

funds. In 1921, also, an independent labor college, called Brook-
wood Labor College, was established at Katonah, New York. It
lasted until 1937 when it foundered on ideological shoals. Some
of its founders were intimately associated with the WEB.

The nineteen-twenties appear very definitely to have been a
period when new departures in workers' education were the order
of the day, a current of intense seriousness in what is sometimes
thought to have been a frivolous decade.

In an effort to exchange experience in residential labor education, a "Joint Administrative Committee for Resident Summer
Schools for Women Workers in Industry" was set up in 1926,
stemming from Bryn Mawr as the name indicates; out of this in
1932 there grew an organization called Affiliated Schools for
Workers, and also a service agency which in turn took the name
American Labor Education Service, Inc., in 1940. The latter continues to operate to the present day. Yet in 1933 workers' education could be characterized as still "fragmentary and unorganized."

Before completing the story of the universities and workers'
education, it will be profitable to examine with care the workers'
education offered during the Great Depression, first by the Federal
Emergency Relief Administration, then by the Work Progress Administration, and finally variously connected with the national defense effort. In some ways this effort to utilize the skills of teachers
on relief was the most remarkable experiment in workers' education
ever made in the United States. It brought federal money to the
support of the task, even if the funds were hedged about with the
restrictions required by their use in a relief program. In one form
or another the experiment continued for ten years, 1933 to 1943,
and left behind a legacy of stimulation for workers' education in
the unions, the public schools, and the universities.[14] Out of it
grew also the idea of a permanent, federally-financed, Labor Extension Service, stemming from the Department of Labor (on an
analogy with the Agricultural Extension Service stemming from
the Department of Agriculture). Although from 1942 to 1950
a skilfully directed campaign was put on to realize the aim, which
had the support of Senators Estes Kefauver, Wayne Morse, and
Elbert Thomas and, especially in 1950, President Truman, the
effort in considerable measure foundered on the conflict between

the AF of L and the CIO, and is little likely to be revived until labor unity is fully achieved.

Like all governmental activities, and especially all New Deal activities, the promotion of workers' education by marrying it to relief required the co-operation of many people beside those who did the actual work. The central figure was unquestionably Hilda Smith who brought to the task many of the ideas she had tested at the Bryn Mawr school. Indeed, it was at the summer school for 1933 that the idea as a whole was hatched and it was Miss Smith who had the patience and stamina to carry it into action.

Miss Smith began work on September 25, 1933, assigned to the office of Dr. L. R. Alderman, Specialist in Adult Education in the Office of Education, who was in charge of an Emergency Education Program, and had already in the previous month begun to use relief funds for teaching unemployed illiterates. Miss Smith formulated *her* program for presentation to Harry Hopkins, Administrator of the Federal Emergency Relief Administration, as follows:

> The teaching emphasizes economic and social problems related to the experience of the workers.

> Its objective is independent thinking, based on a full knowledge of the facts.

> Freedom of teaching and discussion are taken for granted.

> The right of workers to organize and bargain collectively is recognized.

> The classes are organized as democratic groups with the teacher as a leader and one of the group, not as an authority.

> Special training should be given to supervisors and teachers of this program.

> While this is a specialized field of adult education, cooperation and coordination with other projects and with community agencies is desirable.

> It is hoped that the Workers' Education Project will stimulate interest in the economic and social problems of the day and develop a sense of responsibility for their solution.

To judge by past experience in workers' schools and classes, workers will ask for instruction in the following fields:

Current events	Consumer problems
Labor history	Health education
Labor laws	Parliamentary law
The Wages & Hours Act	Public speaking
Social Security	Labor and the community
Unemployment compensation	
The NRA codes	

With variations and elaborations, these ideas ruled the work of the ten years.

Of the manifold administrative difficulties encountered in translating the policy statement into action, practically nothing can be said here. Rather the emphasis must fall on selected aspects of the story which, in one way or another, have a permanent relevance.

There was a constant need to define and defend the very idea of *workers' education*. An early effort to define it was:

This phase of adult education is designed to meet the special needs of wage earners who have had little formal schooling. Its chief purpose is to stimulate an active and intelligent interest in the economic and social problems of the times, and to develop a sense of responsibility for their solution. In contrast to the broader curriculum scope of general adult education, topics of study are for the most part confined to industrial and labor problems of particular concern to the worker.

The rationale, in fact, had two facets: workers' education sought to satisfy the needs of workers *qua* workers, and it was of necessity to be conducted on the (relatively low) level of educational achievement characteristic of workers. In practice this meant the teaching of much narrowly utilitarian and highly perishable information—how to understand an NRA code, where to find a free clinic, how to fill out an income tax blank—while on the other and more important side there was a tendency to leap over the alleged boundaries and take a look at the arts.

Nevertheless, it was unquestionably true that a special approach to worker-students was necessary, particularly in beginning work with them. Their abilities had to be assessed, their needs had to be formulated, and the two sensibly related and translated into a pedagogical approach. This placed a heavy load on the teachers. Special training was indispensable; and to supply it in some reasonable measure fully justified the expenditure of immense quantities of energy in surmounting the hurdles set up by the relief situation. The assumption that any teachers from any level of the educational system could without special training be successfully set to teaching adults was recognized to be false. But the ideal of a properly trained staff was not achieved. To be sure, Miss Smith aimed very high indeed. Here are her criteria for teachers:

A sympathetic understanding of labor.

Experience in a trade union or other contacts with workers' groups.

Knowledge of economics.

Knowledge of his own subject and ability to communicate it.

Knowledge of teaching techniques.

Willingness to learn from the students and relate teaching to their experience.

Intellectual integrity.

A broad, cultural perspective, free from prejudice.

Interest in students as individuals and belief in their desire to learn.

Warm, attractive and sympathetic personality.

A sense of humor.

No wonder sardonic bystanders referred to Miss Smith's "integrated paragons," but as a prescription for perfection the statement has its points.

There was, too, the problem of supplying teaching materials. In the particular case under review, this was a very difficult business for three reasons: first, because funds for materials were strictly limited by regulations governing the spending of relief money; second, the need was believed to be for especially simple materials, calculated for use by the audience as defined—thus limiting choice among the items offered; and, third, the ideological implications naturally had to be closely watched.

The search for simple materials (usually sought in pamphlet form) is one upon which adult educators seem to be perpetually engaged and the production of such materials seems to be perpetually under way. A neurotic anxiety about the specific intellectual gravity of the materials to be used pervades the field, yet surely the simple truth was uttered a few years ago by T. R. Adam when he wrote, "The traditional book, when all is said and done, remains the strongest cornerstone of continued education." [15] If adult students are to be sheltered from the "traditional book" (i.e., the "trade" book of the bookshops and the libraries), then entry into the world of adult discourse is going to be indefinitely delayed. Overanxiety about materials appears to be related on the one hand to a low assessment of the intelligence of the prospective customers, and on the other to an obscure wish to coddle and protect them from the harsh struggles of the intellectual market place.

Miss Smith and her people were much concerned to achieve a reasonable intensity of impact. This they found could be best attained under residential conditions, available however only to women—hence the crack popular among Miss Smith's co-workers: "she, she, she camps." The camps established seem to have been rather more successful *educationally* than the C.C.C. camps for young men established under a different administration, but they had less measurable importance in any other terms—and it was the "other" values of the C.C.C. camps that justified *them*. Nothing comparable to the conservation work of the C.C.C. was done. It was also conclusively demonstrated that *where* the nonresidential classes were held was of major importance. It was a distinct handicap in the earlier months that most classes had to be held in public schools, using chairs and desks designed for adolescents. When it became possible to use community houses, settlement houses, union halls, libraries, and so on, the results were better. A relaxed atmosphere, adult chairs and desks, the right to smoke—these things weighed heavily on the side of good results. But wherever the classes met, the best form of class organization was the small, informal discussion group.

Unluckily no definitive statistics were ever compiled. On the money side the whole venture was of course tangled with relief, which made the figures of doubtful significance, even the figures for funds contributed by nonfederal governments and private organizations. It is perhaps worth recording, however, that the General Education Board of the Rockefeller Foundation granted the Workers' Education Bureau and the Affiliated Schools for Workers about $70,000 each to assist in the work. All told 36 states conducted workers' education activities, 17 throughout the years 1934–38 when FERA or WPA backed the enterprise.[16] Teachers came and went, as in all relief activities; about 2,000 were employed at the peak, which came in 1937; and about 1,700 teachers were actually given six-week special training courses. Perhaps a million persons were enrolled as students, about two-thirds of them men, and most of them unionized workers, but with a heavy representation of nonunion people. The program won strongest support in the Middle West, encountered the most suspicion in the East, and had the least success in the South.[17]

Returning now to the universities and workers' education, we must retreat to 1931 when Rutgers University initiated its "on-campus resident institute for workers," on a pattern established by Norman C. Miller. The Workers' Education Bureau collaborated in the project. This venture stimulated similar enterprises in many states. As World War II drew to a close, a number of industrial-relations or labor-management institutes or schools were set up at both the state-supported and private universities; some but not all of these undertook workers' education as a phase of their program. By 1951 the following universities were concerned with workers' education in one way or another: Alabama, California (both at Berkeley and Los Angeles) Chicago, Harvard, Illinois, Indiana, Cornell, Penn State, Rhode Island, Roosevelt,[18] Rutgers, and Wisconsin. There was no uniformity of purpose, organization, or method. Some schools made a broad approach to workers' education, others took a specialized line. The extension divisions sometimes had to carry the burden of noncampus classes. A frequent emphasis was on leadership training rather than rank-and-file teaching. The work always conformed rather closely to the prevailing interpretation of union needs. But all of it required university-union collaboration for worth-while results. There was no logical escape from Kerrison's conclusion that it would be foolish of labor "to accept education instruments below the standards of public universities. . . ."

Adult Education as an Omnium Gatherum

$\mathbb{A}$T ANY GIVEN TIME in the United States there will be in existence an unknown but undoubtedly large number of clubs, societies, and less formal groups whose activities require members to have a special knowledge of certain issues or problems to which they are currently giving attention with a view to ameliorative or remedial action. To convey the required knowledge for action, the organizations use one method of adult education or another, or a combination of several: they circulate printed matter, provide talks and lectures, devise discussion groups. In addition, such organizations, either as a continuing policy or intermittently, try to interest their members, with the purpose of individual improvement, in other aspects of public affairs about which it is thought they should be informed as citizens. Here, too, adult education methods are used, with the action part of the program working itself out chiefly in voting behavior. Customarily, such organizations have been to some extent tied together intellectually by a monthly magazine reflecting the serious interests currently being cultivated.

Speaking very generally, these activities have for many years added tremendously to the range and bulk of adult education with-

out satisfactorily increasing its depth and penetration; but their
existence has been a constant encouragement to adult educators
to hope that they could one day be improved into more solid adult
education enterprises. They have appeared to be ready-made, but
not tailor-made, outlets for programs of greater substance and significance than the routine operations of the organizations have
seemed to require. Their existence has been a standing challenge,
both to ambitious leaders within the organizations and to outsiders
with presumptively good programs to offer. Moreover, efforts to
improve the programs have been stimulated by the well-supported
observation that the existing programs appear so much better and
stronger when viewed at the planning level at national headquarters
than when actually in use at the local level. To find the secret of
unimpeded, intensive communication all down the line would be a
major contribution to adult education procedures.

This has been one of the frontiers of adult education on which
fascinating skirmishes have constantly been fought. Many organizations could be cited illustratively. The selection made here must be
arbitrary, not at all exhaustive, and least of all the result of any
scientific sampling.

Since voluntary association to effect public improvements is an
ancient American habit, and self-improvement an equally ancient
personal activity, organizations like those to be discussed here may
reasonably claim as at least collateral ancestors the societies suggested by Cotton Mather in *Essays to Do Good* and Benjamin
Franklin's Junto. However, the continuity has never been exactly
established and we must here be satisfied with picking up the story
just after the Civil War when in 1868 Jennie June Croly—mother
of Herbert Croly, founding editor of *The New Republic*—started
in New York City a club for women called Sorosis, a social and
study club of a kind fairly common. Mrs. Croly's club, however,
has special significance in that in 1889 it took the lead in calling
a national convention of women's clubs at the Madison Square
Theatre in New York City. Ninety-seven clubs were invited to
send delegates and sixty-one responded. This group voted to form
a national federation; the committee on the constitution and organization was staffed by women from New York, Indiana, New
Jersey, Minnesota, Rhode Island, Illinois, and Pennsylvania. At
the ratification convention the next year delegates from seventeen

states were present; and at the first Biennial Convention at Chicago in 1892 there were 297 delegates from 185 clubs in 29 states. Thus arose the General Federation of Women's Clubs.

Now of course there are women's clubs and Women's Clubs, and by selecting the General Federation clubs for mention, nothing invidious is intended. It simply offers an opportunity to make the point that while education was never the sole purpose, the General Federation encouraged educational activities from its earliest days. As far back as 1869, Mrs. Croly tried (unsuccessfully) to get the New York Sorosis to concern itself with public education, reformatories, sanitary reform, female labor problems, and so on—subjects which would have had to be studied before action could be recommended or taken. Looking back in 1950, the General Federation stated that in education it took pride in its work for kindergartens, home-economics courses in public schools, college scholarships, the founding of the New Jersey College for Women, and, in adult education specifically, the founding of public libraries, 85 per cent of those in existence having had Women's Club support in their beginnings.

For the rest, the Women's Clubs contributed strongly to a wide variety of reforms, including child-labor laws, the establishment of the United States Women's Bureau of the Department of Labor, reduction of maternal and infant mortality, prison reform, narcotic control, and conservation. They also provided their members with opportunities to inform themselves about international relations, homemaking, art, music, literature, and drama. (This may seem preternaturally solemn to those whose image of women's-club members was formed by Helen Hokinson's cartoons, or the description of the Thanatopsis Club in Sinclair Lewis' *Main Street,* but let it stand. It is the substantive aspect of the record.)

Antedating the emergence of the General Federation was the American Association of University Women, founded in Boston in 1882 by Marion Talbot and Ellen H. Richards to deal with the needs of young women in obtaining and then making use of college education. Called at first the Association of Collegiate Alumnae—the present name was adopted in 1921—the idea of such an organization made a wide appeal and by 1912 branches coast to coast and abroad had been established. In 1951 there were 1,177 branches and 120,675 members. In 1920 an International Federation of University Women was founded in London. The American Association's purpose is: ". . . uniting of the alumnae of different institutions for practical educational work, for the collection and publication of statistical and other information concerning education, and in general for the maintenance of high standards of education." The focus, then, is on "structured" education and its improvement, but in doing its work, the Association also gives attention to the continuing educational needs of its own members, as in questions of foreign policy, by the establishment of study groups in the local branches, and by general publicity and discussion.

What is today the National Congress of Parents and Teachers was founded in 1897 as the National Congress of Mothers by Mrs. Theodore W. Birney, with the collaboration of Mrs. George Hearst. Beginning at the national level, the organization today is rooted in the local Parent-Teachers Association, the familiar PTA's. The name implies the central interest: the public schools and the mutual interest of parents and teachers in their welfare. Closely associated with the National Education Association, the National Congress has given currency to many of the NEA's ideas. It offers the membership study programs, based on the reading of prepared materials, varying the specific subject matter each year, but covering the preschool child, the school-age child, and the adolescent.

In 1901 two wealthy young women, Mary Harriman (later Mrs. Charles Carey Rumsey) and Nathalie Henderson (later Mrs. Joseph R. Swan) founded in New York City what they called the Junior League, with a membership of eighty-five drawn from the year's debutantes. From that beginning has grown what is now a nationwide organization called the Association of the Junior Leagues of America (founded 1921). The fundamental idea behind the Junior Leagues has always been to instill into the minds of the members, all young women from well-to-do homes, a sense of social responsibility. For that reason it was altogether natural that at first much emphasis was placed on social-service activities, an interest still to the fore. But in the course of time other interests were added, notably, from our standpoint, education. Thus, from a society designed to provide young ladies of leisure with ideas about how to make themselves useful to their communities, the

Junior Leagues have become another vehicle for carrying adult education to a specialized but significant public.

As the suffrage movement gained its victory in votes for women, the National American Women Suffrage Association, headed by Carrie Chapman Catt, had $25,000 in its treasury and no obvious task left to perform. Out of that contretemps grew the League of Women Voters of the United States, founded in 1919. Mrs. Catt intended that it should undertake the political education of the new women voters, work for "new legislation" of interest to them, and combat voter apathy. Originally conceived as a five-year enterprise, the League is still in very lively existence. Political education remains central to its purpose, and it conducts a continuous and vigorous program in that area.

Also in 1919 there was founded the National Federation of Business and Professional Women's Clubs. It was an outgrowth of an effort by Newton D. Baker, then Secretary of War, to make better use of woman power in the war effort. To accomplish this end, a War Work Council, staffed largely by personnel from the YWCA, was set up to survey resources. When the emergency ended, the suggestion for a permanent organization of business and professional women was seized upon and, again with YWCA help, turned into a reality. Today there are 160,000 members organized into some 2,700 clubs and there is an International Federation with headquarters in Switzerland. This organization has tended to draw its membership from those well-placed working women who in years past would have been attracted to the General Federation Clubs, now more apt to attract the homemaking, or leisured, women. In addition to taking a primary interest in working conditions and such issues as "equal pay for equal work," it has encouraged study groups among its members, using specially prepared materials and covering such fields as international and national public affairs, health and safety questions, and vocational training.

Turning now to organizations of men, only three out of perhaps twenty-five or thirty, will be cited here: Rotary, Kiwanis, and Lions —all central organizations with thousands of local luncheon clubs scattered across the country. The three cited account for a large proportion of the membership of clubs of the kind. In all cases the membership is overwhelmingly made up of businessmen.

The luncheon-club idea dates from around 1910 when the Rotary International was established with 16 clubs, the oldest dating only from 1905. The Kiwanis International was set up in 1916; and in 1917 the Lions International. The great period of expansion for all three was the nineteen-twenties; they all suffered reverses in the Great Depression; but by 1950 they were back to predepression levels of membership.

Basically the luncheon clubs are social organizations in which a somewhat strenuous bonhommie is cultivated. It is this aspect of them that has from time to time attracted the shafts of satirists, notably Sinclair Lewis, whose Mr. George Babbitt was passed off as characteristic of the membership. But they are also service clubs —the Lions appear to have pioneered the service idea—and since "service" is a well-scuffed word of many connotations in the American vocabulary, it is obligatory here to notice carefully what service means to the clubs. It means, in brief, unselfish concern for welfare, and embraces both the expenditure of money and time on worthy undertakings. The clubs, for example, take a special interest in supporting the churches "in their spiritual aims," in work with boys and girls, in work with underprivileged children, in vocational guidance, in "civic improvement," health and welfare activities, work with the blind, and a wide variety of other causes of the "good works" variety. Guidance for these pursuits reaches the local clubs from national headquarters in the form of easily grasped printed materials, and there is thus involved a minimal amount of adult education, but an evaluative assessment in educational terms is excessively hard to make. The clubs measure *their* results in terms of service. Equally elusive is what by way of adult education is accomplished by the talks on public affairs customarily given by outsiders at the luncheon meetings, since adult educators are from away back skeptical of the worth of brief, isolated lectures. Nevertheless, it is on this well-organized serious side of the clubs that adult educators must find their foothold, whether operating from within the organizations or from outside.

It may appear odd, even outrageous, to bring in at this point such organizations as the YMCA, the YWCA, and the YM and YWHA, but the justification is that they are basically religious-social organizations, with educational interests, great or small.

They are not in any instance *primarily* educational organizations. Their origin can be accurately indicated by a quotation from the official history of the YMCA, written by C. Howard Hopkins:

> Begun among white collar workers for themselves, the city YMCA's remained with few exceptions the creatures of that economic class. . . . When urban degradation reached such depths as to elicit evangelical concern, the YMCA could flourish as a counterattraction to vice, alcoholism, delinquency, crime, and a whole train of evils that rose with the modern city, a large proportion of whose population was comprised of young men. Unlike the Wesleyan revivals of the eighteenth century in Britain and the Great Awakening in America that appealed to the working classes, the revivals of the nineteenth century that created the YMCA's among a host of institutions and reforms were directed to and influenced mostly the middle-class, city-dwelling Americans and the residents of small towns and villages.[1]

The YMCA first appeared in England in 1844 and was established in the United States in 1851. The YWCA in America dates from 1858. And the YM and YWHA date from 1874.

The YMCA drifted into education in seeking to meet the needs of its members. It started out in the eighteen-fifties with Sunday schools and Bible classes, soon added libraries and reading rooms which flourished until the nineties, supplemented these by lecture series, and shifted emphasis to classes during the eighties. Up to about 1895 the classes were mostly in elementary-school subjects with some attention to higher grade work; after 1895 the emphasis changed to commercial, technical, and manual-training subjects where it has since mostly rested. The great period of expansion on the latter basis was from 1900 to 1915. So elaborate and extensive did YMCA educational work become in some instances that a movement to obtain academic recognition for it developed, leading to the "hiving off" of some of the schools as independent institutions, of which Northeastern University in Boston may serve here as the example. However, the YMCA did not by such developments lessen its concern for adult education. Within its established subject-matter limits, the YMCA schools are still among the major adult education enterprises of the time.

The YWCA's education activities have been much more limited in scope. While they have involved the discovery and use of adult education methods, they have never assumed the general-utility shape characteristic of the YMCA. They have mostly remained far more obviously within the confines of the organization's purpose of "realizing in our common life those ideals of personal and social living to which we are committed by our faith as Christians."

The New York YMHA-YWHA, on the other hand, has developed a cultural program of a very high order indeed, and on the side of poetry, at least, unique in the world. Under the direction of John Malcolm Brinnin, use is made each season of a modern version of one of the oldest of adult education devices—one that goes straight back to the Greeks: that of having poets and other literary artists read their own works in public. To be sure, there is a fair continuity of history of this sort of thing in America. Authors' readings had a vogue before the Civil War; it was through them that Americans got personal acquaintance with Charles Dickens and William Makepeace Thackeray, for example. Again in the eighties, authors' readings were popular and Mark Twain was the most popular reader. Charles Laughton and other actors give readings in our day. But at the YMHA-YWHA within a single season readings have been given by Dylan Thomas, Marianne Moore, Robert Frost, W. H. Auden, Edith and Osbert Sitwell, and Rene Char, as poets; Truman Capote, Arthur Miller, and Noel Coward, as dramatists; Katherine Anne Porter, Elizabeth Bowen, and Joyce Cary, as fiction writers; and I. A. Richards, critic, as reader-and-commentator on John Keats. This is richness indeed. The literary emphasis, is, moreover, complemented by activities in music, art, and the dance, both on the side of instruction and professional performance.[2] And the whole is still environed by the traditional Y stand-bys, the gymnasium work, the handball, the billiards, the social-welfare activities. The cultural program illustrates to perfection that adult education need not on all occasions be characterized by a drab and dusty utilitarianism. It also is, and ever-increasingly should be, a vehicle for the dissemination of the highest aesthetic pleasures and profoundest insights into the human condition.

Although only related to the YM-YWHA activities by a common cultural emphasis, this seems a logical place to discuss the use of great books in adult education, and "Great Books" specifically. The name "Great Books" is both a challenge and a misfortune, and to some bulls in the educational china shop nothing less than a red flag. At bottom what we have here is a very simple idea: that adults can profitably read the classic books of mankind—or at least of the Western European cultural tradition—and with worth-while results explore their implications in discussion. Such reading and discussion have always been a characteristic, but not sole, activity of the intelligentsia, both academic and lay, and it is only its promotion among the public-at-large that makes Great Books a striking venture.

Of course there is no possible agreement on just what great books are *the* great books; and Great Books evades the issue by not using the definite article. However the fact that Great Books is associated with the names of Robert M. Hutchins and Mortimer Adler, and they with a particular philosophy of education aggressively expressed, causes the simplicity of the basic idea, and its indisputable value, to be obscured by the cloud of dust that philosophy raises in educational circles. Even the disclaimer of knowing what *the* great books may be escapes notice in the rush to demonstrate that Great Books reflects their philosophical bias. As a matter of fact, the submission of Great Books to untrammeled group discussion makes it impossible to know, let alone guarantee, at what conclusions the discussants will eventually arrive.

The idea of using great books, or more modestly, very good and influential books, in education—even in adult education—is not peculiarly the property of the Great Books people. Benjamin Franklin has been claimed as the "putative father" of the idea— Franklin of the Junto. We have noticed that the reading of classics was basic to the scheme of workers' education devised by Thomas Davidson. More specifically, at a meeting of the American Library Association in 1919, Alexander Meiklejohn, then president of Amherst College, advocated the group reading of classic works by adults under library leadership; and John Erskine, novelist and professor, acclimatized the idea as an independent inspiration, perhaps stimulated by knowledge of the Oxford way of teaching, at Columbia College from 1919. In the late twenties the Erskine idea was carried into adult education by the People's Institute, then flourishing in New York under the direction of Everett Dean

Martin.[3] Clifton Fadiman has written that he and other products of the Erskine regimen took the idea into adult education in the spirit of cultural missionaries. The Erskine idea suggested the radio program "Invitation to Learning," first broadcast May 26, 1940, and a Sunday morning fixture thereafter.

Meiklejohn was director of The Experimental College at the University of Wisconsin from 1927 to 1932 and his version of the great books approach was given a thorough workout there. Robert M. Hutchins began to hold seminars in great books at the University of Chicago in the early 1930's. Late in the decade the idea was again blown up to full curriculum dimensions, by men influenced by both Hutchins and Meiklejohn, at St. John's College, Annapolis, Maryland. Meiklejohn himself took the idea with him to San Francisco in 1933 and it was used by him there in the adult education promoted by The School for Social Studies which functioned for over a decade. The streams of influence flowing from Hutchins and Meiklejohn came together again in Washington, D.C., when in 1945 the Public Library launched a group reading plan on the great books pattern. Meiklejohn and Scott Buchanan of St. John's were directly concerned as consultants and Hutchins provided the money to launch the scheme from a special fund for educational experiments he then had in hand. Later, direction in Washington was taken over by John W. Powell who had directed The School for Social Studies in San Francisco.[4]

Meanwhile at Chicago, Hutchins and Adler were working out *their* idea of Great Books at the University, with adults in the forefront of their minds. This scheme of reading and discussion was first offered to the general public in collaboration with the Chicago Public Library late in 1945. In 1946 the University turned the scheme over to Great Books Foundation, and the Foundation soon started to promote the idea coast to coast.[5]

A moment's reflection on this record will make clear that Great Books is but one version of the idea of using the reading and discussion of great books in adult education. Considering the character of most of the great books it would occur to a thoughtful teacher to use, there is more warrant for submitting them to reading and discussion by adults than by adolescents in college. This statement refers the reader, even if obliquely and invidiously, back to the opinions of Plato and Aristotle on what studies should be reserved to, or at least undertaken by, adults. Nor is the range of great books a circumscribed one, confined to books ambiguously known as classics. At San Francisco, Meiklejohn, avoiding text-books, digests, and "par excellence any material created expressly for adult classes," set his groups to reading "Plato and Dewey, Veblen and Adam Smith, Marx and John Strachey, the Beards and the Lynds, Freud and the anthropologists, Theodore Dreiser and John Dos Passos and Thomas Wolfe, Henry Adams and Lincoln Steffens," or books which thousands of adults have in the ordinary way read anyway, without benefit of adult education classes.

This suggests what is unquestionably true: that the group reading of great (or good, or representative) books and discussion of them is a highly flexible adult education device, and on the record, a very good and fruitful one. Great Books is one use of it, to date the most conspicuous, but others have gained recent recognition also: for example, the program of the American Foundation for Political Education (founded 1947), and the American Heritage program of the American Library Association (launched in 1951). The significant contribution of this approach is to introduce into the enduring world of adult discourse more and more adults who may, on analogy to the experience of Monsieur Jourdain, be surprised to find themselves there, able to do the reading, and able profitably to debate the issues raised.

Efforts of adult educators to use mass communications in their work can be approached from either of two angles: either the use of mass-communications mechanisms as pedagogical tools under "classroom" conditions, or the use of mass communications to reach audiences at large in competition with the commercial communications of the same kind. As an example of the first we have the moving pictures, of the second the radio. Television is still too new to permit a meaningful assessment of its significance in adult education.

The discussions of moving pictures and radio in adult education which follow are focused on that subject alone—their place in *adult education*. The remarks are not to be read as implying any judgment on the intentional or accidental educational activities and significances of commercial movies and commercial radio. Into that vast and complex field the writer does not choose to enter. He is exclusively concerned with the use of movies and radio by educators, not with the educational activities of the commercial people. The latter he believes should properly be viewed as a phase of the education of adults in our society, not of adult education as it is defined and discussed here. It is fervently to be hoped that some wise and wary person will write an exhaustive book on the role of the mass communications in the education of adults, but to date this has not been done and such materials as can be found, full as they may be of brilliant flashes of insight, are far from conclusively authoritative.

The story of adult education by radio [6] is such a mixture of elements that it is difficult to write about it without giving an unbalanced impression of dismal failure. One of the major critical studies of the American radio heads the chapter on educational radio, "The Light that Failed." [7] Failure there has been, if the criterion is the gap between potentiality and actuality, yet the net result of thirty-odd years of effort is far from discreditable to those who matched their belief in the instrument with a willingness to work hard for its use.

In the beginning the educators were at one with Lee de Forest in seeing the radio as "a noble agency for the diffusion of education and culture," [8] as, indeed, were some of the commercial pioneers, and much money (chiefly supplied by the Carnegie and Payne foundations), time, and hard thought was put into promoting educational radio. A remarkable number of colleges and universities, usually in their departments of physics, had early worked in wireless communications, beginning with the dot-and-dash type before World War I, and going on into modern broadcasting after the war; and some of them made valuable technical contributions. From laboratory experimentation and classroom instruction in electrical communications, it was an easy step to broadcasting to the general public. When it became necessary to take out licenses to broadcast, a very surprising number of institutions took them out, but few survived as broadcasters for very long.

Between 1921 and 1936 a total of 202 broadcasting licenses were granted to 168 different educational institutions of all levels of the hierarchy, 28 of them getting two, even three licenses at various times during the decade and a half. The great year for obtaining licenses was 1922 when 73 were taken out, and in the four years following demand continued active: 1923, 39; 1924, 38; 1925, 25; 1926, 10. Thereafter the demand dropped off for a long time.

Loss or abandonment of licenses began simultaneously with the granting of them. Even in 1922, 7 were lost; the worst year was 1925, when 37 were given up; and thereafter the attrition was constant. Three educational institutions out of ten during the first fifteen years lost their licenses within a year of their granting; only one-third of those which obtained licenses were able to hang onto them for three years or more; and but 20 licenses out of the 202 granted 1921–1936 were held for the entire period. By 1934 Morse A. Cartwright, Executive Director of the American Association for Adult Education, which had pioneered the idea of using radio in education, had concluded that "The stations owned and operated by educational institutions seem unlikely to throw much light on the problem." He was then looking to the use made of free time on the commercial stations.

On January 1, 1937, only 38 institutions held licenses. In August, 1937, Levering Tyson, for a number of years director of correspondence teaching for Columbia University, who had played a conspicuous role in the intensive campaign to make educational sense of the new instrumentality, wrote:

> Throughout all this checkered history the educator, traditionally regarded as impractical and idealistic, has had a difficult time. Suddenly there was placed in his hands a powerful weapon for the distribution of intelligence. In attempting to use it he found himself immersed in a new species of mud. So far no one has been able to discover a means for extricating him.

The composition of this "new species of mud" varied from place to place, but certain fairly constant elements were noticeable. The institutions had a difficult time financing the cost of technical improvements which came so rapidly. After it was made plain that advertising was to make radio a rich business, the pressure of commercial interests to take over the channels or times assigned to educational stations was often very intense. The methods used to "put on the heat" were not always scrupulous. Educational institutions all too readily succumbed to the lure of a promise of time on a commercial station if they would abandon their own station. The Federal Communications Commission (founded 1934) and its predecessor bodies were, on the record, unsympathetic to the educational stations; they not only favored commercial stations, but also badgered the educational people by shifting them to poor places on "the band" and shifting them often. The institutions retaining their own stations failed to develop any viable philosophy of the place of the radio in the educational structure. Too little attention was given by educational broadcasters to the techniques of broadcasting, with the result that the material was often presented unattractively to audiences conditioned by the commercial station methods.

It was on the thirty-eight stations which had succeeded in surviving all of the handicaps to the beginning of 1937 that the future of educational radio depended. All were, of course, AM stations and, retrospectively, that seems to have been one of the difficulties. Only when FM channels became available for educational stations after 1945 was there (following a pause during which many critics got worried at the slowness with which applications came in)[9] a great increase in the number of educational stations. How many educational stations were on the air in 1951 is not easy to determine exactly, but certainly over one hundred. And more were on the way. By that time the overwhelming majority of educational stations were FM. FM gave educational broadcasting a new opportunity, and by the time it came along, the educational leaders were a bit clearer about the place of radio in their repertory of instrumentalities.

The coverage of educational radio has, even after the great expansion following World War II, been spotty. Even as more and more stations came on the air, there remained many thousands of people to whom educational radio was simply not available. There were in the early fifties at least a dozen states in which there was only one station, usually not of a power to cover the whole state. Moreover, educational stations were ordinarily on the air for a limited number of hours a day, not always hours when fully employed people could listen. Of only a few states could it be said that anything like statewide coverage, either from one or several stations, had been attained. These were, speculatively, Alabama,

California, Florida, Illinois, Indiana, Iowa, Kansas, Louisiana, Michigan, Ohio, and Wisconsin. Only one state—Wisconsin—had a statewide *network*. Highly regarded individual stations included those of the University of Wisconsin, Michigan State College, Cornell, the University of Florida, the University of Illinois, and the municipal station of the City of New York. In an effort to link up the stations there was developed in 1950 what was subsequently called the Tape Network. This was initiated by Seymour N. Siegel of the New York municipal station when he made available to other educational stations a limited number of tape recordings of very desirable programs. When the work outgrew the resources of the New York station—as it did very quickly—the Network became a co-operative enterprise of the National Association of Educational Broadcasters, with headquarters at the University of Illinois.[10] It continued to enjoy a lively growth.

The national impact of educational radio has always been very difficult to estimate, not only because of spotty coverage, but because the kind of research-in-depth that is needed to measure the impact of mass communications has never yet been carried out on a large scale. Educational stations have thus far learned very little about their audiences on any basis, and least of all in terms of their educational impact. For that reason, any account of what the educational stations have customarily broadcasted tells only *that,* not what the materials have really meant to the receiving audience. In the 1948 *Handbook of Adult Education,* H. B. McCarty, Director of Radio Education, University of Wisconsin, summarized the range of content about that time as follows:

> Regular university courses direct from the classrooms are featured by several of the stations. Agricultural information and home-making programs are prominent on the schedules, and, in addition, the stations present courses of instruction specially written and produced in the studios—courses in world affairs, history, geography, literature, foreign languages, atomic science, international relations, community living, parent education, and a host of other subjects.

But with all possible local ingenuity, it had long been obvious that programing was a fundamental problem of the isolated stations, only to be solved by drawing upon resources outside the educational institution with which the station was associated. The Tape Network contributed precisely at that point.

While better programs were a big lift, they did not solve the problems of educational broadcasting in all particulars. To get a reasonable view of the situation it is necessary to know how the educational broadcasters see themselves after all the years of experimentation. To convey some idea of that we may quote an NAEB statement (*my italics*):

> The NAEB Tape Network is predicated on the simple belief that the use of radio exclusively for entertainment and the selling of merchandise is a serious waste of a major national resource. In addition to these uses, radio broadcasting is capable of being *an important instrument in the dissemination of information, opinion, discussion, and interpretation essential to the solving of today's complex problems.* Radio can also provide, and on a vast scale, *meaningful cultural experiences.*

These remarks can reasonably be assumed to mean that educational radio is a means of extending the parent institution's influence, and that therefore the activity can properly be viewed in much the same light as university extension. If this is true, then it is, by implication at least, subject to the same criticism that university extension attracts. What the President's Commission on Higher Education had to say about university extension is cited fairly fully a few pages farther on. In brief, the Commission accused the institutions of higher education of not taking sufficiently seriously their responsibilities for adult education. Radio has been slighted in the same fashion and for much the same reasons.

There is, however, an important difference between the usual university extension activities and radio. Broadcasting, unlike extension work, is a one-way flow of communication and tends to induce passivity in the listener. This is the crux of the criticism of most mass communications by those concerned to judge them in educational and cultural terms and, naturally, criticism is largely directed at the initiators of the "flow." They determine what the passive recipients receive. Passivity is not an attitude of mind conducive to satisfactory educational experiences. It must be successfully countered before education can properly proceed. The minds of education's customers must be active, their critical powers on the alert.

Now educational radio is an effort to invade the mass communications field in a fashion competitive with, or supplementary to, commercial radio. Since this is true and since its appeal is to a minority audience, or perhaps a congeries of minority audiences, or even "the individual, and special groups" (we do not really know, the question not having been intensively studied), the presumption is that the audience is, as signaled by its acceptance of educational broadcasts, less passive and more critical than the audience for commercial mass communications (as portrayed in Gilbert Seldes' *The Great Audience,* for instance). But this does not allow educational radio to escape the fact that it is, as radio, a one-way flow to its audience. Nor is there any easy way to evade this fact. Listening groups—i.e., groups of people who gather to listen to broadcasts and then discuss them, the education inhering in the discussion and its quality turning upon the quality of the group leadership—have never really caught on, though isolated successes have been achieved.

Educational radio then is an effort to establish a one-way flow at some educational level—public school, college, university—from the station to an audience of unknown dimensions and character. The origin of the flow, the intent in establishing it, and the effect it may have on the flow of radio communications in general, must justify the operation. It extends the university into the area where mass communications find their audience, it competes for attention there, and insofar as it gains it, justifies itself by injecting into the babel of sounds, a few notes presumably appealing to the educated, and perhaps seductive to the not-so-educated. Whether or not educational radio can ever do more is an open question. If this is not a sufficient rationale, then the case for it breaks down. In the writer's opinion, it *is* a sufficient rationale.

What will happen to educational radio when educational television is fully established is as difficult to anticipate as the probable role of commercial radio when commercial television is fully developed; but early indications were that no complete transfer from educational radio to educational television was likely.

Moving pictures have been used by adult educators chiefly as visual or audio-visual supplements in classrooms or discussion groups, though they are, in one of their phases, the stock-in-trade of the groups interested in the aesthetics of the film. The mechanical means of bringing movies to audiences—the projector—lends itself to a far more selective use of this communications mechanism than radio broadcasting. As many writers have noted, people in general enjoy pictures—they are visual-minded. Hence the popularity of the movies, picture newspapers, picture magazines, and the vogue of photography, both as a profession and a hobby. But like radio, the communication "flow" of the moving pictures is one way and it too induces, or does not disturb, passivity.

The educational problem was to make full use of the movies as an audio-visual instructional aid while breaking up the passivity induced by the one-way flow. Back in the twenties, Alvin Johnson proposed to do this by showing the movies and then having them discussed.[11] This idea is one that would naturally occur to anybody reflecting on how to use the movies in education, so it certainly was not originated by Johnson. Nobody, however, seems to have been in any great hurry to use the movies educationally in a systematic way, for what seems to have been the first extensive, closely observed, experiment in the use of films-plus-discussion came as late as 1941–43 under the auspices of the Joint Committee on Film Forums, the collaborating organizations being the American Film Center, the American Library Association, the American Association for Adult Education, and the American Association for Applied Psychology. In 1946 Glen Burch ventured a definition of a film forum: "The film forum may be described as a variant of the forum method in which a film relating to the topic to be discussed is used instead of a speaker to prepare a group for discussion." From experiments like that cited, and from the demonstration in the armed services wartime adult education program of the high utility of the film as an instructional instrument, several conclusions were drawn, conspicuous among them the points that films shown without discussion can be dangerous on the side of indoctrination; that only carefully selected or, better, specially made films are provocative of discussion; and that leadership is absolutely indispensable if any discussion at all is to be developed —the better the leadership, of course, the better the discussion.

Moreover, "forced" and apparently purposeless discussion is un-fruitful, so that only discussion that flows naturally from the film shown and that links up with interests already present in the minds of the audience is truly creative.

In recent years, therefore, the focus of attention has been on the careful selection or production of films for discussion, on prob-lems of discussion leadership, and on improving the quality of the discussion by the use of supplementary printed materials. Thus the movie is not to be viewed as an end-in-itself in adult educa-tion, but as a pedagogical aid which seems to be attractive to a very large number of people.

It is noticeable that in the cases of the radio and the movies adult educators were very late in really learning how to use them for their purposes. Their broad social impact was determined by the commercial users and their impact through adult education has never been more than peripheral. It will be interesting to see what role the adult educators will play in television where their chances of getting a good, early and firm foothold seemed, as this was writ-ten, rather better than in the case of the movies and radio.

Organizing the Adult Educators

BEFORE THE NINETEEN-TWENTIES, efforts to create national organizations in adult education had been confined to fractions of the field. Conspicuous examples had been the National Lyceum, founded in 1830; the Chautauqua, founded in the 1870's; the National Association of University Extension, founded in 1915; and the National Education Association's Department of Adult Education, founded in 1921. No attempt had been made to create a national organization to gather all varieties of adult education into a single fold to co-ordinate efforts, promote the idea, or influence standards, until the American Association for Adult Education was founded early in 1926. This organization functioned for fifteen years with steady vigor and continued for another ten years to occupy the field, but with diminishing impact. Its life ended in 1951 when it was absorbed into a new national organization, the Adult Education Association of the United States of America.

A quick look at adult education about the time AAAE appeared would have convinced almost anybody that such an organization was needed, not to create adult education *de novo,* but to give it a lift and a sense of direction. The need was widely recognized. For instance, in 1924 Nicholas Murray Butler, President of Columbia, wrote: "The education of youth is suffering from over-organization,

276

from over-administration, and from hysterical over-emphasis. The continuing education of the adult, on the other hand, is suffering from lack of organization, from imperfect administration, and from no emphasis at all." [1] Looking at the situation from a different coign of vantage, William S. Learned of the staff of the Carnegie Foundation for the Advancement of Teaching found in a report published that year that "a very great amount of so-called adult education is now proceeding at every turn," but that it lacked both *purpose* and *cumulative sequence*.[2] Mr. Learned argued that both were urgent needs—in his view to be injected under library leadership—because:

> . . . the American adult is not generally trained . . . in the technique indispensable to self-education, namely, the getting of ideas independently from books. Furthermore, he has on leaving school no clear conception of a curriculum in all or any branches of learning whereby, on following a definite sequence of ideas contained in books, he may arrive at a mature comprehension of that field.

Since, then, adult education was "proceeding at every turn," but in an unorganized and underadministrative fashion, so that no proper emphasis was placed upon it, the consequence was that thousands who might have profited from it, lived their lives in effective ignorance of it. There was work to be done in putting adult education on its feet.[3]

The challenge to try to make something more of adult education than had been done up to that time was taken up by Frederick P. Keppel, who, in October 1923, had become president of the Carnegie Corporation. Mr. Keppel worked out the ideas of using Carnegie funds in two fields not hitherto cultivated by the Corporation, adult education and the arts. He had been dean of Columbia College from 1910 to 1917 and by virtue of that position had served on the University's Administrative Board of Extension Teaching during the same years. He thus had some knowledge of adult education when he began to consider it as a field for Corporation action. Moreover, he had the precedent of Mr. Carnegie's view of libraries as a principal adult education resource. He had discovered in the Corporation's files a memorandum by James Rowland Angell, long president of Yale and a predecessor of Keppel's in the presidency of the Corporation, asking in effect, Why not adult education as a field of Corporation activity? And he had been much impressed by W. S. Learned's report which had originally been a staff memorandum of the Carnegie Foundation and which Mr. Keppel himself had caused to be published by a commercial house.[4]

Mr. Keppel's work at Columbia had made him well acquainted with James Earl Russell, dean of Teachers College from 1897, and a redoubtable educational statesman. Teachers College had pioneered extension at Columbia, and Russell had from the beginning been sympathetically concerned with it. Russell's view in the twenties was that "The aim of adult education is to inspire grownups to be something more than they are now and to do their work better than they now do it; at its best it leads to constantly increasing richness of life, better appreciation of what life offers, greater satisfaction in the use of the mind and body and better understanding of the rights and duties of one's fellow man." [5] When Keppel decided to look into adult education systematically with the intent of putting Carnegie money into the field, he called a conference in New York in June, 1924, out of which grew an Advisory Committee on Adult Education to the Corporation with Russell as chairman and Charles A. Beard, Everett Dean Martin, Alfred E. Cohn, C. R. Dooley, and E. C. Lindeman as members of the executive committee.[6]

The Advisory Committee supported a proposal to carry out studies of selected areas of adult education under the general direction of Morse A. Cartwright,[7] recommended that the Corporation focus its interest chiefly on nonvocational adult education, and further suggested that it be concerned only with leisure-time adult education. The research quickly revealed a great deal of activity in adult education and a widespread interest in it. The next step, which did not need to wait upon the publication of the studies, was to discover what sentiment there was for a national organization, and what kind of organization was wanted. Under the general direction of the Executive Committee of the Corporation's Advisory Committee, a national conference was held in Cleveland, Ohio, October 16-17, 1925. There it was agreed that a national body appeared to be wanted, but that sentiment needed further assessment. There followed regional exploratory meetings in New York

City (November 23, 1925), San Francisco (February 8-9, 1926), Nashville, Tennessee (February 19, 1926), and Chicago (May 24, 1926). At each regional meeting the proposal for a national organization was supported and committees of seven nominated to attend a national meeting to form one. This meeting took place at Chicago on March 26-27, 1926, under the chairmanship of Leon J. Richardson, director of extension at the University of California. Out of it came the American Association for Adult Education, whose object, as stated in the constitution:

> . . . shall be to promote the development and improvement of adult education in the United States and to cooperate with similar associations in other countries. It shall undertake to provide for the gathering and dissemination of information concerning adult education aims and methods of work; to keep its members informed concerning the achievements and problems of adult education in other countries; to conduct a continuous study of work being done in this field; and to publish from time to time the results of such study; to respond to public interest in adult education and particularly of study groups whether within or without regular educational institutions; and in other ways to cooperate with organizations and individuals engaged in educational work of this nature in the task of securing books and instructors; and to serve in such other ways as may be deemed advisable.

To govern the Association there was a Council of one hundred and an Executive Board of eighteen, of whom nine formed the Executive Committee. Headquarters were set up in New York in May, with Morse A. Cartwright, a member of the Executive Committee, as Director.[8] Effective power was in the hands of the Executive Committee and the Director. The presidency of the Association was an honorary position, the incumbents symbolizing in some sense the kind of patronage it was thought valuable for adult education to have.[9] The other offices and posts were filled over the years by men whose names are a kind of who's who in adult education for the twenty-five years the Association existed. For fifteen of those years the Carnegie Corporation underwrote the greater part of the administrative costs of the Association.

The history of the Association from its founding in 1926 to its

dissolution in 1951 has never been intensively studied and it is
difficult to formulate a summary version of the story without that
kind of review at hand. The story falls into two sections of unequal
length, one extending from 1926 to 1941, when the Carnegie Corporation underwrote expenses, the other from 1941 to 1951, when
the Association was dependent solely on membership fees.

It seems from the record that the Association had defined its
function by the end of its first decade beyond much expectation of
later change. In the Director's report for 1935–36 (which reviews the history up to that time), the rhetorical question, "What
remains to be done in the years to come?" draws the reply, "The
answer appears to lie in unremitting effort to progress upon the
way already blazed." What was that way?

The AAAE was not an operating agency in the sense that it
offered adult education courses to the public. Rather it was a
"supplemental agency." As the 1927–28 annual report put it, it
was an agency "which should aid other agencies, whether such
agencies were community, state, regional or national in scope." It
sought to avoid dictating form of organization, method of instruction, content of courses. It served as a "central clearing house of
information," sponsored and sometimes conducted "studies, experiments, and researches in adult education." It was a kind of publishing agency for the field. It "spread the word" about adult education
by interpreting, explaining, and clarifying it in personal interviews,
publications, and conferences (including annual conferences, partly
for the membership, partly for the general public), but it eschewed
propaganda for adult education. It sought to advance the common
interests of those active in the field, investigated the common problems, and cultivated common purposes.

Yet the Association, at least as its views found expression in the
writings of the Director, was not flabbily neutral. In the 1935–36
Annual Report, we find the Director telling the world that he had
expressed views in previous reports on

> . . . qualitative versus quantitative success, on the use of
> propaganda methods, on the difficulty of combating special
> pleaders, on "money changers in the temple," on the incon-
> sequence of definitions and formulae, on the folly of super-
> imposition, on the necessity of harmony as between the cultural

and vocational points of view, on the dangers of inflation in the adult education idea, on progress without sensationalism, on the principles of discriminatory thinking among both leaders and led, on the retroactive effects of adult education ideals upon formalized education for the young, upon professional standards and the elimination of claptrap and charlatanism.

It is clear from the way he states the questions what the Director's views on these issues were.

In the course of its life the Association was responsible for an enormous increase in the literature of adult education. Apart from publications which served the needs of the moment only, it brought out an exceedingly valuable magazine (which to this day has not had a successor of equal worth) and either was responsible for, or had a hand, in the production of numerous books and pamphlets reporting research or recounting experiments. Its quarterly *Journal of Adult Education* was published from the January number of 1929 to the end of 1941. The books for which it was in whole or in part responsible cannot all be named here. A few titles still of interest to the general reader may be cited illustratively. Many of the books, it should be noted, are still of live interest to specialist students, for whom they were planned in the first instance.

Adult Learning, by Edward Lee Thorndike and others (1928), a work of major influence on thinking about the feasibility of adult education in its psychological aspects.

Handbook of Adult Education in the United States, first issued in 1934, edited by Dorothy Rowden. The pioneer comprehensive guide to the American field. Subsequent editions, 1936 and 1948. All are primary indices to the state of American adult education at the dates of issue.

Leisure: A Suburban Study, by George A. Lundberg and others (1934). A pioneering study in the consumption of leisure, a subject which, twenty years later, is still the object of lively study.

The American Way, by John W. Studebaker (1934), the key book in the boom in forums during the Great Depression.

Adult Education in Action, edited by Mary L. Ely (1936), a selection of material from the quarterly *Journal* depicting American thinking about adult education during the previous decade.

During the first ten years, much of the material published was exploratory in nature, designed to outline and define the field. At the end of the decade (partly as a result of a cue from the Carnegie Corporation), a shift was made to the problem of standards and the matter of objectively measuring and evaluating accomplishments. In 1937, therefore, the Association began the publication of a series of volumes under the general title, "The Social Significance of Adult Education" which, when it was completed in 1941, totaled twenty-seven small volumes. The series was written by various hands, not all professionally concerned with adult education, after both library and field work. In perspective, the series is as uneven in quality as the field it reported and evaluated, but perhaps a quarter of the volumes—it would be highly invidious to name them—still strike a critical reader as of the first class. The series was rounded off in 1944 with James Truslow Adams' *Frontiers of American Culture: A Study of Adult Education in a Democracy,* a disappointing performance both as to the information and thinking. Following 1941, the publication program of the Association declined sharply in volume, but less sharply in significance. Some very acute reports were issued, notably Glen Burch's study of the difficulties of organizing communities for adult education.

While the Association was closely associated with the Carnegie Corporation, it was in a position to recommend to the Corporation projects in the field of adult education for support. Not only did the money for research and publication thus come to hand and pass either through the Association's accounts or directly to the beneficiary, but many adult education enterprises also thus received subsidies vital to either their initiation or their expansion. The Corporation, additionally, made grants from 1926 to 1941 in the field of adult education quite apart from any recommendation of the Association, both at home and abroad (as in Canada, Australia, and New Zealand). Between the years 1926 and 1941, the Corporation fed into the field of adult education a total of almost five million dollars.

The climactic year in the Association's history was 1941. In that year the whole question of the future of relations between the Carnegie Corporation and the Association was intensively reviewed by a committee of trustees at meetings held from mid-April to mid-May. This was in accordance with the Corporation's policy of reviewing the relation at five-year intervals. The 1941 committee reported to the Executive Committee of the Board of Trustees as follows:

The Corporation since 1925 has expressed an active and continuing interest in adult education. This interest has been made evident through grants totaling some four and one-half million dollars. These grants have been for the maintenance of an adult education association with its program of publication, research, study, and experimentation, and of promotion of the cause of adult education; for the support and encouragement of local demonstrations, projects and experiments; for careful recording of experience and wide-spread diffusion of knowledge as to results.

Acting as a center of interest for adult education, the American Association for Adult Education has received from the Corporation, at the beginning of successive five year periods, ample funds to carry on a program which the Association has varied in emphasis from period to period, aiming always to keep in active contact with a changing world. Its purpose steadily has been to conduct a library and clearinghouse of information, to serve as an encourager of intelligent and well directed effort in the field, and to act as an informed analyzer of the forces calling for adult education and of the efforts put forth in various forms and places to meet these demands throughout the United States and elsewhere.

The Corporation Committee and the representative of the Association have recently made a careful and conscientious audit of experience during the last fifteen years. The Corporation Committee invited the Association to appoint, through its regular procedures, a committee of its directors to make, to the Corporation Committee, a statement of their views as to the future relationship of the Corporation to the Association and to adult education. This was done at a joint meeting held on May 6, 1941.

After extended study and discussion of all the considerations involved, the Corporation Committee now believes that the Corporation can best serve the cause of adult education during the next decade by providing funds not for the continuation of the program initiated in 1925 and developed to date, but for the establishment of a limited society, institute, or other organization devoted to intensive study of the opportunities, problems, materials and methods of adult education and to the training of leaders and competent workers. This agency would derive its support from a single ten-year grant from the Corporation, but would otherwise be entirely separate from the Corporation. It would take form either as an independent agency or as an integral part of an outstanding university or other recognized and existing educational agency identified with the training of leaders and with research. It would undertake, in its consideration of the problems and practices of general education, to enlist the cooperation and services of the best available minds, and would attempt also to serve as a leader in sustained thought and effort in the field.[10]

The suggestion made in the final paragraph quoted above was carried out. The Corporation arranged the establishment at Teachers College, Columbia, of an Institute of Adult Education to carry on with research and study as successor in the field to the Association. To support the Institute for ten years, the Corporation granted Teachers College $350,000. At the same time the Director of the Association, Mr. Cartwright, was appointed Professor of Education at Teachers College, where he also became Executive Officer of the new Institute. Moreover, he retained his post as Director of the Association, of which, however, he was an unpaid, voluntary servant. Mr. Cartwright resigned all his posts in 1949 because of ill health and retired to California.

During the war years the Association, its staff much reduced, was chiefly concerned with questions of morale among civilians and members of the armed services. In 1945 it began to inquire into the current and probable postwar state of adult education. It discovered that, whatever the setbacks of wartime, the prospects were that there would be a great and rapid expansion once the fighting ceased. Since as far as the consumers were concerned, adult education came to a focus in the communities, the Committee on the Future Policy of the Association concluded that:

> Adult education opportunities are everywhere inadequately provided for and unevenly distributed among their potential users. As a first step, therefore, the individual community must be encouraged and helped (1) to determine its particular adult education needs; (2) to ascertain and evaluate the adult education programs already available to its residents; (3) to discover discrepancies between such programs and the total adult educational needs of the community; (4) to develop interested and willing learners; (5) to identify and develop community leaders who are themselves also learners; and (6) to unite the efforts of both learners and leaders in planning and establishing suitable adult educational opportunities.

> The Committee on Future Policy believes that the American Association for Adult Education can achieve this objective to stimulate and guide adult education at the local level only by distributing its efforts throughout the country. It cannot be achieved through the efforts of the Headquarters staff alone, though the active participation of the Association's officers, Executive Board, and Executive Council must be assumed. The working cooperation of the rank and file of the entire membership must be enlisted.

It was in this fashion that the Association proposed to deal with the problems of adult education in the environment created in America by World War II.

Before the war it had beyond a doubt contributed a very great deal to giving the field self-consciousness; to bringing the several parts into friendly communication (with occasional lapses); to building up and circulating validated knowledge of the field and relevant to its special tasks; to stimulating research into the problems of adult teaching and learning; to keeping the field from succumbing to its perennial menaces, special interests, crackpots, and hobbyhorse riders; and to the creation and propagation of standards of performance, *but it had failed to find a way deeply to root itself*

IN QUEST OF KNOWLEDGE

either in the field or in American life. It was not able to demonstrate that it could supply from its own roots the kind of vitality lent artificially to it by the Carnegie Corporation's funds. In its own judgment—quoted above—adult education in America at the close of World War II was still "inadequately provided for and unevenly distributed," a poor base on which to found a viable national organization.

The Carnegie activities, of which the AAAE in retrospect now appears as but one, had concluded with the field in that condition, even though vastly improved over the situation circa 1924.[11] A trustee of the Corporation, Mr. Henry James, wrote in an appreciation of Mr. Keppel published in 1951: "He saw, years ago, that education need not stop at the college level or at any particular age, and so he led the Carnegie Corporation to pour a great deal of money into experiments and demonstrations in adult education. What was learned was sometimes learned at high cost. But the results have been so significant that I believe we are now, with respect to adult education, years further ahead than we would be if Keppel had not explored so widely and given so lavishly." [12]

In the late forties the time had come for new leadership to assert itself. As we shall see in the next section, there was recognition of the need for it, and also the highest recognition thus far of the importance of adult education in American life, at the topmost levels of educational and foundation thinking.

Beginning in 1949, conferences were held throughout the country to discuss the formation of a new national organization. On May 13-15, 1951, two hundred persons active in adult education met in Columbus, Ohio, and established the Adult Education Association of the United States of America. (The actual founding day was May 14.) The new Association absorbed the membership of the American Association for Adult Education and the Department of Adult Education of the National Education Association, and these organizations were dissolved. Professor Howard McClusky of the University of Michigan was elected the first president. As for the role of the foundation in the new situation, the Ford Foundation had established the Fund for Adult Education on the previous April 5 against a background of thinking to which we now turn.

22

American Perspectives of the 1950's

Examining the position of adult education in the average American community in the late nineteen-forties, Glen Burch found that the service had "never developed an institutional pattern"; that this arose from the "diffusion of responsibility for the provision of adult education"; that much of what was provided was marginal to the larger purposes of the suppliers and was apt to reflect the ends of an agency rather than the needs or demands of the customers; that all the varieties needed for a rounded program were rarely to be found in any single community and were sometimes hard to come by anywhere in the nation; and that the co-ordination of what existed and the filling up of even the obvious gaps was a difficult task, rarely if ever successfully executed. "In any given community," Burch wrote, "a public school might be responsible for providing opportunities for vocational adult education, home-making, naturalization and citizenship, and night-school classes; a local YMCA or YWCA might offer classes in arts and crafts and hobby subjects; a local men's or women's club might sponsor a community forum; and the public library might conduct book-discussion groups. In only rare instances . . . was any substantial proportion of these activities carried on by a single community-supported program." [1] Our concern here is to use Burch's shorthand portrait as a taking-off point for a discussion of the intellectual climate of the time with reference to the future of adult education in America. Burch suggested candidly where America was. Where did America think it was going?

Actually, it was a time of high optimism. Recognition of the importance of adult education seemed to be more widespread than ever before, not only among professional adult educators but also among educational statesmen taking a broad view of the whole field of education. Polls showed that many millions of Americans were enrolled in the adult education projects that existed, and that when people were queried about their wishes and intentions about adult education, a hearteningly high proportion said they would, all things being equal, enroll for courses in the future. The proportion ready to respond seemed to be increasing. Old hands in the field, therefore, were in a mood to ignore their past disappointments; and the young and inexperienced were prepared to rush in enthusiastically. The nineteen-fifties opened with the general expectations that the nation was about to enter a dynamic period in the history of adult education. It is for some future historian to report what actually happened.

Why did this upsurge of optimism occur? The writer's skill at socio-psychological diagnosis is not sufficient to allow him to risk dogmatism in reply, but he has noticed in his studies that upsurges of interest in adult education have historically been associated with periods of acute social disturbance, including aftermaths of major wars. When people's lives are upset, they appear to seek for knowledge, perhaps in the hope of gaining a better understanding of the situation in which they find themselves. Some of the best adult education ventures in history have arisen as responses to challenges from inside or outside the nation. In Denmark, for example, adult education was adopted in the 1860's to fend off the collapse of Danish culture under the pressure of Germany. In Sweden the same response was made to a challenge of social disintegration illustrated by declining population, poverty, and widespread chronic drunkenness. (Temperance societies spearheaded much of the work.) In telling the British story we have shown how adult education often served the needs of those striving for social improvement through political action. The challenge was bad social circumstances, the response education for action to remedy them.

In the American situation we are trying to illuminate there was the element of social disturbance all right: World War II and the succeeding Cold War. There was, too, a challenge of major dimensions: the challenge of Soviet communism. The response was, of course, the resolution to defend the country and its democracy. Since the best defence-in-depth was considered to be education, and since the choices at any level would obviously be made by adults, the most immediately useful variety of education was argued to be adult education.

A contingent factor was that during World War II extensive experiments in adult education on a mass basis had been made in the armed services; these had made an enormous impression on adult educators and provoked a resolution to see to it that something of the same sort was available to all citizens in the time of peace to follow. The armed services had used correspondence study, library services, the radio, off-duty classes, unit schools, orientation programs, University Centers (i.e., *ad hoc* universities in foreign countries in the post-armistice period), and occupational counseling. Free use was made of audio-visual aids. Techniques to facilitate rapid learning were much cultivated. Professor Cyril Houle in a study of what was done selected the following "implications" as the most important:

1. Interest in education on the part of adults is widespread.

2. A large number of service people were introduced to education as a part of their adult experience and want to continue learning if opportunities are present for them to do so.

3. The more education mature people acquire, the more they are likely to want.

4. Adult education programs are especially successful when opportunities for recreation are limited and when educational facilities are readily available.[2]

It was against some such background as has been suggested that adult education was viewed in the late forties. The famous Harvard report of 1945, *General Education in a Free Society,* argued for adult education, though its focus was on the high schools and colleges. No opinion was offered on which of the various possible sponsors should take chief responsibility for it, but there was no question left in the minds of readers that the committee felt strongly that without it, "general education in a free society" would be woefully incomplete, especially when that society was played upon by mass communications of unprecedented technical virtuosity.[3] The committee said:

> Like the high-school curriculum, the movies and radio, not to speak of magazines and newspapers, have adapted themselves to the enormous range of taste and intelligence which exists in the general public, catering quite consciously, often quite cynically, to one or another level. This variety is necessary and within limits good. But, as in the case of the high school, it carries with it the possibility of division between class and class because tastes will have been so differently formed. It also carries the possibility of personal frustration, when people struggle against influences which they scarcely know how to escape. Doubtless wisdom has always been the fruit of the tree of good and evil. But one need be no soft paternalist to believe that never in the history of the world have vulgarity and debilitation beat so insistently on the mind as they now do from screen, radio, and newsstand. Against these the book or movie which speaks with authentic largeness to the whole people has no easy victory.

Adult education, then, was argued necessary both for perennial and emergency purposes, to protect the intellectual independence of the people, as came out forcibly when the committee defined its ideal of the adult educator (*my italics*):

> ... the salvation of the community depends upon those individuals whose education gives them the moral and intellectual strength to stand out when necessary against the majority. *It may be added that such are precisely the men and women for whom an adequate system of adult education should find work to do as teachers.*

A more specific approach to the question, at least in terms of where chief responsibility should rest, was made in *Higher Educa-*

tion for Democracy, the report of the President's Commission on Higher Education, transmitted December 11, 1947.[4] The Commission argued that "the colleges and universities are the best equipped of all the agencies, from the standpoint of resources, to undertake the major part of the job." This led the Commission to argue that the colleges and universities should be expected to assume a far larger share of the burden than they ever have historically and, indeed, than it may ever prove wise to have them assume. However, the discussion was predicated on a thesis widely accepted, and in its anxiety to meet the situation head-on, the Commission may have been tempted to overplay its particular hand: "the crucial decisions of our time may have to be made in the near future. Education for action that is to be taken, for attitudes that are to be effective, in the next few years must be mainly adult education."

Looking at the current situation in higher education the Commission took a highly critical line:

> The present status of university extension services makes it painfully clear that colleges and universities do not recognize adult education as their potentially greatest service to democratic society. It is pushed aside as something quite extraneous to the real business of the university.
>
> This attitude is fostered by the necessities of adult education. It takes place outside regular college hours and usually off campus. It makes use of faculty members in other units of the university, and for these men extension and correspondence courses are usually extra chores they agree to add to their regular teaching loads in order to supplement their inadequate incomes. In this frame of mind, many of them candidly get by with as little expenditure of energy as possible.[5]

At about the time the Commission was considering the situation, 40 per cent of university-extension courses were of junior college level, 52 per cent at senior college level, 1 per cent at the graduate level, and 7 per cent not of college level. The level however was not an entirely relevant criterion, if by it one meant merely that college courses were repeated to adults. Much of adult education, the Commission observed, is "stultified by the idea that adult education consists merely of the transmission to mature people of campus courses developed to meet the needs of adolescents." On this vital point, however, the Commission had little to say in terms of content but rather, in harmony with the current set of the pedagogical mind, emphasized method.

It was implicitly recognized that adults live their intellectual lives in an environment of mass communications, but the Commission was more concerned to utilize the mass communications devices in education than to assess their impact when used commercially. (These remarks can nevertheless be found in the Report: "The motion picture industry with its almost limitless possibilities has as yet assumed little responsibility for any outcome except entertainment." "Newspapers and magazines vary from a high degree of helpfulness to a high degree of harmfulness.") The Commission criticized the failure of adult educators to make full use of radio, the movies, filmstrips, transcriptions, mock-ups, and other audio-visual aids, thus indicating an interest in profiting from practices used in armed services education during the war.

The current state of affairs, the Commission declared, could not "be permitted to continue. The colleges and universities should elevate adult education to a position of equal importance with any other of their functions. The extension department should be charged with the task of channeling the resources of every teaching unit of the institution into the adult program."

Prescribing for the future the Commission envisaged adult education as serving these ends:

It can help to round out the education provided by elementary and secondary schools and by other types of institutions; advance the individual in essential knowledge and skills; provide facilities for self-expression and appreciation in the arts; disseminate information regarding recent developments in fields such as government, economics, the physical and natural sciences; provide opportunities for discussion, at the adult level, of issues, vital to national life and to international relations; and give to both the older and younger generations a more adequate basis for understanding their mutual problems.[6]

Far from being incompatible with the proper ends of higher education, it was argued that the suggested ends of adult education should be accepted by the colleges and universities as a justification of their support in a democratic society. The Commission insisted that *all* institutions of higher education should in some degree become community institutions; and it argued strongly for the multiplication of junior colleges, community institutions par excellence and admirable bases for adult education. Although exact figures for expenditures on adult education could not be found, the Commission reasoned from an Office of Education figure of thirty-five million dollars for "extension" in 1939–40, that the colleges and universities should plan to spend one hundred million dollars a year in the future on adult education.[7]

To assist the expanded program, the Commission recommended that new machinery be set up at the state and national levels. In the states, provision should be made for councils charged with the tasks of conducting continuous studies of adult education—its needs and interests, the training of teachers and leaders, the preparation of instructional materials, the evaluation of what is going on, the stimulation of experimentation in instructional methods and subject matters, and the stimulation of constant expansion. At the national level, the Commission asked for a strong division of adult education in the Office of Education, a national council of educators associated with the division, a special commission on the use of radio and moving pictures in adult education; and federal money, distributed through the Office of Education, to support adult education, this last repeating a recommendation of an Advisory Committee on Education made a decade earlier.

A very different approach to the field was made by the Study Committee that reported to the Ford Foundation in 1949 on policy and program.[8] Here the problem was viewed from the angle of a private philanthropic organization. Of the five areas for action suggested in the Committee report, only the fourth—"Education in a Democratic Society"—is pertinent here. The Committee's emphasis throughout the discussion was on value-creating, not informational or vocational, education—on liberal education. It was stated:

The Foundation should support activities directed toward:

A. The discovery, support, and use of talent and leadership in all fields and at all ages.

B. The clarification of the goals of education and the evaluation of current educational practices and facilities for the better realization of democratic goals.

C. The reduction of economic, religious, and racial barriers to equality of educational opportunity at all levels.

D. The more effective use of mass media, such as the press, the radio, and the moving picture, and of community facilities for nonacademic education and for better utilization of leisure time for all age groups.

E. The assistance of promising ventures in education making for significant living and effective social participation.

F. The improvement of conditions and facilities for scientific and scholarly research and creative endeavors, including assistance in the dissemination of the results.

G. Improving the quality and ensuring an adequate supply of teachers in pre-school, elementary and secondary school education, and in colleges, universities, and centers of adult education.

The place of adult education in such a program is abundantly clear. In the Committee's mind it was an integral part of a fully developed educational system. For example, the Report stated:

An important function of our schools which is largely disregarded is education for the adult population. Institutional thinking customarily interests itself less in adult education than in the education of youth—even to the extent of assuming that graduates will, in the remaining forty or fifty years of their lives, acquire by themselves all the further learning they will need. Experience shows this assumption is unfounded. Moreover, as many of society's most crucial decisions will be made in the years immediately ahead, we cannot with safety neglect the very people upon whom we must depend for the shaping of democracy's destiny.

In addition, it was recognized that the adult lives in an intellectual environment heavily influenced by mass communications:

The Committee and its advisors paid considerable attention to the less-publicized types of education in our society which exist outside the schools. The formative and continuing influences of the home, the church, the school, college and university have been profoundly modified by the enormous development of such mass media as the newspaper, the magazine, cheap books, the moving picture, radio, and television. The motives which lead to the development of these means of communication are primarily commercial, and the media themselves tend to neglect the constructive educational influences which they might exert. Because the effects of these media are so strong upon the individual and so pervasive from early childhood to the end of life, they present many major problems for society, as well as for the individual. Their potentialities for constructive use of leisure time are immediately apparent. The necessity to elevate these media to appropriate educational standards is a serious challenge, since democracy may survive and grow only as its people acquire sane, realistic values and develop high capacity to reason for themselves.

In the discussion of what the Foundation could do in education, the point was developed more fully as follows:

Considerable stress has previously been placed upon the high degree of public apathy prevailing in this country and on the lack in the lives of many persons of a realistic and meaningful sense of values. While the causes of these conditions are far from clear, many of the Committee's advisors believe they bear an important relation to the content of mass communications. Further, the mass media play a profound role in the general education of youth, and have an effect in many instances far more powerful than that of our schools themselves.

Since the channels of mass communications—newspapers, magazines, inexpensive books, radio, movies, and television—are privately controlled, those who manage such enterprises should have a real sense of public responsibility. They must exercise a high regard for the effects upon their audiences of what they disseminate. Even though the mass media are restricted by the commercial considerations which make them possible, there exist means of leverage which should be supported. For one thing, important results might flow from a greater collaboration between researchers in public taste and interests and the persons in charge of mass communication media. Also, cooperation with non-commercial organizations concerned with mass communication offers promise. Additional opportunities are to be found for supporting individuals and groups who are interested in the artistic or educational effect of their efforts but who lack the financial resources required for continued activity. Commissions of inquiry, awards, and critical reviews have had notable effects in all these directions, and other techniques may be devised.

. . . .

As with the mass media, large unused potentialities exist in other nonacademic educational facilities for cultural enrichment and for the better use of leisure time. We have not utilized to the full such community resources as the forum, little theatres, concerts, libraries, and museums.[9] Adult education can be greatly furthered by the more effective use of such community facilities as well as by improvements in the content of mass communications.

This discussion made it quite obvious that in the Committee's view the problems confronting adult education could be but imperfectly understood without a sound knowledge of the mass media, and that adult education could not be entirely satisfactory without improvements in the mass media. It was practically obligatory on this reasoning for adult educators not only to understand the mass media in terms of their effects on their customers—itself a difficult and complicated job not yet satisfactorily executed—and to use mass-communication technical facilities, audio and visual, in educational work, but also to be prepared to "do something" about moderating the deficiencies of commercial mass communications and to assist in *their* utilization educationally. This emphasis was rather different from that of the President's Commission on Higher Education, which was satisfied with insisting alone on the use of the audio-visual devices in the educational process. When, then, the Ford Foundation divided the field of education and assigned to a Fund for Adult Education "that part of the total educational process which begins when schooling is finished" it was only to be expected that emphasis should fall not only on liberal, value-creating, adult education but also on the mass media of communications. However, no dogmatic prescription about who should sponsor adult education activities was offered.

Meanwhile the professional adult educators had surveyed the field in the light of the research that had been done through September, 1949.[10] It was found that there was still a confusion in many minds "between what is education and what is something else—propaganda or recreation. . . ." It was not commonly recognized that "adult education is something less extensive than the education of adults." Adult education, it was suggested, was a matter of "deliberate programs carried out by groups or agencies," not the complicated matter of accidents, by-products, and inadvertencies which make up so much of the education of adults. As an educational undertaking, adult education was still fighting for a recognized place, not only in the community (as we have noted Burch contending), but also in the educational world of which it was indisputably a part. It was asking for parity with elementary, secondary, and higher education, but parity had not yet been granted. Reflecting the imperfect differentiation and definition of the field, it was still true that "only a relatively small number of people engaged in adult education call themselves adult educators." There was, of course, no clear, widely accepted location of responsibility for programs; nor were the responsibilities of agencies long in the field—like the public schools—at all clear even to the agencies themselves. The field had never been rationalized; it was a jungle; it was notably recalcitrant even to minimum rationalization, as within particular segments like that sponsored by public educational institutions of various levels; and perhaps it should not be rationalized by plan at all.

While the subject matter of adult education was recognized to be "as broad and complex as the knowledge and understanding of mankind," much of the ground remained uncovered by existing programs in spite of the vast number of groups and agencies in the field. Moreover, while adult educators had made considerable progress in ordering content in a fashion suitable for adults, the escape from the tradition of borrowing directly from elementary schools, secondary schools, colleges, and universities was not yet entire.

A help toward the establishment of adult education as a thing-in-itself was the marked weakening of the notion that its primary task was to remedy deficiencies in the education of individuals at various levels of schooling, but it was recognized that remedial work would always remain *one* of the tasks of adult education as far into the future as anybody could see.

On this showing, neither urgent calls to wider action, nor optimism about future prospects could conceal the fact that the leaders and workers in the field had much to do to get their own house in order.

Their general thinking in the late forties was reported to have been characterized by recognition of the need to "seek democracy deliberately," a view which coheres very well with the suggested genesis of the prevailing optimism; by an emphasis on the need to develop "vital" communities—i.e., both to seek the point of departure for adult education in the concrete circumstances of the people at the community level and to judge results largely in terms of improvement in the community "tone"; by a concentration of interest on the management of groups for maximum educative effectiveness; and by the conviction that the ultimate goal was "the development of more mature adults."

If the literature of these "trends" of thought could be examined, it would be found to contain in each instance old and new elements, entertaining cases of violent hobbyhorse riding, and a general overconcentration on ways and means rather than on questions of substance and ends. Democracy, certainly; but what is democracy? Why could so highly intelligent a man as E. M. Forster give it but two cheers? [11] Emphasis on the community, of course; for it is in the community that adult education necessarily takes place, not in the stratosphere. But where does a reasonable recognition of the claims of the community end and community-worship, a fetishism as disastrous as state-worship, begin? [12] Comprehension of the creative management of groups, beyond a doubt, particularly the relation of the members to the leader; but is the aim to learn how individual men can best be educated in groups (an inescapable necessity to some unknown extent), or is it to promote something rather distasteful called group-thinking which points unmistakably to that public menace, the mass man? And what, oh what, is a mature man? Is not the danger that a predefined pattern, consciously or unconsciously formulated, will be imposed on men of a wide variety of potential maturities? Is there really a pattern of the mature democratic man, as there is alleged to be one of the Soviet man, and if so, who defined him and who planned his planners, and what was their purpose?

PART V

ADULT EDUCATION:

IDEA AND REALITY

The Road Ahead

THE IDEA of adult education has a way of appearing more attractive than the practice at any particular moment. Looking closely at the practice, one has a strong feeling that this collection of trees simply does not naturally make a wood and that no amount of verbal ingenuity can conjure one into existence. The feeling that there is a gap between idea and practice afflicts the professionals as well as outside observers. The professionals seek to exorcise the resulting distress by giving an intense loyalty to that fraction of the field to which they are personally committed and a much weaker allegiance to the field as a whole. The trees have a meaning fairly easy to define in exact terms; the wood of which they are theoretically a part has only that meaning which finds expression in a loose, diffuse rhetoric lacking in any very specific reference. The whole seems forever to be less than the sum of the parts, the wood less impressive than particular trees in it, the reality markedly inferior to the idea.

Progress toward making the wood of adult education as admirable to the view of all observers as some of the individual trees now are, can only come as more trees worthy of admiration grow through the underbrush and reach toward the sky, and as trees now growing strongly are pruned by well-aimed criticism and enriched by skillful grafting.

The points of growth in American adult education in the early nineteen-fifties were commonly identified as the public-school programs, the programs of the community colleges, university extension, and the library programs—or, in short, those programs stemming from established education institutions, mostly as additions to the "structured" educational system. If it is the number of customers one has in mind, this identification is probably correct, but if considerations of quality are to be taken into account, emphasis must also be placed on the creative contributions of privately managed and supported programs, often experimental, which when proved successful and rewarding will enrich all adult education culturally. Any really candid observer of adult education in America today will feel strongly that progress in numbers within the existing framework is somehow less important than progress in the cultural enrichment of the field. What we need today is education-in-depth as a defence-in-depth against the tragic life in which, God wot, so many villains flourish. Yet such an observer will know that continued multiplication of numbers is far more certain than general cultural enrichment of programs.

Since adult education is but one of the mechanisms at work bringing to wayfaring men the knowledge and understanding they need to manage their lives, the whole of the cultural problem cannot be understood within the framework of adult education itself, nor can the best focus for its activities be determined by adult education criteria alone. At this moment in human history, the useful citizen is the man who brings expertness and efficiency to his vocation and who acts wisely in his private and public life. Adult education thus far has done its best job in promoting expertness and efficiency in vocations, its least remarkable job in cultivating wisdom in the management of private and public affairs. It is now painfully obvious, however, that until we bring our interest and concern for wisdom at least to equality with our concern for vocational skill, we run the risk of catastrophic disaster at some unidentifiable moment in the future. This being just about an inevitable conclusion from any analysis of the general situation in which man today finds himself, it follows that adult education, insofar as it may be regarded as a responsible activity, should today be deeply concerned to correct the characteristic imbalance it has long suffered and give particular attention to those subjects which will contribute to the wise management of private and public affairs.

What are those subjects? The writer takes a wider view of them than some may regard as justifiable. He thinks they are the humanities, the social sciences, the arts, and science.

On the record, it is clear that the managers of adult education have had least success in making these fields of interest continuously parts of their programs. Sporadic appearance and disappearance has characterized their history. This would seem to mean that they have rarely been found by wayfaring men to meet needs as urgent as those served by vocational studies. The common reason given by adult educators for the general failure to promote them successfully is that the customers will not "buy" them. However, evidence is now multiplying that market resistance is diminishing, but it is not at all clear either that adult education is responsible for this or that it is taking advantage of the fact.

Certain it is that American adult education (at least since the decline of Chautauqua's influence) has had very little to do with the vast diffusion and acceptance of superior music in America. Nor can it be said that the vast increase of interest in painting— whether on the side of those who find aesthetic pleasure in viewing pictures in museums, at shows by living artists, in portable reproductions,[1] or in personally-owned pictures hung in their homes; or on the side of those who are experimenting in making pictures of their own—owes much to adult education. Rather these developments appear to flow from great changes in the cultural climate which the late Frederick P. Keppel, who took a keen interest in these matters, dated from *circa* 1876–1893, with a marked change in a favorable direction beginning after World War I.

Similarly with the humanities and the social sciences. Insofar as these have made their way forward in recent years as fields of interest for adults, the progress is more to be attributed to the writing activities of academicians and nonacademic intellectuals, than to anything adult educators have done systematically to sustain and promote such studies.

The case of science is a trifle ambiguous. Certainly there has been no lack of effort on the part of adult educators to diffuse knowledge of science as fact, or knowledge of currently prevailing theories—this task, as we noted, was assumed very early in the history of adult education and stimulated its growth—and even more energy has gone into diffusing knowledge of the facts and theories of science in their vocational usages. But these are not the aspects of science with which we are concerned here. Rather our concern is with instruction of the kind that would give incisive insight into the ways in which the minds of great scientists have operated, what they were like as persons, and which would convey an enduring understanding of science *as method*. To be sure, adult educators cannot be heavily blamed for their failure to utilize this approach for the simple reason that it has but lately been explored in a preliminary way, notably by James Bryant Conant and some active teachers of the history of science. But certainly if adult educators are wise, they will soon seize upon it, if only to insure that more of the denizens of a scientific civilization are intelligent about science than is now the case.

All the evidence points to the conclusion that the time is at hand to exploit as growing points for the cultural enrichment of adult education: music, the plastic arts, the humanities, the social sciences, and science (as defined). Long ago, during the American Revolution, John Adams wrote from Paris to his wife Abigail: "My duty is to study the science of government that my sons may have the liberty to study mathematics and science. My sons ought to study geography, navigation, commerce, and agriculture in order to give their children a right to study philosophy, painting, poetry, music, architecture, sculpture, tapestry, and porcelain." [2] Surely it is not entirely fanciful to argue that we have today reached the last stage in John Adams' suggested progression. (Adult educators also like to recall that John's grandson Henry devoted but some thirty pages of *The Education of Henry Adams* to his schooling and over four hundred to his education as an adult.)

This speculation opens up both an attractive and a frightening vista, for the possibility of enriching the culture of wayfaring men is vastly heartening in this day of pessimistic talk about mass-culture of a low grade; but the problems of discovering how to deal with these fields in such a fashion as to capture and retain the interest of an appreciable number of adults are frighteningly complex. Work on these problems has barely begun, even though great pioneers like Thomas Whitney Surette in music and John Cotton Dana in the plastic arts, both of whom worked in adult education, are already figures of the past. But nothing ventured, nothing gained. If adult education is ever to capture its proper place in the national community, it is precisely on the side of quality that it most needs to be venturesome.

To deal with the task successfully, adult education will have to deal forthrightly with some very difficult internal problems, notably the problems of personnel, leadership, and money.

It has already been said in passing that surprisingly few of those who are today engaged in adult education are trained specifically for the teaching of adults. Either on the one hand they are trained to teach children or adolescents, or on the other they have no pedagogical training at all; and in both cases, as Professor Wilbur Hallenbeck has pointed out, "they were pushed into their jobs by circumstances." [3] Moreover, only a fraction of the workers, whatever their training, are occupied full-time with adult education, either as of the moment or on a career basis. For the teachers as for the clientele, adult education is usually a detour on the way to somewhere else. Until lately the greatest single concentration of full-time, trained adult teachers was in Agricultural Extension. Today it is a reasonable speculation that professional training is far more common (but not universal) among the directing and supervising personnel of adult education than among the personnel, whether part- or full-time, actually dealing with adults in classes, discussion groups, etc. Plainly there is an acute need to increase the number of workers in adult education who have training for the work, for it is well known that many people are put off from adult education by the poor quality of the instruction.

The annoying fact, however, is that although it is a quarter-century since such specialized training was first offered,[4] it is still far from clear of what the training should consist. All too often it is simply training in method. The writer is going to take advantage of his status as an outsider with regard to education to say quite bluntly that method is far from enough. American teachers of teachers have lost sight of the wisdom of A. N. Whitehead's remark, "Some of the major disasters of mankind have been produced by the narrowness of men with good methodology." The American people have suffered bitterly and unnecessarily from the depredations of men and women, notably engineers and teachers, well instructed in methodology, but imperfectly educated otherwise. The time has come when it is vital that we find out how to insure that our teachers are educated. We must beware of those educators whose sole content is method; it is extremely difficult to take seriously people who call themselves educators but about whom it is impossible to gain the conviction that they are educated. This is not an argument for ignorance of method, but rather an argument for a proper evaluation of method.[5] In any reasonable perspective, teachers should at least be well-instructed in the subjects they assume to teach, at most be well-educated, and in either case professionally competent (which means, privy to the best pedagogical methods). The sequence of qualities is deliberately meaningful. Nowhere is this more vital than in adult education, for there is small hope that adults are going to take seriously the call to lifelong education if they suspect that those assuming to educate them have small claim to being educated themselves. Adult education must strive constantly to enlist better teachers, more of them, more on a full-time basis, and more on a career basis. The historical record shows what a wide range of indisputably educated men and women have taken a hand in the work in times past, and this by itself gives hope for the future.

The transition from personnel to leadership seems easy, but some confusion is bound to arise from the specialized way in which adult educators are now using the word "leader." It is pointless to interrupt the flow of the argument here to analyze the particularistic usage, so it will instead be stated that here "leader" is used only in the traditional sense as referring to men and women who show the way—to those who, by their superior attainments or characteristics of personality, convey to others a sense of being worthy of special allegiance; and also to those who are worthy of acceptance by men with their critical faculties alive as guides to thought and action in the present and toward the future.

Adult education needs such leaders at all levels and in all wings of its activities. Much turns upon what kinds of leaders it gets and accepts. The writer shares the opinion of those whose view Robert Luke has phrased as follows: "Adult education as a field will never be able to exert itself until it is led—not by program technicians as at present—but by the physical scientists, political leaders, theologians, writers, economic philosophers, artists and others who are responsible for directing (or giving expression to) current influences in public opinion, moral values, and artistic standards in American life today." Only leaders so described can give cohesion to a highly fragmentized field like adult education where the whole has such a striking tendency to be less than the sum of its parts. The old AAAE was on the right track when it selected presidents who in some sense were of the character just suggested, for quite apart from any active leadership they may have given to AAAE, they had great symbolic value to adult education as an activity. Their presence in office let the public know that men of stature regarded adult education as very important.

Moreover, if there is one thing that adult education needs more than any other if it is to do its proper work, it is the confirmation of its collaboration with the intelligentsia, academic and lay, which has characterized its history—the writer has been at pains to scatter names freely through this essay to illustrate this point—from the earliest days to the present time. The intelligentsia of the United States spend an unconscionable amount of time bemoaning the fact that communication between them and the people is difficult, if it is not assumed to have broken down altogether. Surely adult education offers one means for re-establishing or confirming communications between the two groups; and perhaps at some future date a man of the stature of Emerson will once again try out his essays as talks to, or bases of discussion with, adults assembled to learn. If this is ever to happen again, every effort must be put into strengthening adult education in its cultural phases. Linked with those who conserve, create, and advance the moral and cultural values of America, adult education will be helped to gain the strength and stature it must have to do its proper work of cultural diffusion.[6]

There is no single, simple answer to the money question. It will be recalled that the President's Commission on Higher Education expressed the opinion that the institutions of higher education should spend a hundred million dollars a year on extension. Up to the present time this has not been done, but it is fairly certain that a good deal more than a hundred million has been spent on adult education of all kinds in recent years.[7] Yet even this vast expenditure is not enough.

Such expansion of adult education as takes place in the future from such bases as public schools, community colleges, universities, and libraries will in part be financed from public taxes and in part from students' fees. Most other expansion will probably depend on students' fees. Some money will be supplied by foundation grants.

Lurking here is a three-part question: Should adults, in most instances self-supporting members of the community, pay for their own adult education at rates which will make the service self-supporting? Or should they be able to claim it as a "free" service, the cost to be a charge on public revenue or private philanthropy? Or should it be a matter of nominal fees plus public or private subsidization? Unless one detects a moral issue lurking here, as the writer does not, it would seem reasonable to let expediency rule and allow all three modes of financing the field continue simultaneously, the choice among them to be dictated by circumstances, with possibly a bias in favor of fees large enough to make the venture self-supporting. Especially will it be necessary for private ventures to be in a position to command fees; and the health of the field depends in considerable measure upon the number and strength of private, experimental, ventures. At all levels of its activities, adult education and adult educators should be able to command that kind of support which will allow them to maintain their independence and self-respect, able to stand up straight, strong, and free.

Shrewd readers who have followed the writer to this point will have been wondering whether he has not been writing lately without reckoning on the attitudes of the final arbiters of adult education, the customers, actual and potential. Not at all. What has been written has been written in full consciousness of the fact of "apathy" (however defined or explained), of those difficulties inherent in bridging the gap between high and popular culture (including the language bar), of the difficulty of demonstrating the high utility of the nonutilitarian, of the difficulty of surmounting a sense of cultural inadequacy in the customers, of the need for exorcising the notion that age makes learning impossible, and of the trials involved in dealing with persistent persons called yearners (not learners.)[8] These burdens have not been forgotten. Rather they have been carefully filed under the label *Permanent Challenges to Adult Educators*. They are the difficulties to which the flesh of adult educators is inescapably heir; they perpetually cast their dark, enigmatic shadows over the adult educator's world. They cause the adult educator to select as his private hero, not Hercules cleaning out the Augean stables with celerity, but Sisyphus of Corinth eternally rolling his stone up the hill.

Notes

PART I. ADULT EDUCATION AND ITS SOCIAL CONTEXT

Chapter 1. DEFINITION AND IMPLICATIONS

1. Lyman Bryson, *Adult Education* (New York, 1936), p. 3.
2. F. A. Cavenagh (ed.), *James and John Stuart Mill on Education* (Cambridge, England, 1931), pp. 132-133.
3. *General Education in a Free Society* (Cambridge, Mass., 1945), p. 256.
4. Lundberg, Komarovsky, and McInerny, in their pioneering book —George A. Lundberg, *et al., Leisure: A Suburban Study* (New York, 1934)—presented the following conclusions on leisure use in West-chester County: "We have found that seven broad categories of activity today occupy ninety per cent or more of the leisure time of nearly all people in the area we have studied. The most important and common of these activities is the daily ceremonial of eating with its attendant sociability. . . . The feeding complex, together with that of 'visiting' which it largely overlaps, occupies almost half of the total leisure of most people. . . . The remainder of people's leisure is variously dis-tributed between reading, public entertainment, sports, radio, motoring, and a multitude of miscellaneous items." (p. 365.) Adult education found its place among the miscellaneous items.
5. Victor Grove, *The Language Bar* (New York, 1950).

PART II. ADULT EDUCATION HAS DEEP ROOTS

Chapter 2. PRELITERATE MAN LEADS THE WAY

1. M. J. Herskovits, *Man and His Works* (New York, 1951), pp. 39 f.
2. E. A. Speiser, "The Beginnings of Civilization in Mesopotamia,"

311

Journal of The American Oriental Society, Supplement, 1939, pp. 17-31.

Chapter 3. THE GREEKS ON THE EDUCATED ADULT

1. Werner Jaeger's *Paideia: The Ideals of Great Culture* is very briefly quoted several times in this chapter. An English translation in three volumes has been published (New York, 1939–44).
2. H. D. F. Kitto, *The Greeks* (A Pelican Book), p. 219.
3. Oxford, 1913.
4. A. J. Toynbee (ed.), *Greek Historical Thought* (A Mentor Book), p. xxiii.
5. A. E. Taylor, "Socrates," *Encyclopaedia Britannica* (14th ed.), XX, 918.
6. J. B. Bury, *A History of Freedom of Thought* (New York, 1913), p. 30.
7. A. E. Taylor, *Socrates* (Boston, 1951), pp. 165-166.
8. A. E. Taylor, *Platonism and its Influence* (Boston, 1924), pp. 59-62.
9. As translated by W. D. Ross in *The Basic Works of Aristotle*, ed. Richard McKeon (New York, 1941), pp. 935 ff.
10. John L. Stocks, *Aristotelianism* (Boston, 1925), pp. 89-90.

Chapter 4. ROME: A PROBLEM IN CULTURAL DIFFUSION

1. Valuable insights into the situation under the Romans (and the Greeks, too) are to be gained from a reading of Moses Hadas, *Ancilla to Classical Reading* (New York, 1954).
2. Jerome Carcopino, *Daily Life in Ancient Rome* (New Haven, 1940).
3. It is suggestive of the differentiation of the intelligentsia according to the audience served that in the time of the Emperor Vespasian when the "philosophers" were expelled from Rome for subversion, they were divided into (1) nonteaching philosophers, (2) professors, (3) public lecturers, and (4) popular, or street, philosophers.
4. Comparable cases are those of Koine in late Greek times and of English in our own time. The compulsory learning of Russian in the satellites of the USSR is obviously intended to open up more and more minds directly to Soviet "culture," an implicit recognition of the point made here.
5. M. I. Rostovtzeff, *Social and Economic History of the Roman Empire* (New York, 1926), pp. 486-487.

Chapter 5. EDUCATING MEDIEVAL MAN: THINGS HEARD AND SEEN

1. See L. J. Sherrill, *The Rise of Christian Education* (New York, 1944), especially p. 186.
2. Gilbert Highet, *The Classical Tradition* (New York, 1949), p. 538.
3. A. R. Myers, *England in the Late Middle Ages* (A Pelican Book), p. 62.
4. G. R. Owst, *Literature and Pulpit in Mediaeval England* (Cambridge, England, 1933).
5. On the impact of itinerant preachers in the fifteenth century see J. Huizinga, *The Waning of the Middle Ages* (Anchor ed., 1954), pp. 12-14, 277.

Chapter 6. TOWARD MODERN TIMES

1. The printed book began the process which, when the newspaper and the magazine, and the radio and television were added, became what is currently called mass communications. Printing signalized, as Schramm has pointed out, a swing of the balance "from the long centuries of spoken first-hand communication toward visual and second-hand communication on a large scale. The importance of the development in the nineteenth century is that some of the limits were taken off communication; it was extended, over the heads of the specially privileged and the specially able, to the masses who had need of it. And the importance of the recent electronic developments is that the balance of the communication channels is again swung back toward spoken and seemingly first-hand communication, although to fantastically large audiences." [Wilbur Schramm (ed.), *Mass Communications* (Urbana, Ill., 1949), p. 3.] This is the communication context of modern adult education. See also Bernard Berelson and Morris Janowitz (eds.), *Reader in Public Opinion and Communication* (Glencoe, Ill., 1950).
2. D. C. McMurtie, *The Golden Book* (New York, 1931), pp. 167-168.
3. Lyman Bryson, *The Drive Toward Reason* (New York, 1954).
4. Quoted in J. U. Nef, *War and Human Progress* (Cambridge, Mass., 1950), p. 232.

PART III. THE BRITISH RECORD: ADULT EDUCATION IN AN INDUSTRIAL SOCIETY

Chapter 7. SHALL THE LABORING POOR BE LITERATE?

1. Quoted in J. A. Thomas, "The Man Who Taught His Nation to Read," *Fundamental and Adult Education,* IV, No. 4 (October, 1952), p. 8.

2. David Williams, *A History of Modern Wales* (London, 1950), p. 147.

3. W. J. Warner, *The Wesleyan Movement in the Industrial Revolution* (London, 1930), pp. 230-231.

4. W. F. Lloyd, *Sketch of the Life of Robert Raikes* (New York, 1879), pp. 83-84.

5. *Ibid.,* p. 86.

6. J. W. Hudson, Ph.D., *The History of Adult Education* (London, 1851).

7. Bristol, England, 1816.

8. J. W. Rowntree and H. B. Binns, *A History of the Adult School Movement* (London, 1903).

Chapter 8. THE UTILITARIAN APPROACH: SDUK AND MECHANICS' INSTITUTES

1. See Cavenagh, *op. cit.*

2. John Stuart Mill, *Autobiography* (New York, 1924), p. 63.

3. Printed in full in C. F. Harrold (ed.), *Essays and Sketches by John Henry, Cardinal Newman* (New York, 1948), pp. 173 ff.

4. The sponsors of the University of London (founded 1828) included the following persons identified with adult education: Jeremy Bentham, James Mill, Lord Brougham, George Birkbeck. The University was designed to counter the Oxford and Cambridge influence and promote the utilitarian approach of its founders, using Scottish organizational forms.

5. The prospectus of the Edinburgh School of Arts (one of the several alternative names of mechanics' institutions), published in 1821, declared: "The great object of this Institution is to supply, at such expense as a working tradesman can afford, instruction in the various branches of Science which are of practical application to mechanics in their several trades, so that they may the better comprehend the reason for each individual operation that passes through their

hands, and have more certain rules to follow than the mere imitation of what they have seen done by another. It is not intended to teach [trades] . . ."

6. On the vexed question of popularization, Birkbeck declared in 1800: "Whatever the arrogance of learning may have advanced, in condemnation of superficial knowledge, and however firmly persuaded I may be that the people cannot be profound, I have no hesitation in predicting that vast benefit will accrue to the community by every successful endeavor to diffuse the substance of great works; which cannot be perused by the people at large; thereby making them reach the shop and the hamlet, and converting them from unproductive splendor to useful though unobserved utility."

7. Harriet Martineau (1802–1876) was the author of *Illustrations of Political Economy* and other works popularizing economic orthodoxy. In her day she was enormously influential.

8. J. L. and B. Hammond, *The Bleak Age* (A Pelican Book, 1947), p. 146.

9. *Ibid.*, p. 166.

10. *An Essay on The History and Management of Literary, Scientific, and Mechanics' Institutions* (London, 1853), pp. 65-66. It is, of course, impossible to say exactly when the English mind became mature enough to allow ideas to be evaluated by the free competition of the market place—i.e., by free discussion—but it is notable that both John Stuart Mill and Walter Bagehot, writing during the last half of the nineteenth century, regarded public discussion as the essential characteristic of liberal democratic society.

11. Thomas De Quincey, writing on the problem of self-education in the early eighteen-fifties, said: "Lectures? These, whether public or private, are surely the very worst modes of acquiring any sort of accurate knowledge; and are just as much inferior to a good book on the same subject, as that book hastily read aloud, and then immediately withdrawn, would be inferior to the same book left in your possession, and open at any hour, to be consulted, retraced, collated, and in the fullest sense studied." However, lectures do have a place in adult education, though perhaps a minor one. The writer found no treatise on "the lecture" in England, though he is well aware that many of the great literary figures gave lectures, e.g., W. M. Thackeray, William Hazlitt, Thomas Carlyle, etc.

12. Quoted from J. W. Adamson, *English Education, 1789–1902* (Cambridge, England, 1930), p. 41.

Chapter 9. SEARCH FOR A FIRM BASE FOR ADULT EDUCATION

1. Hammond, *op. cit.*, p. 236.
2. *Ibid.*, p. 203.

3. Substance in G. C. Martin, *The Adult School Movement* (London, 1924), pp. 135-137.

4. See article "Christian Socialism" in *Encyclopedia of the Social Sciences*, III, 449.

5. A. E. Dobbs, *Education and Social Movements, 1700–1850* (London, 1919), p. 183.

6. F. D. Maurice, *Learning and Working* (Cambridge, England, 1855), p. 170.

7. Quoted in M. E. Sadler (ed.), *Continuation Schools* (Manchester, England, 1908), p. 42.

8. Quoted in Adamson, *op. cit.*, p. 168.

9. Ministry of Reconstruction, Adult Education Committee, *Final Report* (London, 1919), p. 25.

10. See James Stuart, *Reminiscences* (London, 1912), pp. 150-165.

11. B. A. Yeaxlee, *Spiritual Values in Adult Education* (Oxford, England, 1925), I, 279. The range of subjects was wide: ancient and modern history and literature, natural science, political science, economics, and art.

12. On Toynbee, see F. C. Montague, *Arnold Toynbee* (Baltimore, 1889). The final quote is at p. 42.

Chapter 10. EDUCATING WAYFARERS AT THE UNIVERSITY LEVEL

1. Although this characterization ("university level") has been subjected to criticism, as, for example, in the great adult education *Report* of 1919 (see note 9, chap. 9, *supra*) described below, it seems to have survived the passage of time as a convenient bit of shorthand. In the 1919 *Report* we read that "the standards of work done in a university, ranging from that of a passman to that of the scholar, are so various as to make such a phrase meaningless." Apparently the irreducible meaning of the phrase is that the work, whatever its actual quality, is carried out under university auspices.

2. Quoted in Sadler, *op. cit.*, p. 46.

3. Albert Mansbridge in Sadler, *op. cit.*, p. 370.

4. The classic statement of the case for Oxford's collaboration in working-class education was *Oxford and Working-class Education: Being the Report of a Joint Committee of University and Working-class Representative on the Relation of the University to the Higher Education of Workpeople*, originally published in 1908 and reprinted as lately as 1951. A wonderfully vivid story of the individual suffering caused by the exclusion of a poor man is Thomas Hardy's famous novel, *Jude the Obscure* (1896). Hardy has Jude say: "I love the place [the University]—though I know how it hates all men like me—the so-called self-taught—how it scorns our labored acquisitions, when it should be the first to respect them; how it sneers at our false quan-

tities and mispronunciations, when it should say, I see you want help, my poor friend!" It is interesting to note that Jude aspired, not to economic and political knowledge, but to classical and theological learning. At the crisis of the novel is this passage: " 'Nothing can be done,' he replied. 'Things are as they are, and will be brought to their destined issue.' She paused. 'Yes! Who said that?' she asked heavily. 'It comes in the chorus of the Agamemnon. It has been in my mind continually since this happened.' 'My poor Jude—how you've missed everything!— you more than I, for I did get you! To think you should know that by your unassisted reading, and yet be in poverty and despair.' "

5. Mary E. Stocks, *WEA: The First Fifty Years* (London, 1953).

6. Ministry of Reconstruction, Adult Education Committee, *Final Report* (London, 1919).

7. S. J. Curtis, *History of Education in Great Britain* (London, 1950), p. 472.

8. Asa Briggs, "A Silent Revolution," *The Listener*, L, No. 1275 (August 6, 1953), pp. 213 ff.

9. See *Report of the Ministry of Education, 1950,* chap. V, ¶ 32.

Chapter 11. THE POSITION TODAY

1. W. E. Williams, *The Auxiliaries of Adult Education* (London, 1934).

2. *The Economist,* October 24, 1953, p. 236.

3. Two forceful critical articles on correspondence courses, especially those in technological and business subjects, were printed in *The Economist,* October 4 and 11, 1952.

4. *Adult Education after the War: A Report of an Enquiry Made for the British Institute of Adult Education* (London, 1945), pp. 9-10.

5. *Ibid.,* p. 2. (*My italics.*)

6. See especially Guy Hunter, *Residential Colleges,* "Occasional Papers of The Fund for Adult Education," No. 1 (New York, 1952).

PART IV.   THE AMERICAN STORY: TOWARD CULTURAL DEMOCRACY?

Chapter 12. BEGINNINGS OF ADULT EDUCATION IN AMERICA

1. H. T. Buckle, *History of Civilization in England* (New York, 1880), I, 174-175. The work was originally published in 1857–62.

2. A recent and pertinent illustration of how knowledge can on

occasion be rapidly diffused in the United States is the extraordinary coverage given in newspapers and magazines to *Sexual Behavior in the Human Female* by Kinsey, Pomeroy, Martin, and Gebhard in the fall of 1953.

3. G. M. Waller (ed.), *Puritanism in Early America* (Boston, 1950), p. 12.

4. Other terms applied to the groups are informal, primary, natural, and face-to-face. For a recent discussion of them see H. H. Doddy, *Informal Groups and the Community* (New York, 1952).

5. Adrienne Koch and William Peden (eds.), *The Life and Selected Writings of Thomas Jefferson* (Modern Library ed., 1944), pp. 597-598.

6. Merle Curti, *The Growth of American Thought* (2nd ed., New York, 1951).

7. *The Papers of The Bibliographical Society of America*, 35 (1941, 2nd Quarter).

Chapter 13. JOSIAH HOLBROOK, THE LYCEUM, AND PUBLIC LECTURES

1. In addition to the secondary influence of Bentham through Lord Brougham, there is the interesting fact that John Neal of Maine (who lived for two years in Bentham's household in London, published in America a book of Bentham's table-talk, and filled his novels with Benthamism) was active in the Maine Lyceums and in the national organization. The Benthamite outlook appealed to Americans and the American outlook to Bentham, who, writing to President Jackson, said that he was "more of a United-States-man than an English-man."

2. A pen-and-ink drawing of a Lyceum lecture in 1841, by James Pollard Espy, appears in *The Columbia Historical Portrait of New York* (New York, 1953), p. 173.

3. In his *History of Education in the United States,* cited in C. B. Hayes, *The American Lyceum* (Washington: U. S. Dept. of Interior, Bulletin No. 12, 1932).

4. One of the most illuminating books on the history of lectures the writer has seen is David Mead, *Yankee Eloquence in the Middle West: The Ohio Lyceum, 1850–1870* (East Lansing, Mich., 1951). This book covers institutions, personalities, subject matter of lectures, audience reaction, and so on.

5. A biography of this remarkable man who contributed so much to establishing the tradition of popular education in science on the one hand, and to college and graduate-school scientific education on the other is J. F. Fulton and E. H. Thompson, *Benjamin Silliman, 1779–1864* (New York, 1947). Chapter XI is "Presenting Science to the Public, 1834–1857."

6. With this reference to music we imperceptibly move over into

the field of the support and appreciation of the arts, a matter allied to adult education but more satisfactorily discussed in a wider context than "lecturing." The same reasoning applies also to the drama and the theater, the ballet, painting, etc. Training for both appreciation and participation in the arts is, of course, an important aspect of adult education.

7. What adults? A study of Des Moines, Iowa, forum audiences (1349 persons replying) gave the following occupational breakdown:

Professional	396
Semiprofessional	188
Skilled	213
Semiskilled	66
Unskilled	10
Unemployed	72
Students	91
Housewives	281
Not given	32
	1,349

Of these people 74 reported grade-school education only, 418 high-school, and 857 college education. The data fit very well with observations made elsewhere on the audience for adult education.

Chapter 14. CHAUTAUQUA: THE CULTURAL STRIVING OF SMALL TOWNS

1. These adaptations to changing times are usually associated with the successive leaders. Vincent was succeeded by his son George who was in charge from 1904 to 1915 (and later was successively president of the University of Minnesota and the Rockefeller Foundation). He shifted the emphasis to psychology and the humanities. His successor, Dr. Arthur E. Bestor, in charge 1919–44, emphasized citizenship. In late years the vacation note has been stronger. See *The Chautauqua Jubilee Sketchbook* (Chautauqua, N. Y., 1949).

2. Correspondence teaching of adults has a history running back at least to 1873, when the Society to Encourage Studies at Home was founded in Boston. It never served more than a limited number of persons, mostly housewives. A Correspondence University was founded in 1883 at Ithaca, New York, with professors from thirty-seven colleges—including Johns Hopkins, Harvard, and Wisconsin—collaborating, but with no formal relation to any particular college. William Rainey Harper was a pioneer believer in correspondence teaching. He began his work when he was at the Baptist Union Theological Seminary, took it with him to Yale and Chautauqua, and, eventually, the University of Chicago. The idea began its spread through the universities, in association with extension, in the eighteen-nineties. The private

correspondence schools, perhaps rather better known to the general public, are conventionally dated from 1891, the founding date of the International Correspondence Schools at Scranton, Pennsylvania. Since 1926 the private schools, which have always been most important in vocational training, have been inspected and approved by the National Home Study Council of Washington, D. C. (founded with Carnegie Corporation backing as an offshoot of its interest in adult education), which issues an annual *Home Study Blue Book*.

3. J. H. Vincent, *The Chautauqua Movement* (Boston, 1886), pp. 183 ff.

4. R. T. Ely, *Ground Under Our Feet* (New York, 1938), p. 79.

5. Quoted from A. M. Schlesinger, Sr., *The Rise of the City, 1878–1898* (New York, 1933), pp. 172-173.

6. See *The Letters of William James,* edited by Henry James (Boston, 1920), II, 40-44.

7. William James, *Talks to Teachers* (New York, 1915), pp. 268-271, 273. Permission to reprint granted by Paul R. Reynolds & Son, 599 Fifth Avenue, New York, 17.

8. For the background of Bryan's turn to Chautauqua, see Paxton Hibben and C. Hartley Grattan, *The Peerless Leader: William Jennings Bryan* (New York, 1929), pp. 209-210.

9. Since music was important in all the Chautauquas, the Chautauqua influence on musical taste in America must have been immense, probably the greatest single influence before the coming of the radio. Yet the writer has found no reference to this in any book or article.

10. H. S. Commager, *The American Mind* (New Haven, 1950), p. 407.

Chapter 15. HIGHER EDUCATIONAL INSTITUTIONS AND ADULT
EDUCATION

1. Or, to care for activities stemming from colleges and junior colleges, simply "extension" work. Here the term "university extension" will be used to cover all work of the general character. Usually the work is done at the *college* level.

2. S. Ditzion, *Arsenals of Democratic Culture* (Chicago, 1947).

3. 1890–1900: 236 local centers serviced, of which 45 were in Philadelphia, 110 in Pennsylvania outside the city, 34 in New Jersey, and the rest (47) scattered in Delaware, Maryland, New York, Massachusetts, Maine, Colorado, and Louisiana. See *Ten Years of the ASEUT, 1890–1900* (pamphlet, Philadelphia, 1901).

4. Pamphlet, *supra.*

5. Columbia, Indiana, Iowa State, Pennsylvania State, Harvard, State University of Iowa, California, Chicago, Colorado, Idaho, Kansas, Michigan, Minnesota, Missouri, North Carolina, Oklahoma, Pennsyl-

vania, Pittsburgh, South Carolina, South Dakota, Virginia, and Wisconsin.

6. M. Curti and V. Carstensen, *The University of Wisconsin, 1848–1925* (Madison, Wisc., 1949), p. 559. This work should be consulted on the whole episode.

7. Quoted in James Creese, *Extension of University Teaching* (New York, 1941), p. 54.

8. *Ibid.*, p. 51.

9. In J. R. Morton, *University Extension in the United States* (Tuscaloosa, Ala., 1953).

10. Who among the businessmen pioneered the policy of encouraging and assisting his employees to take advantage of adult education opportunities the writer has not ascertained, but he suggests the possibility that it was John Wanamaker, the Philadelphia merchant.

Chapter 16. TEACHING ADULTS AGRICULTURE AND THE MECHANIC ARTS

1. E. de S. Brunner and E. H. P. Yang, *Rural America and the Extension Service* (New York, 1949), p. 1.

2. The Farm Bureau was first organized at Binghampton, N. Y., in 1913 and spread nationally from a Cornell Farmers' Week in 1919. It was organized on a national basis at Chicago in March, 1920. Aside from *ad hoc* local committees, other organizations involved in, or exerting influence upon, Agricultural Extension are the Farmers' Union (founded 1902), the National Grange (founded 1867), and the buying and selling co-operatives.

3. For Agricultural Extension in its context of general farm policy, see Murray R. Benedict, *Farm Policies in the United States, 1790–1950* (New York, 1953).

4. Carl Van Doren, *Benjamin Franklin* (New York, 1938), p. 178.

5. Quoted from an article, "Elkanah Watson," in *Encyclopedia of the Social Sciences*, XV, 385.

6. Conventionally credit for this act goes to Justin S. Morrill, Senator from Vermont, for his name was attached to it in Congress, but at least equal credit certainly should be given to Jonathan Baldwin Turner, the Massachusetts-born president of Illinois College, Jacksonville, Illinois, who evolved and promoted the idea of "industrial" universities from 1850. During the campaign of 1860 Abraham Lincoln promised Turner that he would, if elected, sign a bill embodying his principles, if it should be passed by the House and Senate.

7. Quoted from Russell Lord, *The Agrarian Revival* (New York, 1939), p. 50.

8. See Joseph Bailey, *Seaman A. Knapp: Schoolmaster of American Agriculture* (New York, 1945).

9. The use of a religious terminology in relation to Knapp's work is entirely *a propos*. He was a deeply religious man, as many who knew him have testified. Once again the relation between religion and adult education can legitimately be emphasized.

10. See Raymond B. Fosdick, *The Story of the Rockefeller Foundation* (New York, 1952), pp. 181-182. Knapp died on April 1, 1911, at the age of 77. It is interesting indeed that his vital work for rural adult vocational education was done when he was over seventy.

11. In *Land Policy Review*, Fall, 1944.

12. Brunner and Yang, *op. cit.* The Report is printed in full as Appendix 1.

13. Charles P. Loomis, *et al., Rural Social Systems and Adult Education* (East Lansing, Mich., 1953). (This study was financed by The Fund for Adult Education.)

14. See W. S. Tryon (ed.), *A Mirror for Americans* (Chicago, 1952), III, 612.

15. The writer found the two books by Charles A. Bennett, *History of Manual and Industrial Education to 1870* (Bloomington, Ind., 1926) and *History of Manual and Industrial Education, 1870–1917* (Bloomington, Ind., 1937), of great use in preparing these brief notes.

16. In the 1948 *Handbook of Adult Education* J. S. Noffsinger, then director of the National Home Study Council stated: "The majority of the students of the home study institutions reside in smaller communities where there are few, if any, evening vocational courses available. The private correspondence school, therefore, represents about the only opportunity for formal schooling in vocational subjects that is open to approximately 75 per cent of the adult population of this country."

17. A discussion of the problem from an international perspective is to be found in the UNESCO publication *Education in a Technological Society* (1952). What it means at the college level can be learned by inquiring about the experiments in introducing science students to the arts, humanities, and social sciences at such institutions as California Institute of Technology, Carnegie Institute of Technology, Case Institute of Technology, Massachusetts Institute of Technology, etc.

Chapter 17. THE PUBLIC SCHOOLS SERVE ADULTS

1. The following percentages report an analysis of the urban audience in 1950–51. The figures are taken from *A Study of Urban Public School Adult Education Programs,* made by the Division of Adult Education Service of the National Education Association on a grant from The Fund for Adult Education, published in 1952. It will be referred to hereafter as the NEA-DAES study.

Foreign born, working on Americanization	7.5
Illiterate, seeking basic skills	2.0
Unskilled, semiskilled, and skilled workers	26.3
Business and office employees	17.6
Professional people	5.8
Housewives	24.2
Physically or mentally handicapped	.4
Not classified above	16.2
	100.0

2. The NEA-DAES study (see above) found that in 1950–51 in urban areas about 65 out of every 100 teachers were trained as teachers, *but not as teachers of adults,* 22 out of every 100 were not trained at all, and only 12 out of every 100 were trained as teachers of adults.

3. Leipziger described this school as "not a trade school, but a technical school." It endeavored "to make *young men* as well as *young artisans.* . . . It works on educational lines to economic ends."

4. Quoted from R. L. Frankel, *Henry M. Leipziger* (New York, 1933), p. 156.

5. E. George Hartmann, *The Movement to Americanize The Immigrant* (New York, 1948).

6. There may be some methodological wisdom buried in the ten volumes of the *Carnegie Studies in Americanization,* financed by the Carnegie Corporation, edited by Allen Burns, and published 1920–23, mostly after the Americanization Crusade had begun to fade, but the basic approach in them was sociological and Hartmann notes that they were directed primarily to social workers.

7. Andrew Hendrickson, *Trends in Public School Adult Education in Cities of the United States, 1929–1939* (New York, 1943), p. 14.

8. One of the Department's earliest campaigns was for the appointment of a specialist in adult education to the staff of the United States Office of Education. In this it succeeded. The history of the appointment was given as follows in a letter to the writer from the Office of Education, dated March 10, 1954: "The position of Specialist for Post High School and General Adult Education was created in 1947 and Dr. Homer Kempfer was appointed October 1 of that year. He resigned October 1, 1952, and the position has not been refilled. In August, 1925, Dr. Lewis R. Alderman was appointed Specialist in Adult Education and served in that capacity as well as that of Chief of the Service Division until August, 1938, when he became Director of the Division of Education of the Works Progress Administration on loan from the Office of Education. He retired in January, 1942, without, I believe, returning to this Office. Between that time and the appointment of Dr. Kempfer, Dr. Maris M. Proffitt, Consultant to the Assistant Commissioner and Specialist in Industrial Arts, carried on some work in the field of adult education."

9. In the NAE-DAES study of 1950–51 (see note 1 above), 16 curriculum areas were used for the reporting, as follows: (1) civic and public affairs; (2) general academic education; (3) Americanization and elementary education; (4) fine arts; (5) practical arts and crafts; (6) commercial and distributive education; (7) agriculture; (8) vocational and technical education other than agriculture; (9) homemaking education; (10) parent and family life education; (11) health and physical education; (12) personal improvement; (13) recreational skills; (14) safety and driver education; (15) remedial and special education; and (16) the inevitable "miscellaneous."

10. F. W. Reeves, T. Fansler, and C. O. Houle, *Adult Education* (Survey for the New York State Regents' Inquiry) (New York, 1938).

11. See Howard Y. McClusky's article in *Review of Educational Research,* XX, No. 3 (June, 1950).

Chapter 18. THE LIBRARIES AS ADULT EDUCATION INSTITUTIONS

1. Quoted in S. Ditzion, *op. cit.*
2. *Ibid.*
3. Quoted in Fremont Rider, *Melvil Dewey* (New York, 1944), p. 88. As early as 1869, Dewey had confided to his diary, "I wish to inaugurate a higher education for the masses." (p. 8.)
4. See Benjamin Fine's news story in *The New York Times,* June 15, 1953, reporting a survey directed by Charles F. Gosnell, New York State Librarian: "More than 53,000,000 persons do not have easy access to books, while 24,000,000 have no public library service of any kind. Of the 3,000 counties in this country, one of every six has no library service. Most of the 7,500 separate library systems of the country are substandard, with insufficient reading materials and inadequate staffs the general rule."
5. The origin of Readers' Advisory Service is a disputed question.
6. See Alvin Johnson, *The Public Library: A People's University* (New York, 1938), pp. 61, 71, 73.
7. *Ibid.,* pp. 8-9.
8. For details of the situation in early 1953, see Helen Lyman Smith, *Adult Education Activities in Public Libraries* (Chicago, 1954). This study, published by the American Library Association, was financed by The Fund for Adult Education.
9. It is rather important to have a clear idea of what a library's public really is if any reasonable understanding of its adult education potential is to be had. According to Bernard Berelson in *The Library's Public* (New York, 1949) it is precisely that aspiring section of the middle class that has chiefly supported adult education since early in the nineteenth century. It is not, as is sometimes assumed—this is even implied by Alvin Johnson in the quotes cited above—an institution serving the mass of the people in any sizable community.

Chapter 19. ADULT EDUCATION IN THE LABOR MOVEMENT

1. See his article "Workers' Education," in *Encyclopedia of the Social Sciences*, XV, 484.

2. Merle Curti, *The Growth of American Thought* (2nd ed., New York, 1951), p. 142.

3. William James, "Thomas Davidson," in *Memoirs and Studies* (New York, 1924). The essay was originally published in 1905.

4. Davidson's highest value was freedom: "A free life is the only life worthy of a human being. That which is not free is not responsible, and that which is not responsible is not moral. In other words, freedom is the condition of morality."

5. A full account of the adventure is to be found in Thomas Davidson, *The Education of the Wage Earners* (edited by C. M. Bakewell) (Boston, 1904).

6. See *ibid.* (*My italics.*)

7. The John L. Elliott Institute of New York City, founded 1942.

8. Mark Starr in his 1951 survey of union education included the Rand School and gave its purpose as "The spread of intelligence as a means of orderly and social progress and the maintenance of freedom of inquiry and teaching in opposition to fascist and communist totalitarianism." See "Trade Union Education Survey," in *Labor and Nation*, Fall, 1951. The survey was financed by The Fund for Adult Education.

9. As the story of workers' education is bound one day to be fully investigated historically, it may be helpful to call attention to the *Memoirs of Alice Henry* (Melbourne, Australia, 1944), published in stenciled typescript, copies of which were distributed to major American libraries by the writer, who knew Miss Henry in her retirement in Australia.

10. Among those who met with Beard to plan the project—the first meeting was held on New Year's Eve, 1920—were Arthur Gleason, Fannia M. Cohn, Professor Henry W. L. Dana, Paul Blanshard, A. J. Muste, Abraham Epstein, and David J. Saposs. See James H. Maurer's autobiography, *It Can Be Done* (New York, 1938), p. 369.

11. See the Starr survey (note 8, *supra*).

12. Quoted in T. R. Adam, *The Worker's Road to Learning* (New York, 1940), p. 53.

13. In addition to Miss Smith, other women who entered actively into workers' education at this time were Alice Shoemaker, Jean Carter, Louise McLaren, and Eleanor Coit.

14. It should not be thought that only federal money was available for workers' education in the decade. Although no exactly comparable figures can be offered, Spencer Miller, Jr., estimated that during the years 1931–38 unions contributed 38 per cent of the money spent, the WPA 24 per cent, liberal sympathizers 20 per cent, foundations 13 per

cent, and state governments 5 per cent. See I. L. H. Kerrison, *Workers'
Education at the University Level* (New York, 1951).

15. Adam, *op. cit.,* p. 120. These remarks should not be read as
critical of efforts to improve the *readability* of materials, the concern
of several individuals and groups in recent years, as for example the
Readability Laboratory financed with Carnegie Corporation funds
through the AAAE and directed by Professor Lyman Bryson at
Teachers College, Columbia, from late 1934 to the end of 1941, and
the "communications" studies of such men as Douglas Waples and
others. The Readability Laboratory illustrated the principles it discovered in a series of books called "The Peoples Library," published
by Macmillan, to which such writers as Bryson himself, H. A. Overstreet, Paul Sears, Mildred Adams, and John Pfeiffer contributed. The
influence of work of this kind on publishers' editorial practices has been
considerable. Yet the writer cannot help feeling that the reprinting as
"paper-backs" of so many excellent books, many of them stylistically
highly readable, but others notably difficult—e.g., Thorstein Veblen's
writings—offers more "material" in inexpensive form for adult education and self-education than any other development in recent years.
The "paper-back" reprints are books that have survived the severe
competition of the intellectual market place.

16. Arkansas, California, Colorado, Illinois, Indiana, Iowa, Kansas,
Michigan, Minnesota, Missouri, New York, North Dakota, Ohio,
Oklahoma, Pennsylvania, Washington, and Wisconsin.

17. For a full account of the adventure in all its phases see the
manuscript report: Hilda W. Smith, "People Come First, A Report of
Workers' Education in the Federal Emergency Relief Administration,
the Civil Works Administration, and the Works Progress Administration, 1933–1943." Prepared for The Fund for Adult Education, 1952.
Unattributed quotations in the discussion are from this report.

18. At Roosevelt College in Chicago there was established a Labor
Education Division, co-equal with the other divisions of the school,
and the only one in America at that time with that status.

Chapter 20. ADULT EDUCATION AS AN *Omnium Gatherum*

1. C. Howard Hopkins, *History of the YMCA in North America*
(New York, 1951).

2. The director of the entire cultural program since 1935 has been
Dr. William Kolodney.

3. This development is reported in *Experimental Classes for Adult
Education* by P. N. Youtz, published by the American Association for
Adult Education in 1927. Among those who participated as leaders in
addition to Youtz were Houston Peterson, Mortimer Adler, Whittaker

Chambers, Richard McKeon, Scott Buchanan, John Storck, Herbert Solow, Moses Hadas, and Clifton Fadiman. The Youtz pamphlet led the American Library Association to publish the book list used, as a pamphlet entitled *Classics of the Western World* for distribution to adult library users.

4. For a discussion of great books, with a short sketch of the background (which is incomplete) see J. W. Powell, *Education for Maturity* (New York, 1949); and for a review of the great books question from the Erskine-Columbia point of view, so to speak, see Jacques Barzun, *Teacher in America* (Anchor ed., 1954), pp. 138-146. In general the Barzun book is excellent, but his discussion of adult education is far below the rest of the book in information, insight, and worth. Mortimer J. Adler's *How to Read a Book: The Art of Getting a Liberal Education* (New York, 1940), has very little about the historical background in it, though mention is made of John Erskine and Robert M. Hutchins, but it is an interesting presentation of an ideological background for Great Books, though not as persuasive as Hutchins' own (see below). Clifton Fadiman prints a brief reminiscence of his early association with the work, particularly useful as capturing the spirit of the venture, in his book, *Party of One* (New York, 1955).

5. In October, 1951, the Hutchins-Adler Great Books were published as a set—a putative ancestor frequently recalled was Dr. Charles W. Eliot's "Harvard Classics" (the "Five-Foot Shelf"), launched in 1909—and unveiled to the public at a dinner at the Waldorf-Astoria Hotel in New York City. Hutchins' introductory volume to the collected edition is the most persuasive statement of his position the writer has ever seen.

6. A full-dress history of educational radio may be published in the next year or two, but these comments were written without benefit of it.

7. Llewellyn White, *The American Radio* (Chicago, 1947).

8. Quoted in W. A. Orton, *America's Search for Culture* (Boston, 1933), p. 245.

9. In *Higher Education for Democracy: A Report of the President's Commission on Higher Education* (1947) we read: ". . . the universities are niggardly and slow. The Federal Communications Commission has set aside twenty bands on the FM spectrum for the use of educational institutions, but the colleges are not taking advantage of the opportunity thus offered them. . . ."

10. This is the professional organization in the educational radio field. It was founded in Washington, D.C., in 1925 as the Association for College and University Broadcasting Stations and took its present name in 1934.

11. Alvin Johnson, *Pioneer's Progress* (New York, 1952), pp. 287-288.

Chapter 21. ORGANIZING THE ADULT EDUCATORS

1. Quoted in John Angus Burrell, *A History of Adult Education at Columbia University* (New York, 1954), p. 84.

2. W. S. Learned, *The American Public Library and the Diffusion of Knowledge* (New York, 1924).

3. This is a proper place to pause over the words "adult education" once again. We have remarked that much that is properly so called has not yet been recognized to be such either by those offering it or those receiving it. In 1935 Morse A. Cartwright, Executive Director of AAAE, put down as the opening sentence of his *Ten Years of Adult Education* (New York, 1935), the words: "Before the month of June, 1924, the term 'adult education' was not in use in the United States of America." But the writer has run upon the use of the term as far back as 1900 in the United States of America. Henry Leipziger's lecture system was described as "adult education" in a magazine of general circulation in that year—*The Forum*, XXIX (May, 1900). It was coming into frequent use by the twenties, as has already been illustrated textually. What Cartwright and the AAAE did was to popularize the term, give it wider currency, not introduce it.

4. In the light of all this, the familiar story of Keppel resolving to develop adult education after reading the British book, *The Way Out: Essays on the Meaning and Purpose of Adult Education,* edited by the Hon. Oliver Stanley (London, 1923), seems vastly overdrawn. Rather it seems likely that the book was but one item stiffening his resolution to go forward with his idea.

5. Quoted in Burrell, *op. cit.,* p. vii.

6. Since the people invited to the conference of June, 1924, may be taken as those who were at that time presumed to be interested in adult education, at least among those residing in or near New York, their names perhaps should be recorded: Charles A. Beard, Mrs. J. C. Campbell, Alfred E. Cohn, Miss Louise Connolly, L. L. Dickerson, C. R. Dooley, Miss Linda A. Eastman, W. F. Hirsch, W. S. Learned, E. D. Martin, S. A. Matheson, Carl H. Milam, Spencer Miller, Jr., J. J. Tompkins, Levering Tyson, Clark Wissler, H. C. Bedford, John Cotton Dana, Ferris Greenslet, Edward C. Jenkins, E. C. Lindeman, Thomas H. Nelson, W. W. Peter, Charles R. Richards, James E. Russell, Mrs. V. C. Simkhovitch; and President Keppel and Morse A. Cartwright, his assistant, from the Corporation.

7. Five studies, published in 1926, dealt with correspondence schools, lyceums and chautauquas, vocational education for young workers, the libraries and adult education, university extension, and a miscellany of other activities, including forums, workers' colleges, and social-settlement educational ventures. Out of this material Dorothy Canfield Fisher composed *Why Stop Learning?* published in 1927 after serialization in *McCall's Magazine*.

8. Mr. Cartwright, as Assistant to President Keppel, played an important role in launching the Association and he was director of it until 1949. He was born in Omaha, Nebraska, in 1890, educated at the University of California, and had had a career as teacher and administrator there—he was, for example, Assistant Director of University Extension 1923–24—before joining the Carnegie Corporation.

9. The first president was Dean James Earl Russell who served 1926–1930 and then became chairman of the Executive Committee until 1936. His successors in the presidency to 1951 were: Newton D. Baker, 1930–31; Felix M. Warburg, 1931–32; Dorothy Canfield Fisher, 1932–34; Edward L. Thorndike, 1934–35; Charles A. Beard, 1935–36; Everett D. Martin, 1936–37; William A. Neilson, 1937–38; John H. Finley, 1938–39; Alvin Johnson, 1939–40; H. A. Overstreet, 1940–41; Harry W. Chase, 1941–42; Alexander Meiklejohn, 1942–43; Austin H. MacCormick, 1943–44; Lyman Bryson, 1944–46; Alain Locke, 1946–47; Harvey N. Davis, 1947–48; Hans Kohn, 1948–49; Morse A. Cartwright, 1949–50.

10. Quoted from document supplied by The Carnegie Corporation. The Committee consisted of Trustees Thomas S. Arbuthnot (Chairman), Walter A. Jessup, Nicholas Kelley, and Arthur W. Page.

11. It should not be assumed that the Corporation finally "abandoned" the field of adult education in 1941. Not at all. It ceased to be a major concentration of interest, but the Corporation continued to make grants which can only be described as for adult education.

12. *Appreciations of Frederick Paul Keppel by Some of His Friends* (New York, 1951).

Chapter 22. AMERICAN PERSPECTIVES OF THE 1950's

1. Mary L. Ely (ed.), *Handbook of Adult Education* (New York, 1950), pp. 281 ff.

2. The full report of the study is C. O. Houle, *The Armed Services and Adult Education* (Washington, 1947).

3. A comprehensive consideration of this question may be found in *Mass Media and Education* (Chicago: National Society for the Study of Education, 1954).

4. Members of the Commission then or later identified with adult education included Sarah G. Blanding, Milton S. Eisenhower, Horace M. Kallen, Harry K. Newburn, and Mark Starr.

5. (Washington, 1947), I, 97.

6. *Ibid.*, II, 59.

7. *Ibid.*, V, 17.

8. *Report of the Study for The Ford Foundation on Policy and Program* (Detroit, November, 1949). The Study Committee members were H. Rowan Gaither, Jr., Chairman; Thomas H. Carroll, T. Duckett

Jones, Donald G. Marquis, William C. DeVane, Charles C. Lauritsen, Peter H. Odegard, and Francis T. Spaulding.

9. This is a mixed bag indeed. Forums and libraries have been discussed earlier. Little theaters have an association with adult education of fairly long standing—the Little Theatre movement dates back to 1906—but it is one that needs clarification both from the standpoint of those who work on production and that of the audience. Evidently the Ford committeemen were thinking of the audiences. There is a large literature on the little theaters, but little on what their wares ordinarily mean, or could mean, in adult education terms. The role of music (concerts) in Chautauqua was noted in passing. Music-making and listening to music have reached a high pitch of development in America in recent years. This is an area in which the commercial radio has a good record. That taste in music develops readily on a wider scale than is true of taste in reading and in pictures has often been noted. Painting was attracting more and more people in the late forties and early fifties, both practitioners and viewers. Visitors to museums of art were multiplying. For data on popular participation in the arts *circa* the date of the Forum, see the reports of speeches at the *Herald-Tribune* Forum, New York *Herald-Tribune*, October 25, 1953. The possible future role of the arts in adult education will be discussed in the final chapter.

10. The remarks following are based on *Review of Educational Research*, XX, No. 3 (June, 1950).

11. E. M. Forster, *Two Cheers for Democracy* (New York, 1951).

12. Uncritical use of the concept of community as the basic yardstick for measuring all things, can obscure the fact that the actual programs very uncommonly reach the entire community. We have emphasized again and again that, historically, adult education has been predominantly a middle-class activity, and still largely remains such. Leland Bradford has remarked, ". . . it would be all too easy for adult educators to assume they had developed a total community program when in effect they had merely tapped middle-class groups."

PART V. ADULT EDUCATION: IDEA AND REALITY

Chapter 23. THE ROAD AHEAD

1. See André Malraux, *The Voices of Silence* (New York, 1953), "I. Museum Without Walls."

2. John H. Mueller, *The American Symphony Orchestra: A Social History of Musical Taste* (Bloomington, Ind., 1951).

3. Mary L. Ely, *op. cit.*, p. 244.

4. The most recent survey of professional training in adult education known to the writer is Elwin V. Svenson, "A Study of Professional
Preparation Programs Offered by Schools of Education" (unpublished
thesis presented for the degree of Doctor of Education at the University of California, Los Angeles, June, 1954). Svenson reported that
Teachers College, Columbia University, pioneered this field when, in
the summer session of 1929, a single course was offered, supported by
Carnegie Corporation funds and the AAAE. Considering the situation
at the time of his study, Svenson differentiated between 14 institutions
which offered some work in adult education and 12 which offered
work for advanced degrees (M.A. or Ph.D. or equivalent). The latter
were University of California at Los Angeles, University of Chicago,
Columbia University, Cornell University, George Washington University, Indiana University, University of Maryland, University of
Michigan, New York University, Ohio State University, State University of Iowa, and the University of Wisconsin. (In a letter, Svenson
called attention to recent developments at the degree level at the
University of California at Berkeley under the leadership of Professor
Jack London.) Of his 12, Svenson selected 7 institutions as doing
perhaps the most impressive jobs at the time of his survey: State
University of Iowa, Ohio State, University of Michigan, Indiana, Chicago, UCLA, and Teachers College of Columbia. Men conspicuously
identified with the work (not necessarily professors of adult education)
were Professor Hew Roberts (Iowa), Professor Andrew Hendrickson
(Ohio State), Professor H. Y. McClusky and Assistant Professor Watson Dickerman (Michigan), Dr. Paul Bergevine (Indiana), Professor
Cyril Houle (Chicago), Professor Paul Sheats and Dr. Abbott Kaplan
(UCLA), Professors Paul Essert, Ralph Spence, and Wilbur Hallenbeck (Teachers College, Columbia). Svenson commented (at pp. 86-87)
that the most important factor determining the value of the training
programs was the personnel conducting them, not the course offerings,
university regulations, etc.

5. A good deal has been said in this book about method, but always
in nonprofessional terms—see the page references under *Method* in
the Index. On the other hand, no effort has been made to present a
systematic, sophisticated history of method, for the writer strongly felt
that this was quite beyond his competence, and better left to a professional to present either in a specialized journal article or a monograph.
It has been suggested by Professor Lyman Bryson that a useful road
into the field is provided by the bibliography to McBurney and Hance,
Discussion of Human Affairs (New York, 1950). The latest methodological approach really to stir the field is that called "group dynamics,"
of which the pioneer was Professor Kurt Lewin (1890–1947). Group
dynamics has especial relevance to the discussion method in adult
education.

6. A brilliant statement of this point is to be found in Randall

Jarrell, *Poetry and the Age* (Vintage ed., New York, 1955), pp. 21-22. A partial quotation reads: "One of the oldest, deepest, and most nearly conclusive attractions of democracy is manifested in our feeling that through it not only material but also spiritual goods can be shared; that in a democracy bread and justice, education and art, will be accessible to everybody. If democracy should offer its citizens a show of education, a sham art, a literacy more dangerous than their old illiteracy, then we should have to say that it is not a democracy at all. . . ."

7. AEA has under way a study of this aspect of the question, but it was not yet available when this was written.

8. The classic critique of this breed of adult education customers is, of course, Flaubert's *Bouvard and Pécuchet*.

Index

Steffens, Lincoln, quoted, 193
Stocks, J. L., quoted, 41-42
Stocks, Mary, quoted, 114; 120
Stuart, James, 103-4
Studebaker, John W., 164, 165, 229
Sturge, Joseph, 94-96
Subject matter, 5-7, 26, 37, 39, 42, 49-50, 58, 59, 65, 71, 83-89, 95-101, 104, 106, 109, 121, 126, 174-75, 188, 194-95, 207, 221, 223, 227-28, 244, 252, 267

Tawney, R. H., 95, 114, 117
Taylor, A. E., quoted, 36, 37, 38-40
Taylor, Bayard, 161, 162
Teachers, 187, 253, 290, 291, 307-8
Temple, William, 112
Thompson, Lawrance, quoted, 148
Thoreau, Henry David, quoted, 159; 161
Thorndike, E. L., 14, 281
Tocqueville, Alexis de, 154
Toynbee, Arnold, 105-6, 107, 112
Tutorial classes, 113-14
Tyson, Levering, quoted, 269

University Extension, 58; in Britain 103-4, 121; in U.S. 163, 172, 180, 183-96, 242-43, 249, 272, 291

Van Hise, C. R., 184, 192; quoted, 193-94
Van Rensselaer, Stephen, 158, 210-11
Varro, 45

Villon, François, quoted, 57
Vincent, George, 184
Vincent, John Heyl, 167-69, 172
Virgil, 46, 49
Visual aids, 32, 48-49, 57, 221
Vocational adult education, 5, 24, 33, 56-57, 84, 98-99, 197-216
Vrooman, Walter, 108, 241

Ward, Lester, 193-94
Washington, George, quoted, 146-47; 199
Watson, Elkannah, 199-200
Wesley, John, 70, 71
White, William, 95-96
Whitehead, A. N., quoted, 307
Williams, W. E., cited, 122
Wilson, M. L., 206
Wilson, Woodrow, 175, 197, 221
Women's adult education, 123, 258-61
Women's Trade Union League, 246-47, 249
Woodward, C. M., 211
Worsdell, Edward, quoted, 95-96
Workers' education, in U.S., 239-56
Workers' Education Bureau, 247
Worker's Educational Assn., 97, 109-15, 119-21
Workingmen's Colleges, 97-102

Yeaxlee, Basil, quoted, 104
YM and YWCA: in Britain, 125; in U.S., 262-64, 287
YM and YWHA, 264

AMERICAN EDUCATION:
ITS MEN, IDEAS, AND INSTITUTIONS
An Arno Press/New York Times Collection

Series I

Adams, Francis. The Free School System of the United States. 1875.

Alcott, William A. Confessions of a School Master. 1839.

American Unitarian Association. From Servitude to Service. 1905.

Bagley, William C. Determinism in Education. 1925.

Barnard, Henry, editor. Memoirs of Teachers, Educators, and Promoters and Benefactors of Education, Literature, and Science. 1861.

Bell, Sadie. The Church, the State, and Education in Virginia. 1930.

Belting, Paul Everett. The Development of the Free Public High School in Illinois to 1860. 1919.

Berkson, Isaac B. Theories of Americanization: A Critical Study. 1920.

Blauch, Lloyd E. Federal Cooperation in Agricultural Extension Work, Vocational Education, and Vocational Rehabilitation. 1935.

Bloomfield, Meyer. Vocational Guidance of Youth. 1911.

Brewer, Clifton Hartwell. A History of Religious Education in the Episcopal Church to 1835. 1924.

Brown, Elmer Ellsworth. The Making of Our Middle Schools. 1902.

Brumbaugh, M. G. Life and Works of Christopher Dock. 1908.

Burns, Reverend J. A. The Catholic School System in the United States. 1908.

Burns, Reverend J. A. The Growth and Development of the Catholic School System in the United States. 1912.

Burton, Warren. The District School as It Was. 1850.

Butler, Nicholas Murray, editor. Education in the United States. 1900.

Butler, Vera M. Education as Revealed By New England Newspapers prior to 1850. 1935.

Campbell, Thomas Monroe. The Movable School Goes to the Negro Farmer. 1936.

Carter, James G. Essays upon Popular Education. 1826.

Carter, James G. Letters to the Hon. William Prescott, LL.D., on the Free Schools of New England. 1924.

Channing, William Ellery. Self-Culture. 1842.

Coe, George A. A Social Theory of Religious Education. 1917.

Committee on Secondary School Studies. Report of the Committee on Secondary School Studies, Appointed at the Meeting of the National Education Association. 1893.

Counts, George S. Dare the School Build a New Social Order? 1932.

Counts, George S. The Selective Character of American Secondary Education. 1922.

Counts, George S. The Social Composition of Boards of Education. 1927.

Culver, Raymond B. **Horace Mann and Religion in the Massa-chusetts Public Schools.** 1929.

Curoe, Philip R. V. **Educational Attitudes and Policies of Organized Labor in the United States.** 1926.

Dabney, Charles William. **Universal Education in the South.** 1936.

Dearborn, Ned Harland. **The Oswego Movement in American Education.** 1925.

De Lima, Agnes. **Our Enemy the Child.** 1926.

Dewey, John. **The Educational Situation.** 1902.

Dexter, Franklin B., editor. **Documentary History of Yale University.** 1916.

Eliot, Charles William. **Educational Reform: Essays and Addresses.** 1898.

Ensign, Forest Chester. **Compulsory School Attendance and Child Labor.** 1921.

Fitzpatrick, Edward Augustus. **The Educational Views and Influence of De Witt Clinton.** 1911.

Fleming, Sanford. **Children & Puritanism.** 1933.

Flexner, Abraham. **The American College: A Criticism.** 1908.

Foerster, Norman. **The Future of the Liberal College.** 1938.

Gilman, Daniel Coit. **University Problems in the United States.** 1898.

Hall, Samuel R. **Lectures on School-Keeping.** 1829.

Hall, Stanley G. **Adolescence: Its Psychology and Its Relations to Physiology, Anthropology, Sociology, Sex, Crime, Religion, and Education.** 1905. 2 vols.

Hansen, Allen Oscar. **Early Educational Leadership in the Ohio Valley.** 1923.

Harris, William T. **Psychologic Foundations of Education.** 1899.

Harris, William T. **Report of the Committee of Fifteen on the Elementary School.** 1895.

Harveson, Mae Elizabeth. **Catharine Esther Beecher: Pioneer Educator.** 1932.

Jackson, George Leroy. **The Development of School Support in Colonial Massachusetts.** 1909.

Kandel, I. L., editor. **Twenty-five Years of American Education.** 1924.

Kemp, William Webb. **The Support of Schools in Colonial New York by the Society for the Propagation of the Gospel in Foreign Parts.** 1913.

Kilpatrick, William Heard. **The Dutch Schools of New Netherland and Colonial New York.** 1912.

Kilpatrick, William Heard. **The Educational Frontier.** 1933.

Knight, Edgar Wallace. **The Influence of Reconstruction on Education in the South.** 1913.

Le Duc, Thomas. **Piety and Intellect at Amherst College, 1865-1912.** 1946.

Maclean, John. **History of the College of New Jersey from Its Origin in 1746 to the Commencement of 1854.** 1877.

Maddox, William Arthur. **The Free School Idea in Virginia before the Civil War.** 1918.

Mann, Horace. **Lectures on Education.** 1855.

McCadden, Joseph J. **Education in Pennsylvania, 1801-1835, and Its Debt to Roberts Vaux.** 1855.

McCallum, James Dow. **Eleazar Wheelock.** 1939.

McCuskey, Dorothy. **Bronson Alcott, Teacher.** 1940.

Meiklejohn, Alexander. **The Liberal College.** 1920.

Miller, Edward Alanson. **The History of Educational Legislation in Ohio from 1803 to 1850.** 1918.

Miller, George Frederick. **The Academy System of the State of New York.** 1922.

Monroe, Will S. **History of the Pestalozzian Movement in the United States.** 1907.

Mosely Education Commission. **Reports of the Mosely Education Commission to the United States of America October-December, 1903.** 1904.

Mowry, William A. **Recollections of a New England Educator.** 1908.

Mulhern, James. **A History of Secondary Education in Pennsylvania.** 1933.

National Herbart Society. **National Herbart Society Yearbooks 1-5, 1895-1899.** 1895-1899.

Nearing, Scott. **The New Education: A Review of Progressive Educational Movements of the Day.** 1915.

Neef, Joseph. **Sketches of a Plan and Method of Education.** 1808.

Nock, Albert Jay. **The Theory of Education in the United States.** 1932.

Norton, A. O., editor. **The First State Normal School in America: The Journals of Cyrus Pierce and Mary Swift.** 1926.

Oviatt, Edwin. **The Beginnings of Yale, 1701-1726.** 1916.

Packard, Frederic Adolphus. **The Daily Public School in the United States.** 1866.

Page, David P. **Theory and Practice of Teaching.** 1848.

Parker, Francis W. **Talks on Pedagogics: An Outline of the Theory of Concentration.** 1894.

Peabody, Elizabeth Palmer. **Record of a School.** 1835.

Porter, Noah. **The American Colleges and the American Public.** 1870.

Reigart, John Franklin. **The Lancasterian System of Instruction in the Schools of New York City.** 1916.

Reilly, Daniel F. **The School Controversy (1891-1893).** 1943.

Rice, Dr. J. M. **The Public-School System of the United States.** 1893.

Rice, Dr. J. M. **Scientific Management in Education.** 1912.

Ross, Early D. **Democracy's College: The Land-Grant Movement in the Formative Stage.** 1942.

Rugg, Harold, et al. **Curriculum-Making: Past and Present.** 1926.

Rugg, Harold, et al. **The Foundations of Curriculum-Making.** 1926.

Rugg, Harold and Shumaker, Ann. **The Child-Centered School.** 1928.

Seybolt, Robert Francis. **Apprenticeship and Apprenticeship Education in Colonial New England and New York.** 1917.

Seybolt, Robert Francis. **The Private Schools of Colonial Boston.** 1935.

Seybolt, Robert Francis. **The Public Schools of Colonial Boston.** 1935.

Sheldon, Henry D. **Student Life and Customs.** 1901.

Sherrill, Lewis Joseph. **Presbyterian Parochial Schools, 1846-1870.** 1932.

Siljestrom, P. A. **Educational Institutions of the United States.** 1853.

Small, Walter Herbert. **Early New England Schools.** 1914.

Soltes, Mordecai. **The Yiddish Press: An Americanizing Agency.** 1925.

Stewart, George, Jr. **A History of Religious Education in Connecticut to the Middle of the Nineteenth Century.** 1924.

Storr, Richard J. **The Beginnings of Graduate Education in America.** 1953.

Stout, John Elbert. **The Development of High-School Curricula in the North Central States from 1860 to 1918. 1921.**
Suzzallo, Henry. **The Rise of Local School Supervision in Massachusetts. 1906.**
Swett, John. **Public Education in California. 1911.**
Tappan, Henry P. **University Education. 1851.**
Taylor, Howard Cromwell. **The Educational Significance of the Early Federal Land Ordinances. 1921.**
Taylor, J. Orville. **The District School. 1834.**
Tewksbury, Donald G. **The Founding of American Colleges and Universities before the Civil War. 1932.**
Thorndike, Edward L. **Educational Psychology. 1913-1914.**
True, Alfred Charles. **A History of Agricultural Education in the United States, 1785-1925. 1929.**
True, Alfred Charles. **A History of Agricultural Extension Work in the United States, 1785-1923. 1928.**
Updegraff, Harlan. **The Origin of the Moving School in Massachusetts. 1908.**
Wayland, Francis. **Thoughts on the Present Collegiate System in the United States. 1842.**
Weber, Samuel Edwin. **The Charity School Movement in Colonial Pennsylvania. 1905.**
Wells, Guy Fred. **Parish Education in Colonial Virginia. 1923.**
Wickersham, J. P. **The History of Education in Pennsylvania. 1885.**
Woodward, Calvin M. **The Manual Training School. 1887.**
Woody, Thomas. **Early Quaker Education in Pennsylvania. 1920.**
Woody, Thomas. **Quaker Education in the Colony and State of New Jersey. 1923.**
Wroth, Lawrence C. **An American Bookshelf, 1755. 1934.**

Series II

Adams, Evelyn C. **American Indian Education. 1946.**
Bailey, Joseph Cannon. **Seaman A. Knapp: Schoolmaster of American Agriculture. 1945.**
Beecher, Catharine and Harriet Beecher Stowe. **The American Woman's Home. 1869.**
Benezet, Louis T. **General Education in the Progressive College. 1943.**
Boas, Louise Schutz. **Woman's Education Begins. 1935.**
Bobbitt, Franklin. **The Curriculum. 1918.**
Bode, Boyd H. **Progressive Education at the Crossroads. 1938.**
Bourne, William Oland. **History of the Public School Society of the City of New York. 1870.**
Bronson, Walter C. **The History of Brown University, 1764-1914. 1914.**
Burstall, Sara A. **The Education of Girls in the United States. 1894.**
Butts, R. Freeman. **The College Charts Its Course. 1939.**
Caldwell, Otis W. and Stuart A. Courtis. **Then & Now in Education, 1845-1923. 1923.**
Calverton, V. F. & Samuel D. Schmalhausen, editors. **The New Generation: The Intimate Problems of Modern Parents and Children. 1930.**
Charters, W. W. **Curriculum Construction. 1923.**
Childs, John L. **Education and Morals. 1950.**

Childs, John L. **Education and the Philosophy of Experimentalism.** 1931.
Clapp, Elsie Ripley. **Community Schools in Action.** 1939.
Counts, George S. **The American Road to Culture: A Social Interpretation of Education in the United States.** 1930.
Counts, George S. **School and Society in Chicago.** 1928.
Finegan, Thomas E. **Free Schools.** 1921.
Fletcher, Robert Samuel. **A History of Oberlin College.** 1943.
Grattan, C. Hartley. **In Quest of Knowledge: A Historical Perspective on Adult Education.** 1955.
Hartman, Gertrude & Ann Shumaker, editors. **Creative Expression.** 1932.
Kandel, I. L. **The Cult of Uncertainty.** 1943.
Kandel, I. L. **Examinations and Their Substitutes in the United States.** 1936.
Kilpatrick, William Heard. **Education for a Changing Civilization.** 1926.
Kilpatrick, William Heard. **Foundations of Method.** 1925.
Kilpatrick, William Heard. **The Montessori System Examined.** 1914.
Lang, Ossian H., editor. **Educational Creeds of the Nineteenth Century.** 1898.
Learned, William S. **The Quality of the Educational Process in the United States and in Europe.** 1927.
Meiklejohn, Alexander. **The Experimental College.** 1932.
Middlekauff, Robert. **Ancients and Axioms: Secondary Education in Eighteenth-Century New England.** 1963.
Norwood, William Frederick. **Medical Education in the United States Before the Civil War.** 1944.
Parsons, Elsie W. Clews. **Educational Legislation and Administration of the Colonial Governments.** 1899.
Perry, Charles M. **Henry Philip Tappan: Philosopher and University President.** 1933.
Pierce, Bessie Louise. **Civic Attitudes in American School Textbooks.** 1930.
Rice, Edwin Wilbur. **The Sunday-School Movement (1780-1917) and the American Sunday-School Union (1817-1917).** 1917.
Robinson, James Harvey. **The Humanizing of Knowledge.** 1924.
Ryan, W. Carson. **Studies in Early Graduate Education.** 1939.
Seybolt, Robert Francis. **The Evening School in Colonial America.** 1925.
Seybolt, Robert Francis. **Source Studies in American Colonial Education.** 1925.
Todd, Lewis Paul. **Wartime Relations of the Federal Government and the Public Schools, 1917-1918.** 1945.
Vandewalker, Nina C. **The Kindergarten in American Education.** 1908.
Ward, Florence Elizabeth. **The Montessori Method and the American School.** 1913.
West, Andrew Fleming. **Short Papers on American Liberal Education.** 1907.
Wright, Marion M. Thompson. **The Education of Negroes in New Jersey.** 1941.

Supplement

The Social Frontier (Frontiers of Democracy). Vols. 1-10, 1934-1943.

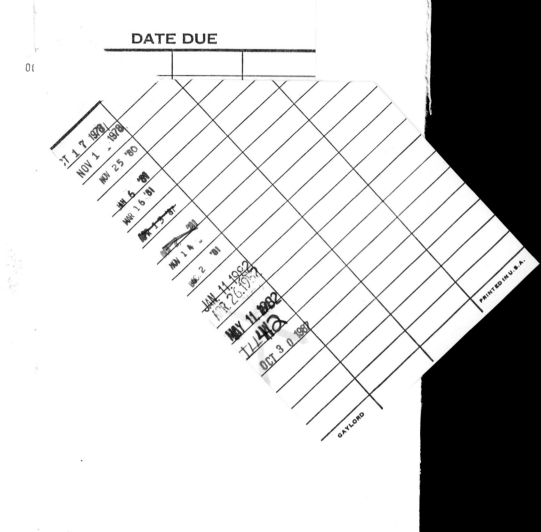